RELATIONAL INTERCULTURAL EDUCATION FOR INTERCULTURAL MINISTRY

Enoch Wan, Mark Hedinger, and Jon Raibley

Relational Paradigm Series of CDRR
Relational Intercultural Education for Intercultural Ministry

Copyright 2024 © Western Academic Publishers

Enoch Wan, Mark Hedinger, Jon Raibley

Cover designed by Mark Benec

ISBN: 978-1-954692-28-2

All rights reserved. Except for brief quotations in critical publications or reviews, no part of this book may be reproduced in any manner without prior written permission from the publisher or author.

CDRR (Center of Diaspora & Relational Research) @ https://www.westernseminary.edu/outreach/center-diaspora-relational-research

Western Academic Publishers

TABLE OF CONTENTS

LIST OF FIGURES vii
CHAPTER 1 Introduction 1
    The background of this book 1
    How this book came about 1
    Background of the co-authors 1
    The purpose of this book 3
    Definition of key terms 3
    Education and Intercultural Education 6
    Underlying Assumptions Behind the Definition of ICE 6
    Theoretical Framework of Intercultural Education 7
    Preliminary Discussion on Secular and Christian ICE 9
    The Readership and Organization of the Book 15

CHAPTER 2 The Breadth of Intercultural Education 17
    Introduction 17
    Educational Scope of Intercultural Education 17
    Historical Scope of Intercultural Education 18
    Summary 25

CHAPTER 3 Theories of ICE and Relational Intercultural Education 27
    Introduction 27
    Theories of Intercultural Education 27
    Theoretical Framework of RICE 31
    Theory of Relational Interactionism 39
    Summary 42

CHAPTER 4 : Biblical and Thematic Foundations Soo Min (James) Park and Jon Raibley 43
    Introduction 43
    Transformational Growth 44
    Transgressional Change 46
    Textual Examples 50
    Theological Components 52

Salvific Grace Leading to Transformation 59

Comparisons of Relational Transformational Change Paradigm and Jack Mezirow's Transformational Learning Theory 65

Summary 69

CHAPTER 5 Understanding Intercultural Education............ 71

Introduction 71

Understanding Ministry in Biblical/theological perspective.................... 71

Relational Ministry... 72

IV. Understanding Intercultural Ministry 77

V. Opportunities for Intercultural ministry.. 81

Summary 81

CHAPTER 6 Characteristics of RICE 85

Introduction 85

Current Trend #1; RICE is relational at its core... 85

Current Trend #2: RICE is process-oriented.. 85

Current Trend #3: RICE deliberately adjusts to complex human interactions.. 86

Summary 87

CHAPTER 7 . Challenges of RICE..89

Introduction 89

Challenge number 1: Ethnocentrism 89

Challenge number 2: Intercultural (Mis)communications 90

Challenge number 3: Emphasis on Attitudes 90

Challenge number 4: Inviting God into a teaching/learning relationship... 91

Challenge number 5: Teaching and Training Oral Learners and Digital Oral Learners... 92

Summary 96

CHAPTER 8 The Practice of Relational Intercultural Education for Intercultural Ministry 97

Introduction 97

Functional and Relational Educational Approaches................................. 97

Relational Intercultural Education 100

Summary 111

CHAPTER 9 Case Study #1 – Relational Language Acquisition.   Karen Hedinger 113

Introduction 113
Definitions 114
Goals of the Language Learner 114
Language Learning Community (LLC) 116
Language Trainer's Role in LLC 118
RLA is More Than LLC 119
Conclusion 119

CHAPTER 10 Case Study #2– Relational Teaching Methods (RTMs). Soo Min (James) Park 121

Introduction 121
Definitions 122
Scriptural Validation and Invalidation of the Five Educational Frameworks 123
Markers of Relational Interactionist Educational Framework 125
Assessment and Delineation of Teaching Methods Based on RI Markers 126
Conclusion and Suggestion for Future Research 134
Works Cited 134

CHAPTER 11 Case Study #3 – Christ-Centered Transformational Education for Second-Generation Chinese Adolescents. Jessie Yin 137

Introduction 137
Definition of Key Terms 137
RICE for Second-generation Chinese Adolescents 138
Christ-Centered Transformational Education 139
Application in Youth Ministry as a youth camp design 141
Feedback from Adolescents' and Parents' Interview 143
Conclusion 144
Works Cited 145

CHAPTER 12 Case Study #4 – The Importance of Names. Robert Aguayo 153

Introduction 153
Cultural Background 154
Intercultural Education Implications 156
Conclusion 160
Works Cited 160

CHAPTER 13 Case Study #5: International Student Ministry (ISM) Workers as Relational Intercultural Educators (RICE-R) in Discipleship of International Students. Estera Piroşcă Escobar 163

Introduction 163
Definition of Key Terms 163
Intercultural Relational Discipleship Process 164
"Being:" ISM Workers and International Students 165
"Belonging:" Key Principles of Discipleship 166
"Becoming:" Maturity in Christ 169
Conclusion 171
Works Cited 171

CHAPTER 14 Case Study #6 Relational Competency-Based Intercultural Theological Education 173

Introduction 173
Traditional Education and Competency-Based Education 173
CBE Characteristics 174
Process of Intercultural Education 180
Conclusions 183
Works Cited 183

CHAPTER 15 CONCLUSION 184

Appendix 1: Two Series of Publication by Enoch Wan 187

Series on Diaspora Missiology 187
Series on Relational Paradigm 187

Appendix 2: Resources for Further Studies 192

Transformative Learning 192
Outcome-Based Education 192
Andragogy 192

BIBLIOGRAPHY 193

LIST OF FIGURES

Figure 1-1. Types of Education 9
Figure 1-2. Umbrella Model of Intercultural Education 14
Figure 1-3. Secular vis-à-vis Christian Intercultural Education 15
Figure 2-1. Interculturally Relevant Variables in Intercultural Education 18
Figure 2-2. Microcultures and the National Macroculture 23
Figure 2-3. Approaches to Multicultural Education in the United States 24
Figure 3-1. Summary of Five Theoretical Frameworks of ICE 27
Figure 3-2. Five Theoretical Frameworks of ICE: Positivist 28
Figure 3-3. Five Theoretical Frameworks of ICE: Relativist 29
Figure 3-4. Five Theoretical Frameworks of ICE: Constructivist 29
Figure 3-5. Five Theoretical Frameworks of ICE: Critical Theory 30
Figure 3-6. Five Theoretical Frameworks of ICE: Relational Interactionist 31
Figure 3-7. The interactive relationship within the Trinity and beyond 41
Figure 3-8. Comparison of Three Paradigms 42
Figure 4-1. Examples of Paul's Influence on the Ephesian Church 46
Figure 4-2. Comparison of 1 John 2:16 and Genesis 3:6 47
Figure 4-3. Comparison of the actions and character of Lot with the residents of Sodom 49
Figure 4-4. Example Scriptural components of transformational growth and transgressional change with relation to Being 53
Figure 4-5. Example Scriptural components of transformational growth and transgressional change with relation to Belonging 53
Figure 4-6. Example Scriptural components of transformational growth and transgressional change with relation to Becoming 54
Figure 5-1. Comparison of Three Paradigms 73
Figure 5-2. Possible Postures of Stimulus and Response 74
Figure 5-3. Christian Ministry Elements 79
Figure 5-4. Illustrations of cultural outworking of 5 relational elements 80
Figure 5-5. Illustrations of Ministry areas in relational intercultural perspective 82
Figure 5-6. Education as relational and as intercultural ministry 83
Figure 8-1 Relational Intercultural Education 100
Figure 8-2. Complexities: possible transgressional change 102
Figure 8-3. Relational Andragogy & Transformative Change: three dimensions 107
Figure 8-4. Program outcomes in cross-cultural training 107
Figure 8-5. Pyramid of Educational Design: from Foundation to Outcomes 109
Figure 8-6. Christian adult transformational learning 110
Figure 8-7. Relational transformation: process & progress 111

Figure 9-1. Characteristics of Genuine Relationship 115
Figure 9-2. Language Learning Community 118
Figure 11-1. Christ-Centered Transformational Education 140
Figure 12-1. Teso sub-region of Uganda 154
Figure 12-2. Ateso Names 156
Figure 12-3. Relational Realism and Transformational Change 157
Figure 12-4. Intercultural Discipleship in Action 159
Figure 13-1. Intercultural Relational Discipleship Process in ISM as an
    Application of RICE 164
Figure 13-2. Themes of ISM Workers as "beings" and Relational Elements . 165
Figure 13-3. Experiences of International Students as "beings" and Relational
    Elements 166
Figure 13-4. Seven Relationships in the Intercultural Discipleship Process in
    ISM 167
Figure 14-1. Comparison between Traditional Education and Competency-
    Based Education 174
Figure 14-2. CBE-oriented Intercultural Education within Relational
    Interactionism 176
Figure 14-3. Interactions in a CBE framework of Relational Interactionism 178
Figure 14-4. CBE Assessment 179
Figure 14-5. The CBE Program Design Process 180
Figure 14-6. Intercultural Leadership Training Program in Relational
    Interactionism 182

CHAPTER 1
Introduction

The background of this book

This book is a sequel of collaborative work between the co-authors in prior publications:

- Enoch Wan & Mark Hedinger, *Relational Missionary Training: Theology, Theory & Practice.* (2017)
- Enoch Wan & Mark Hedinger, "Transformative Ministry for the Majority World Context: Applying Relational Approaches." *Occasional Bulletin*, EMS (2018).
- Enoch Wan & Jon Raibley, *Transformational Change in Christian Ministry.* (2022)
- Enoch Wan, Mark Hedinger & Jon Raibley, Transformational Growth: Intercultural *Leadership, Discipleship and Mentorship.* (2023)

Readers of this book will soon recognize the similarities of this book with the theoretical framework, the theological foundation and practical implementation of the article and three books listed above. In this way, this book is a sequel of the four publications listed above.

How this book came about

The three co-authors met regularly and discussed frequently to explore the practical way of expanding our mutual understanding and professional practice into the field of intercultural education. After months of collaborative efforts, this book is now a reality as a textbook for use in the PhD Program of Intercultural Education at Western Seminary. This book is a continuation of the ongoing research and field practice of "relational interactionism" by the co-authors in Christian ministry, theological education, and mission practice.

Background of the co-authors

Enoch Wan has served on the faculty at Western Seminary for over twenty years, leading three doctoral programs in intercultural studies and intercultural education. He served for two terms as president of the Evangelical Missiological Society and as vice president in various capacities for two decades. Enoch began his research on the paradigms of relational realism and diaspora missiology during his sabbatical as scholar-in-residence at Yale Divinity School two decades ago. Since then, he has published many articles and dozens of books on these two themes.[1]

Mark Hedinger came to this book project after a long history of mission work and study. After living and working in Mexico for twelve years, Mark served in mid-level leadership of a mission agency. In those roles he became convinced of the importance of intercultural training for mission practitioners. After completing a doctorate at Western Seminary under the direction of Dr. Enoch Wan, he eventually joined a mission training program headquartered in Portland, Oregon. That organization, named CultureBound, offers training for intercultural ministry and second language acquisition to intercultural workers sent out from many different nations. Mark also continues to teach intercultural communication and education through Western Seminary and a number of other schools. The key idea that ties Mark together with the other authors of this work is a commitment to the relational perspective. All three authors are convinced that life and ministry are much more aligned with relationships than with methods and techniques. That idea is central to all elements of Mark's ministry, including this book.

Jon Raibley has been employed by Western Seminary since 1988, working with their online education program, and is now a member of their faculty. He has spent 18 months assisting church planters in the Philippines. Under Enoch Wan's supervision, Jon completed Western's Doctor of Education in Intercultural Education program in 2021 and published an article on transformational learning.[2] His dissertation explored the experiences of online students with communities of learning.[3] He continues to teach and to serve in Western's online education department with an emphasis on the transformative influence that Christians can have by being intentional about their interactions with others.

This book has also benefitted from the work of current students and graduates of the intercultural doctoral programs at Western Seminary. Chapters 9 through 14 contain case studies written by students and graduates. Chapter 4, in particular is based on class discussions within a recent doctoral class on "Transformational Change and Intercultural Discipleship." And the entire book benefited from the graphic design work provided by Maureen York, the assistance of Soo Min (James) Park, Dr. Wan's Graduate Fellow, and the formatting work of Karen Hedinger. We appreciate the contributions of you all!

---

[1] See Appendix 1 for a list of publications on the relational paradigm and the diaspora missiology paradigm.

[2] Enoch Wan and Jon Raibley, "Transforming Meaning Perspectives and Intercultural Education," in *Covenant Transformative Learning Theory and Practice for Mission* (Western Seminary Press, 2021), 147–62.

[3] Jon Raibley, "Experiencing Communities of Learning: A Phenomenological Study of Students Enrolled in Western Seminary's Online Master of Divinity Program" (Portland, Oregon, Western Seminary, 2021).

The purpose of this book

The purpose of this book is to introduce the readers to "relational intercultural education" (RICE) for the practice of "intercultural ministry" (ICM).

Definition of key terms

Education

The process of interaction between the teacher/trainer/instructor and the student/trainee/learner during which the latter is transformed relationally in multiple dimensions: cognitive, affective, and behavioral.

Relational Intercultural education (RICE)

- RICE is defined as a "Christian educator participating in God's *missio Dei*[4] to nurture unity (with cultural diversity), mutuality (in communion and sharing), harmony (*shalom*[5] - in spite of ethnic diversity), reciprocity (overcoming barriers, e.g. intercultural communication) amidst interaction of personal Beings/beings within an intercultural context.
- In the context of education, RICE is "the formal/informal/non-formal process whereby the educator interacts relationally with the learner towards development/enrichment in 'being' and 'doing' (i.e. multidimensional such as cognitive, affective, volitional, etc.) within a cross-cultural context."[6]

---

[4] The definition of "mission" is "a process by which Christians (individuals) and the Church (institutional) continue on and carry out the *missio Dei* of the Triune God ("mission") at both individual and institutional levels spiritually (saving souls) and socially (ushering in *shalom**) for redemption, reconciliation, and transformation (Wan, Enoch. *Diaspora Missiology*. 2nd ed. Portland, OR: The Institute of Diaspora Studies, 2014:7). For Enoch Wan's detailed discussion on the definition of "mission," see Enoch Wan, "'Mission' and '*Missio Dei*': Response to Charles van Engen's 'Mission Defined and Described,'" in *MissionShift: Global Mission Issues in the Third Millennium*, eds. David J. Hesselgrave and Ed Stetzer, (Nashville: B & H Publishing Group, 2010d), 41-50.

[5] "*shalom*" is the context of total wellness in which created humanity can reach his/her full potential and properly respond to God and His message relationally (Jer. 29:7, 1 Tim. 2:1-5).

[6] Enoch Wan. "Interculturality and Intercultural Education: The Concept and Definition of 'Culture' at Two Levels." Unpublished manuscript. Western Seminary. 2022: 10.

Intercultural educator
An individual who operates between two or more cultures with an intercultural self-perception and orientation.

Interculturality
Instead of being monocultural, interculturality is both the commitment and competence of someone venturing beyond his/her cultural background and boundary with multidimensional qualities, such as self-identity (psychological), multiculturality (ideational), intentionality (attitudinal) and practicality (operational). Thus, "interculturality" is the quality of an ideal intercultural teacher/trainer, including:

- a subjective construction of identity (psychological),
- a desire to embrace "multiculturality" as a goal for growth (intentional),
- the ability to navigate among different cultural spaces (bicultural and beyond),
- the competence in two or more languages (bilingual and beyond),
- the ability to relate and interact harmoniously with those who are culturally diverse (adaptable and venturesome).[7]

Intercultural Education
Intercultural education is the formal/informal/non-formal process whereby the educator interacts relationally with the learner towards development/enrichment in "being" and "doing" (i.e. multidimensional such as cognitive, affective, volitional...etc.) within a cross-cultural context.[8]

There are four assumptions to accompany this definition:

- Ontologically, the context is delimited to personal beings/Beings; the best way of learning is relational interaction.
- Epistemologically, subjective and objective dimensions are critically different and yet both should be included.[9]
- Theoretically, relational perspective is preferred to other perspectives such as rationalistic, behavioral, communicative, and pragmatic

---

[7] David Luna, Torsten Ringberg, and Laura A. Peracchio, "One Individual, Two Identities: Frame Switching among Biculturals," *Journal of Consumer Research* 35, no. 2 (August 1, 2008): 283, https://doi.org/10.1086/586914.

[8] Enoch Wan offers the definition of "Intercultural Education"(ICE) from a relational interactionist perspective – from Enoch Wan. Unpublished lecture notes from IE701 – Fall 2019.

[9] For detailed discussion on "epistemology of relational paradigm," see Ryan Gimple and Enoch Wan, *Covenant Transformative Learning: Theory and Practice for Mission*. Center of Diaspora & Relational Research (CDRR). 2021

because the purpose of intercultural education is to promote positive change through relational interaction.
- Existentially, "doing" is not to be separated from "being" since there is a dynamic interplay and intricate relationship between the two; yet "being" precedes "doing" and with integration of both.

Intercultural ministry (ICM)
Christian ministry carried out within a cross-cultural context.

Relational interactionism (RI)
An interdisciplinary narrative framework that develops from practical considerations of dynamic interaction of personal Beings/beings, forming realistic relational networks in multiple contexts (i.e., theo-culture, angel-culture, and human-culture) and with various consequences.[10]

Relational intercultural education (RICE)
The formal/informal/non-formal process whereby the educator interacts relationally with the learner towards development/enrichment in "being" and "doing" (i.e. multidimensional elements such as cognitive, affective, volitional...etc.) within a cross-cultural context.[11]

Relational Intercultural Training (RIT)
An interactive process of learning to develop one's attitudes, knowledge, and skills that contribute to one's intercultural relational competency and formation of intercultural identity.

Transformational Growth (TG)
The dynamism and process of positive change, originated vertically from the Triune God and ushered in the relational reality horizontally, through the process of interaction between personal Beings (the Triune God) and human beings (at micro and macro levels) multi-dimensionally, with spiritual, moral, social, and behavioral dimensions at personal and/or institutional levels.[12]

Transgressional Change (TC)
Change caused by the dynamism from the enemy of the Triune God and by fallen nature that is contrary to the attribute of God and His will, His revelation in Jesus Christ and the Scripture, i.e., the opposite of transformational change.[13]

---

[10] Enoch Wan, "Rethinking Urban Mission in Terms of Spiritual and Social Transformational Change" (Missiological Society of Ghana/WAMS Biennial International Conference, Virtual, October 26, 2021).

[11] From lecture notes, Enoch Wan, IS/IE 701, Feb. 4, 2019.

[12] Enoch Wan, Mark Hedinger & Jon Raibley, *Transformational Growth: Intercultural Leadership, Discipleship and Mentorship*. 2023:6.

[13] Enoch Wan, Mark Hedinger & Jon Raibley, *Transformational Growth: Intercultural Leadership, Discipleship and Mentorship*. 2023:6.

Education and Intercultural Education

There are "5 Ps" in education as listed below:[14]

Personnel:
- relational type & role, e.g. teacher/student; trainer/trainee

Purpose:
- progressive change due to learning
- transformational growth; not merely improvement

Process & pattern:
- cognitive pattern – e.g. lineal thought pattern vis-à-vis cyclical
- learning style – e.g. auditory/visual/tactile…etc.
- teaching method – e.g. teacher-centered/student-centered

Program:
- types - formal, informal & non-formal
- curriculum design and pedagogical methodology

Product:
- outcome (outcome-based)
- competence (competence-based)
- personal growth, mutual enrichment, and community development

Underlying Assumptions Behind the Definition of ICE

- "Education is a process in which a learner comes to understand reality (vertical and horizontal relationships) and truth (Truth revealed vertically and truth communicated horizontally) with transformative changes (being & doing)"[15]
- Christian educators and learners rely not merely on human reasoning nor expertise in pedagogy to produce new understanding in the learner; but on the Spirit of God who leads all people into truth (Truth – John 14:6; and truth - John 16:13 NIV) with dynamism for change (Philippians 2:13 – "for it is God who works in you to will and to do…" and Ro 12:1-4 "…transformation…")
- Transformative learning is a matter of allowing the Spirit of truth to transform the heart (Matthew 15:10-2), as well as the mind (Romans 12:1-2) through relationship with God vertically and others horizontally (Ephesians 4:15, 25-32). Pattern of relational interaction, within and beyond the realms of Triune God, angelic and human beings, can be decerned then narratively described.

---

[14] Enoch Wan, lecture notes of IS 701 Intercultural Education. Fall semester 2012.
[15] Enoch Wan, lecture notes of IS 701 Intercultural Education. Fall semester 2012.

Theoretical Framework of Intercultural Education

- Based on Jack Mezirow, *Learning as Transformation: Critical Perspectives on a Theory in Progress.* See Chapter 4 for a comparison of the Relational Transformational Change Paradigm and Jack Mezirow's Transformational Learning Theory
- The "transformative learning" paradigm of Mezirow is applied in addressing the following issues:
  - step-by-step program planning process
  - Christian formation & development
  - psychological health & healing
  - business/job preparedness & re-entry to society with new identity & productivity.
- The philosophy of adult education (andragogy) is distinct and different from the philosophy of childhood education (pedagogy).[16]

In contrast to secular education focusing primarily on learning knowledge, information and skills; relational Christian adult education must focus on "being" and "doing," individually and collectively including assumptions and beliefs that drive their perspectives (or worldviews) leading to a new reality in Christ and new humanity in the Church. (Stevens 2012, 2015)[17] This is in contrast to Mezirow's statement below:

> Central to [the process of helping adults enhance their understandings, skills, and dispositions] is helping learners to critically reflect on, appropriately validate, and effectively act on their (and others') beliefs, interpretations, values, feelings, and ways of thinking...Our human need to understand our experience, the necessity that we do so through critical discourse, and the optimal conditions enabling us to do so freely and fully provide a foundation of a philosophy of adult education.[18]

Mezirow's understanding of adult transformative learning is accomplished through "critical discourse." William N. Isaacs uses the term "dialog" similarly:

> If people can be brought into a setting where they, at their choice, can become conscious of the very process by which they form tacit assumptions and solidify beliefs, and be rewarded by each other for doing

---

[16] Jack Mezirow, *Learning as Transformation*, San Francisco: Jossey-Bass, 2000, 3.
[17] David E. Stevens, *God's New Humanity: A Biblical Theology of Multiethnicity for the Church*. Oregon: Wipf and Stock, 2012; David E. Stevens, "God's new humanity in diaspora: a church of the nations and for the nations," In Pocock & Wan 2015:107-126.
[18] Mezirow, *Learning as Transformation*, 26.

so, then they can develop a common strength and capability for working and creating things together.[19]

- Instead of "critical discourse," we emphasize "interactive learning" at personal level and within the learning community both vertically and horizontally.
- Our paradigm is integrative:
  - being + doing.
  - belief + behavior.
  - personal + collective.
  - individual + communal.
  - convergence of multiple realms: Triune God, angelical beings and human beings.
  - general understanding of "change" = cognition + volition + affection + action.
  - linkage and network created by relational interaction of Beings/being with multiplicity and complexity.
- Christian adult transformational learning
  - transformative change = divine aid + godly teacher's input + Christian learner's positive response. i.e. adults (willing to grow and change) by entering a relational community can experience positive change through interactive learning vertically and horizontally
- Uniqueness of the relational paradigm (in contrast to conventional Christian approaches)
  - Not individualistic; but collective: Trinity=3 & interdependent
  - Not personally private: pattern of relational interaction - observable and discernable, social and community based, can also be narratively described.
    a) The Son's deference to and dependence on the Father (Jn 4-8, 12)
    b) The Father testifies for the Son at baptism and transfiguration
    c) The Holy Spirit testifies to the Father and the Son (e.g. Jn 14:16-31; 15:26-27; 16:13-14; Acts 1:8)
    d) The Father sent the Son (Jn 17:6-8, 18, 21)
    e) The Incarnation: Father's will, virgin Mary from the HS
    f) HS came down to the Son at baptism...Jesus at crucifixion gave up the spirit
    g) The resurrection of the Son: Father raised Him (Gal. 1:1, Eph. 1:17,20), H.S. raised Him (Romans 8:11)
  - Multi-directional: Not unilineal in process of pedagogy (teacher as a learner; growing together)

---

[19] William N. Isaacs, "Taking Flight: Dialogue, Collective Thinking, and Organizational Learning," *Organizational Dynamics*, no. 2 (Autumn 1993), 25.

- Multi-dimensional Not unidimensional in progress (not merely knowledge or behavior or etc. only)
- Characteristics of this approach:
    a) Ontological convergence of spheres (interplay and overlapping), e.g. the scenario of Chapters 1 and 2 in Job: dialogue of Jehovah with the accuser
    b) Pedagogical confluence in dynamic interaction (interactive throughout)
    c) Transformational change is the anticipated positive outcome.

There are various types of education as shown below:

MODE OF DELIVERY			DEVELOPMENT	
FORMAL	IN-FORMAL	NON-FORMAL	TRADITIONAL	NON-TRADITIONAL
taught from fixed curriculum & syllabus; diploma, degree	flexible format & adaptive process	Unstructured, fluid,	Face-to-face, teacher-centered, unidirectional, passive process	Computer-mediated, Interactive, student-oriented

Figure 1-1. Types of Education[20]

Preliminary Discussion on Secular and Christian ICE

In this book, "intercultural education" (ICE) is generically defined as "education within a cross-cultural context." There are clear differences between the secular view and Christian perspective on ICE.

Secular View on ICE

The Intercultural Education Network offers a definition:

Intercultural education promotes the understanding of different people and cultures. It includes teachings that accept and respect the normality and diversity in all areas of life. It makes every effort to sensitize the learner to the notion that we have naturally developed in different ways. It seeks to explore, examine, and challenge all forms of "isms" and xenophobia, while promoting equal opportunity for all. Intercultural education works to transform not only the individual but the institution as a metaphor and mechanism for the transformation of society."[21] In a fairly recent conference on intercultural education, this sort of definition was used to create the aim of the conference: "Acquiring increased awareness of subjective cultural context ("worldview"), including one's own, and

---
[20] Enoch Wan, lecture notes of IS 701 Intercultural Education. Fall semester 2012.
[21] Intercultural Education Network, https://ien.inclusion.msu.edu/node/130.

developing greater ability to interact sensitively and competently across cultural contexts as both an immediate and long-term effect of exchange."[22] Secular intercultural education seeks, partly, to combat racism, both within and across national and ethnic units. Below are samples of secular views on ICE:

- Grant, Carl A., and Agostino Portera, eds. *Intercultural and Multicultural Education: Enhancing Global Interconnectedness.* 1st ed. Routledge Research in Education, Book 39. Abingdon: Routledge, 2013.

  A collection of twenty-one essays exploring education within a context where multiple cultures exist and may be in conflict. The authors are from around the world, and do not agree on the definition or preference of the terms 'multicultural' and 'intercultural,' though many do prefer to see 'multicultural' as a description of the situation, and 'intercultural' as an attempt to create understanding and cooperation between cultures. Many address the political implications of failing to achieve this level of understanding. The history and description of current educational status of the various nations are interesting, although as a collection the redundancy and, in some cases, the political posturing, become tiresome.

- Gundara, Jagdish. *The Case for Intercultural Education in a Multicultural World*. Mosaic, 2015.

  Gundara's text is a collection of ten articles and addresses mostly presented between 2006 and 2014. He makes helpful distinctions between 'multicultural' and 'intercultural' approaches, but the essays are tediously repetitive and poorly edited. To someone interested in a single article representative of Gundara's views and goals, I would suggest 'Issues of Religious and Cultural Diversity in Modern States,' pages 203-221.

- Hoopes, David S. *Intercultural Education*. Bloomington, IN: Phi Delta Kappa Educational Foundation, 1980.

  A brief fastback publication that presents the role of intercultural education as a bridge between various local or 'traditional' cultures to a national or 'modern' culture to a global or 'postmodern' culture. The booklet contains helpful sections on the aims and processes of

---

[22] Defining, Measuring, and Facilitating Intercultural Learning: A Conceptual Introduction to the IJIE Special Issue. In M. J. Bennett (Ed.), State of the Art Research on Intercultural Learning in Study Abroad and Best Practice for Intercultural Learning in International Youth Exchange. Special Double Issue of *Journal of Intercultural Education*, 2009, 3.

intercultural education, although an updated version of the contents would be helpful.

The National Council for Curriculum and Assessment (NCCA) in Ireland defined intercultural education as

> ...education which respects, celebrates and recognises the normality of diversity in all areas of human life. It sensitises the learner to the idea that humans have naturally developed a range of different ways of life, customs and worldviews, and that this breadth of human life enriches us all. It is education, which promotes equality and human rights, challenges unfair discrimination, and promotes the values upon which equality is built.[23]

This council continued by describing what intercultural education is also about:

> ...respecting cultural difference and promoting anti-racism, it is not simply the knowledge of a variety of cultures. It aims to counter misconceptions and negative stereotyping of different cultures, religions and nationalities and seeks to develop an appreciation of other cultures in the context of a critical appreciation of local/Irish cultures. Intercultural education celebrates the positive aspects to cultural diversity as well as drawing attention to the power differences between groups and societies[24]

Jane Knight notes the role of intercultural education as internationalization which she defines as "the process of integrating an international, intercultural, or global dimension into the purpose, functions or delivery of postsecondary education."[25]

Christian View on ICE

A biblical understanding of intercultural education will differ in significant ways from its secular counterpart. Primarily, whereas the latter has the agenda of fostering cultural understanding, equality and a global community, a biblical approach will attempt to create a mutual understanding of Scripture as citizens of the kingdom of God.

In his book, *Teaching Across Cultures*, James Plueddemann writes, "Teaching that is pleasing to God builds on all of God's truth and fosters the development of learners into all God intended them to become."[26] Referring to himself as an educational "developmentalist," Plueddemann believes that

---

[23] "Intercultural Education | DICE Project," accessed February 27, 2019, http://www.diceproject.ie/de-ice/intercultural-education/.
[24] Intercultural education in the primary school. Irish National Teachers' Organization, Dublin 2004.
[25] Jane Knight, "Updating the Definition of Internationalization," n.d., 2.
[26] James E. Plueddemann, *Teaching Across Cultures: Contextualizing Education for Global Mission* (Downers Grove, IL: IVP Academic, 2018), 2.

"theological assumptions have profound educational implications"[27] but that we can easily be in conversation with those who do not share such assumptions since "many of the educational principles in [the book] are commonly accepted by the broader educational community."[28] In regard to intercultural education, there is much on which both secular and faith-based educators can agree, but there are also fundamental differences.

Of concern to secular educators is the problem of elevating one culture over another, and the desire to level the playing field by giving everyone a voice. Christians who are committed to Scripture as the final authority and who hold to certain theological assumptions, believe that the Voice has already spoken through His Word (the Incarnate Christ and the canon), and that every other voice is simply an echo or an affirmation. In this light, we could define Christian intercultural education as "the intentional fostering of faith across cultures in the Triune God through the authority of Scripture, striving to create shared understanding by affirming the learning processes and perspectives of both learners and teachers from their unique cultural contexts."

Like the secular approach, this definition recognizes that truth is perceived and practiced uniquely in different cultures, and thus the global community is interdependent, gaining from (and even requiring) the unique lens of each learner or teacher. However, unlike its secular counterpart that easily esteems "my truth" as one of many possibilities (especially in a postmodern world), and in which "authority" may lie in either the individual or in the community, the Christian individual and community has made an *a priori* decision to submit to the authority of a Triune God and Scripture.

In his award-winning book, *Exclusion and Embrace*, Miroslav Volf comments on social agents versus social arrangements. As one who experienced the destruction of his homeland, and who happens to be situated epistemologically in the story of Scripture, he is somewhat pessimistic about the possibility of pursuing harmonious social arrangements as an end. Commenting on various options for gluing together a fragmented humanity, Volf writes,

> They offer a proposal for how society (or all humanity) ought to be arranged in order to accommodate individuals and diverse groups with different identities living together – a society that guards universal values, or that promotes the plurality of particular communal identities, or that offers a framework for individual persons to go about freely making and unmaking their own identities... In contrast I want to focus on social agents. Instead of reflecting on the kind of society we ought to create in order to accommodate individual or communal heterogeneity, I will

---

[27] Plueddemann, *Teaching Across Cultures*, 4.
[28] Plueddemann, *Teaching Across Cultures*, 5.

explore *what kind of selves we need* to be in order to live in harmony with others.[29]

Volf's basic premise is that "the scandal of the cross" is the only true means to creating mutual understanding across national, ethnic and cultural divides. The starting point for Christian intercultural education is consistent with all of Christian life: we begin with the cross. Humbled before the Word of God, who humbled himself before the world, we have been given ears to hear the basic Truth about heaven's culture. The Communicator has spoken first about his self-giving and sacrificial love, and this voice now echoes through all the tribes and tongues that bow before him.

We have discussed two differences between Christian and secular education: truth claims of Scripture and the "scandal of the cross." There is also a third distinction - the availability of the Spirit of God in Christian education to guide both learner and teacher. Stephen and Mary Lowe state, "If this kind of social influence is taking place among human beings connected in a social network, should we not expect that even more powerful forms of influence are possible among Christians connected in a spiritual network empowered by the Holy Spirit?"[30] A critical part of Christian intercultural education is depending on the Holy Spirit to produce spiritual transformation in the lives of both instructors and students.

The goal of Christian ICE, in contrast to secular ICE, is to help Christians reach an intercultural understanding and intercultural mindset within a

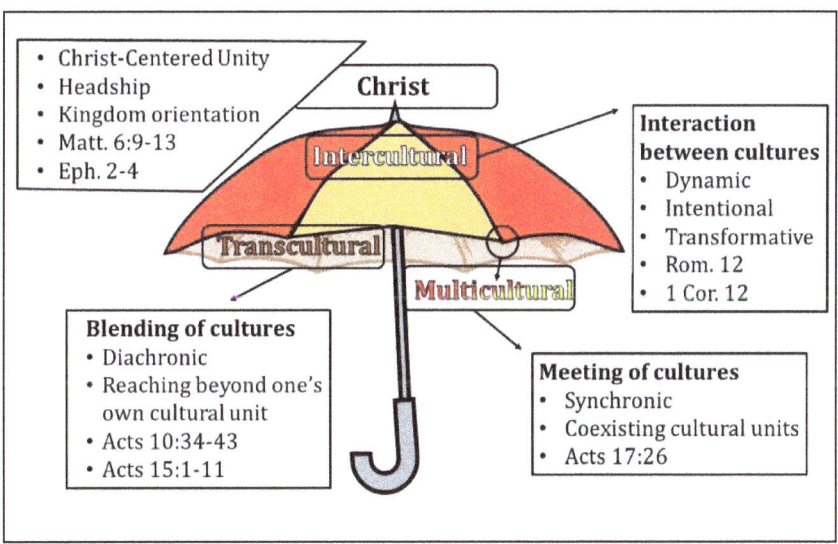

---

[29] Miroslav Volf, *Exclusion and Embrace, Revised and Updated: A Theological Exploration of Identity, Otherness, and Reconciliation*, Updated edition (Nashville: Abingdon Press, 2019), 20–21. Emphasis in original.

[30] Stephen D. Lowe and Mary E. Lowe, *Ecologies of Faith in a Digital Age: Spiritual Growth through Online Education* (Downer's Grove: IVP Academic, 2018), 220–21.

ministry context. This intercultural understanding and mindset operate as an umbrella which covers and includes aspects of multicultural and transcultural approaches as shown in the figure below:

Figure 1-2. Umbrella Model of Intercultural Education[31]

In this model, "intercultural" is understood under an assumption of the "unity above diversity" concept seen in the Trinity in Wan's Relational Realism Paradigm. The umbrella model seeks to center all cultures and ethnicities toward a Christ-centered unity. Under this ultimate reality and focus, the vertical relationship between Beings and beings is the vertical drive which transforms different cultures toward the Kingdom culture. The horizontal relationship between beings is the dynamic which helps different cultures and ethnic groups interact. This vertical drive can be understood through the soteriological perspective that Christ is drawing and giving His people a new identity in Him and thus unifies all nations; while this horizontal dynamic can be understood as the directional reaching out from God's people towards those who do not know God yet. Therefore, in the umbrella model, multiculturalism is no longer pluralism, but is the underlying purpose for the diversity, and trans-culturalism is no longer direction-free transition and connection between different cultural and ethnic groups, but it is transformation with one ultimate vertical goal. Together, transcultural and multicultural approaches are covered under the intercultural umbrella, with a pinned focal point on top, which is Christ.

The table below is a comparison of a secular view with a Christian view on Intercultural Education.

---

[31] Adapted from Ai Chen (Noel) Chiu, "Key Parameters of Establishing Frontline LGBTQ Outreach" (Portland, Oregon, Western Seminary, 2021), 175.

TYPE / AREA	SECULAR	CHRISTIAN	
		BIBLICAL	KINGDOM-ORIENTATION
Culture: big picture	"Cultural relativism; all cultures are equal and there is no ideal, standard culture"[32]	God created diversity; "culture is a gift from God"[33]	Lordship of Christ = ultimate authority over & embodiment of God's desired culture on earth and in heaven.
Why ICE	Equity and inclusion; global citizenship; correcting inequities and history of oppression for minority cultures and ethnicities. Equality among cultures with no idea, standard, or objectively superior culture	Desire for balance in vertical and horizontal relationships; God helps to reconcile and unite[34], "Human sin, alienation from God [and others], God's commandment to love the Lord and the neighbors"[35]	Human sin and the resulting rebellion against God alienated humanity from his Kingdom
What for	"Intercultural Education aims to go beyond passive coexistence, to achieve a developing and sustainable way of living together in multicultural societies through the creation of understanding, of respect for and dialogue between the different cultural groups."[36]	Knowledge of the truth,[37] Prepare students for success in a diverse world; prepare students for eternity,[38] providing supportive opportunities for diverse students to move towards transformation of awareness, attitudes, feelings, and knowledge	Repentance and reconciliation with God through Christ first and humanity second. God's Kingdom is eternal and glorious
How	Interaction and learning with/from others; creating educational policies; incorporating intercultural themes into curriculum and co-curricular activities; promoting intercultural and bias trainings; providing bilingual or other innovative programs	Understanding the Biblical foundation of diversity; interacting and learning from God, self, and others; "Practicing biblical principles, applying the fruits of the Spirit to or within each person's life"[39]	The atoning death of the crucified Christ redeemed sinners, ushering in God's dominion over all. People conquered by the Kingdom will bear the fruits of the Spirit.

Figure 1-3. Secular vis-à-vis Christian Intercultural Education

The Readership and Organization of the Book

This is an introductory textbook for teachers and trainers serving interculturally. It is also a handy reference for intercultural educators who serve domestically in multicultural contexts or abroad in intercultural circumstances.

This chapter has defined key terms associated with relational intercultural education and distinguished between secular and Christian approaches to intercultural education. In Chapter 2, we will explore the breadth of intercultural education by examining some of the commonalities of education across cultures, and some of the key themes that characterize the history of intercultural education.

Chapter 3 discusses the theoretical frameworks behind the approach that we are proposing for relational intercultural education. In Chapter 4, we look at the elements of relational Christian ministry in general, and intercultural relational Christian ministry specifically. Chapters 5 and 6 look at trends and challenges of relational intercultural education, while Chapter 7 explores the practical implications of implementing a relational approach to intercultural education. In Chapters 8 through 14, we have invited practitioners of relational intercultural education to share the challenges they have encountered, and their suggestions for ministering well from this approach.

Our hope is that this book will help you see the distinctives of, and rationale for, a relational approach to Christian ministry, particularly when that ministry includes intercultural education. And we pray that your use of these principles will be used by God for His glory and the growth of His Kingdom.

---

[32] HeeKap Lee, "Building a Community of Shalom: What the Bible Says about Multicultural Education," *International Christian Community of Teacher Educators Journal* 5, no. 2 (2010): 14.

[33] Carver T. Yu, "Culture From an Evangelical Perspective," *Transformation* 17, no. 3 (2000): 82—85.

[34] Nyaradzo Mvududu, "Culturally Responsive Teaching: The Bible Tells Me So" (2009): 5.

[35] Lee, "Building a Community of Shalom," 6.

[36] UNESCO Education Sector, "UNESCO Guidelines on Intercultural Education" (2006): 18.

[37] Paul G. Hiebert, *Anthropological Reflections on Missiological Issues* (Grand Rapids, Mich: Baker Academic, 1994).

[38] Paul G. Hiebert, *Anthropological Reflections on Missiological Issues* (Grand Rapids, Mich: Baker Academic, 1994).

[39] Lee, "Building a Community of Shalom," 6.

CHAPTER 2
The Breadth of Intercultural Education

Introduction

In this chapter, we will examine the breadth of Intercultural Education, in terms of educational and historical scope. We first examine some elements of learning that are shared across cultures but are addressed differently in those various societies. We will then take a brief look at the history of intercultural education and some of the various goals and approaches that have been used to increase understanding across cultures.

Educational Scope of Intercultural Education

The human activity of learning is both highly personal and highly cultural. As humans, we literally teach one another how to learn. And yet as humans we also have preferences based on our own individual strengths and weaknesses. Table 2-1 shows some of the variables that can be seen in teaching/learning across cultures.

Variables Categories	Educational Elements	Interculturally Relevant Variables in Educational Contexts
General	Media preferences	Oral; Textual; Digital oral
	Languages of culture	Interaction between instructor, learner and the learning group: does it follow the social cues of learners or of instructors? The "translation" of words, body language, use of space, time, etc.
	Situated placement of emotional involvement	Some cultures see emotion as situated "within" the person; most cultures see emotion as situated between people – a construction that is created between people
	Time factors	Age of instructors; Age of learners; Expected duration of learning sessions; Expected duration of learning process (including possible iterative processes); Expected maturation time for learning to take root
Teaching	Social posture of teacher	Expectations vary; can include: Controlling; Dialog; Influence; Resource
Learning	Social posture of learner	Various approaches: Obedient/ compliant; Dialog; Curious/engaged; Self-directed
	Learning domains	Cognitive; Affective; Behavioral; Relational
	Nature of learners	Individuals who are both responsible for their own learning and gain the benefit from what is learned; Groups which motivate individual achievement and which focus on collective value

Variables Categories	Educational Elements	Interculturally Relevant Variables in Educational Contexts
		of learning;
Outcomes	Outcomes of education	Skill and knowledge for financial or technological advance; Skill, knowledge, empathy building for relational interaction and human support.
	Learning impact[40]	Learning that: Produces no change; Produces Incremental change; Challenges existing assumptions; Shifts beliefs; Leads to transformation

Figure 2-1. Interculturally Relevant Variables in Intercultural Education

Historical Scope of Intercultural Education

Terms for Intercultural Education

Kenneth Cushner and Jenifer Mahon note that "the concept of 'intercultural' is not new to the field of education."[41] In this book, we are examining intercultural education based on the philosophical foundation of relational interactionism, which explores the various consequences of the connections and interactions between personal beings. These beings can include the divine Members of the Trinity, who have been in an eternal network of relationships that we refer to as the 'theo-culture.'[42] By definition, any self-revelation or instruction from the Trinity to angels or humans crosses cultural boundaries, and we could conclude that intercultural education began with God's first communication to angels.

Cushner and Mahon use a more recent example of intercultural education, pointing to Comenius in the 1600s, who "proposed a pansophic college based on ideas of pedagogical universalism, or the belief that a multiplicity of perspectives not only was foundational to knowledge acquisition but also encouraged mutual understanding between people of differing backgrounds."[43] It is challenging, however, to point to a specific point in history at which intercultural education was first proposed as a desired approach to teaching. This difficulty is partly due to the various terms that have been used to describe the efforts. Akirah Bradley, for example, divides U.S. history into the following terms and time periods:

---

[40] from Gregory Bateson, *The Logical Consequences of Learning and Communication*. Chicago: Univ of Chicago Press, 2000.

[41] Kenneth Cushner and Jennifer Mahon, "Intercultural Competence in Teacher Education: Developing the Intercultural Competence of Educators and Their Students: Creating the Blueprints," in *The SAGE Handbook of Intercultural Competence* (Thousand Oaks, CA: SAGE Publications, Inc, 2009), 305.

[42] Wan, "Rethinking Urban Mission in Terms of Spiritual and Social Transformational Change."

[43] Cushner and Mahon, *Intercultural Competence in Teacher Education*, 305.

1. Intercultural Education Movement 1924-1941
2. Intergroup Education Movement 1940s-1950s
3. Legislating "Change" Movement 1950s-1960s
4. Ethnic Studies Movement 1960s-1970s
5. Multiculturalism Movement 1980s-1990s[44]

Other historians see more fuzziness within the terminology. Lauri Johnson and Yoon Pak, for example, state:

> Historians have chronicled a variety of terms that refer to efforts by teachers and teacher educators to increase group understanding and combat racial and religious intolerance. Montalto, who researched the history of progressive organizations such as the Service Bureau on Intercultural Education from 1924 to 1941, used the term intercultural education but also referred to diversity work during this period as intergroup, interhuman, human relations, and ethnic studies.[45]

European countries that have large numbers of immigrants have also incorporated intercultural approaches to education. Johnson and Pak note that "The specific term intercultural education faded in the U.S. context but was taken up in Europe by the early 1980s to refer to pedagogical approaches aimed at improving the interaction between diverse cultural groups in response to increasing immigration from the former colonies of Africa and Asia to Western Europe."[46]

Goals of Intercultural Education

The lack of a clear historical timeline is also caused by the fact that educators have had competing goals and have used competing methods in dealing with multiple cultures. Some of the goals that teachers in the United States have pursued in intercultural education include the following:

1. Assimilation.

Philip Gleason discusses the complicated interplay between the concepts of pluralism and assimilation in U.S. history. He states, "Pluralism, generally speaking, affirms the existence and persistence of diversity and prescribes its preservation. Assimilation is associated with unity; it concerns itself with and generally approves of the processes by which various elements have been

---

[44] Akirah Bradley, "A Time to Intervene: A Historical Overview of Pedagogical Responses to an Unjust Society," *The Vermont Connection* 28, no. 1 (January 1, 2007): 71.
[45] Lauri D. Johnson and Yoon K. Pak, "Teaching for Diversity: Intercultural and Intergroup Education in the Public Schools, 1920s to 1970s," in *Review of Research in Education* (SAGE Publications, 2019), 2, https://doi.org/10.3102/0091732X18821127.
[46] Johnson and Pak, *Teaching for Diversity*, 3.

blended into the overall national culture."[47] Gleason's article explores the nuances of these two concepts, and the ways in which the terms' definitions and implications changed over the years. He does note, however, the way in which assimilation was used around the turn of the twentieth century to enforce conformity to the dominant culture: "… while assimilation was an elastic term that could accommodate a wide variation of interpretations, it became more closely identified with a narrow nativistic insistence that immigrants had to conform themselves closely to the prevailing American norms before they could be considered satisfactorily assimilated."[48]

Elwood Cubberly, the dean of Stanford's School of Education, for example, wrote in the early twentieth century, "Our schools are, in a sense, factories, in which the raw products (children) are to be shaped and fashioned into products to meet the various demands of life. The specifications for manufacturing come from the demands of twentieth-century civilization, and it is the business of the school to build its pupils according to the specifications laid down."[49] Cubberley feared the eugenic impact of immigration, portraying non-white and Eastern European immigrants as inherently inferior to the Anglo-American population.[50] A tragic example of this assimilation occurred at many of the federal boarding schools for Native American students, starting in the 1870s:

> At the federal boarding schools, which were located in white communities, children were given Anglo names. Their native languages and cultural practices were forbidden. Their strict educations included language lessons and studies in subjects like manual labor, housekeeping, and farming, and students were usually required to help keep the school self-sufficient by laboring there when they were not in the classroom.[51]

2. Appreciation

Franz Boas was an anthropologist who criticized his fellow scholars for comparing cultures to an assumed absolute standard of civilization. Milton Bennett notes that this approach created a hierarchy of cultures from 'savage'

---

[47] Philip Gleason, "The Odd Couple: Pluralism and Assimilation," in *Speaking of Diversity: Language and Ethnicity in Twentieth-Century America.* (Johns Hopkins University Press, 2019), 49, https://muse.jhu.edu/pub/1/oa_monograph/chapter/2412200.
[48] Gleason, "The Odd Couple," 50.
[49] "Larry Cuban on School Reform and Classroom Practice: Schools as Factories: Metaphors That Stick | National Education Policy Center," accessed December 28, 2023, https://nepc.colorado.edu/blog/schools-factories.
[50] "Ellwood Cubberley | Stanford Eugenics History Project," Eugenics at Stanford, accessed December 28, 2023, https://www.stanfordeugenics.com/ellwood-cubberley.
[51] "A Century of Trauma at U.S. Boarding Schools for Native American Children," History, July 9, 2021, https://www.nationalgeographic.com/history/article/a-century-of-trauma-at-boarding-schools-for-native-american-children-in-the-united-states.

to 'civilized.' He states, "Colonialists and other cultural imperialists were using this idea and the mistaken notion of "social Darwinism" to fuel their assumption of cultural superiority. Boas pointed out the ethnocentrism of this stance and argued that cultures could only be understood in their own terms – a position that became known as cultural relativism."[52] John Dewey argued against the traditional approach to didactic education:

> I believe it is also a social necessity because the home is the form of social life in which the child has been nurtured and in connection with which he has had his moral training. It is the business of the school to deepen and extend his sense of the values bound up in his home life. I believe that much of present education fails because it neglects this fundamental principle of the school as a form of community life. It conceives the school as a place where certain information is to be given, where certain lessons are to be learned, or where certain habits are to be formed. The value of these is conceived as lying largely in the remote future; the child must do these things for the sake of something else he is to do; they are mere preparation. As a result they do not become a part of the life experience of the child and so are not truly educative.[53]

The writings of Boas, Dewey, and others led to the formation of the Intergroup movement. Harriet Zilliacus and Gunilla Holm state that this approach sought to increase appreciation between cultures. "The so-called intergroup education emerged already when African Americans competed with Whites in the northern states and Mexican Americans competed with Whites in the western states in the U.S. for jobs and housing after WWII. This intergroup education was aimed at reducing racial tensions and increasing understanding between the groups."[54]

James Banks quotes G.W. Allport, "who theorized that contact between groups will improve intergroup relations if the contact has the following characteristics:

a. The individuals experience equal status;
b. They share common goals;
c. Intergroup cooperation exists; and

---

[52] Milton J. Bennett, "A Short Conceptual History of Intercultural Learning in Study Abroad," in *A History of U.S. Study Abroad: 1965 - Present* (Forum on Education Abroad, 2010), 3, https://www.idrinstitute.org/wp-content/uploads/2018/02/short_conceptual_history_ic_learning.pdf.

[53] John Dewey, "John Dewey My Pedagogic Creed," *School Journal* 54 (January 1897): 77–80. Article Two: What the School Is."

[54] Harriet Zilliacus and Gunilla Holm, "Multicultural Education and Intercultural Education: Is There a Difference?," in *Dialogues on Diversity and Global Education*, 2009, 11.

d. The contact is sanctioned by authorities, such as teachers and administrators, or by law or custom."[55]

Horace Kallen advocated for a cultural pluralism approach, affirming that "each ethnic and cultural group in the United States has a special contribution to make to the variety and richness of American culture and, thus, provided a rationale for those Jews who wish to preserve their Jewish cultural identity in the American melting pot."[56]

Zilliacus and Holm note that the Council of Europe's 2008 statement of policies and recommendations for intercultural education is divided into two areas of focus:

> (1) inclusion and participation, which includes centrally both pluralism and equality, and (2) learning to live together. The latter implies a feeling of belonging to a wider community, which is based on mutual respect and a shared belief in dialogue…The goal for intercultural education "is to incorporate all students into the plural society, by giving a new idea of history, geography, language, culture, philosophy, humanity and society."[57]

3. Perspective Transformation

Banks describes a transformative approach to multicultural education as one in which "the structure of the curriculum is changed to enable students to view concepts, issues, events, and themes from the perspective of diverse ethnic and cultural groups."[58] His description of the Civil Rights Movement serves as an example of a period of history that transformed the perspectives of teachers and students. He writes,

> A major goal of the Civil Rights Movement of the 1960s was to eliminate discrimination in public accommodations, housing, employment, and education. The consequences of the Civil Rights Movement had a significant influence on educational institutions as ethnic groups – first African Americans and then other groups – demanded that the schools and other educational institutions reform curricula to reflect their experiences, histories, cultures, and perspectives.[59]

---

[55] James A. Banks, "Diversity, Group Identity, and Citizenship Education in a Global Age," *Educational Researcher* 37, no. 3 (April 2008): 129–39, https://doi.org/10.3102/0013189X08317501, 135.

[56] "Kallen, Horace Meyer," in *Jewish Virtual Library* (jewishvirtuallibrary.com), accessed December 26, 2023, https://www.jewishvirtuallibrary.org/kallen-horace-meyer.

[57] Zilliacus and Holm, "Multicultural Education and Intercultural Education," 9.

[58] James A. Banks, "Approaches to Multicultural Curriculum Reform," *Trotter Institute Review* 3, no. 3, Article 5 (June 1989): 19.

[59] James A. Banks, "Multicultural Education: Characteristics and Goals," in *Multicultural Education: Issues and Perspectives* (John Wiley & Sons, 2010), 6.

He further illustrates the goals of a transformational approach with the graphic shown in Figure 2.2. He uses it to describe microcultures that

> ... consist of unique institutions, values, and cultural elements that are nonuniversalized and are shared primarily by members of specific cultural groups. A major goal of the school should be to help students acquire the knowledge, skills, and attitudes needed to function effectively within the national macroculture, their own microcultures, and within and across other microcultures.[60]

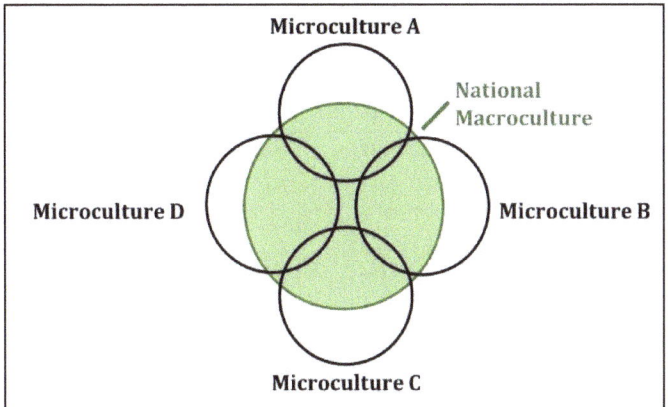

Figure 2-2. Microcultures and the National Macroculture[61]

---

[60] Banks, Multicultural Education, 11.
[61] Banks, Multicultural Education, 11.

Approach / Elements	Benevolent Multi-culturalism	Cultural Understanding	Cultural Pluralism	Bicultural Education
Purpose of Multicultural Education	To equalize educational opportunities for culturally different students	To teach students to value cultural differences, understand the meaning of the culture concept, and accept others' right to be different	To preserve and extend cultural pluralism in American society	To produce learners who have competencies in and can operate successfully in two different cultures
Proponents	Mainstream educators	Subordinate minorities, immigrant minorities, mainstream educators	Subordinate minorities.	Non-English mother tongue minorities
Precondition	Rejection of cultural and genetic deficit models	Immigrant minorities' demands for ethnic studies	Rejection of majority enforced cultural assimilation	Rejection of majority enforced cultural assimilation
Underlying Value	Compatibility of home and school cultures	Cultural under-standing and cultural relativity	Preservation and extension of ethnic groups	Reciprocal learning
Target Population	Culturally different students	All students	Subordinate minority-group students	All students
Intended Outcomes	Equity in educational benefits	Respect and acceptance of others' right to be different	Increased power for minority groups	Bicultural competencies

Figure 2-3. Approaches to Multicultural Education in the United States[62]

In 1976, Margaret Gibson evaluated various approaches to multicultural education, which fall into the perspective transformation approach. She compares four of them as shown in Figure 2-3, then proposed a fifth conceptualization of multicultural education, stating it "stems from an anthropological perspective on both education and culture and, unlike the others, does not equate education with schooling or view multi-cultural

---

[62] Margaret Alison Gibson, "Approaches to Multicultural Education in the United States: Some Concepts and Assumptions," *Anthropology & Education Quarterly* 7, no. 4 (1976): 7, 15.

education as a type of formal educational program."[63] She then elaborates on these approaches:

> Each of the first four approaches tends to restrict its view of culture to the culture of an ethnic group. This leads to unintentional pigeonholing and stereotyping of students. The fifth approach recognizes that there may be a culture shared by members of an ethnic group. Indeed, it is this shared competence which provides members with a common sense of ethnic identity. But members of the ethnic group will also acquire competence in the cultures of other sets and clusters of people. Such a perspective leads to an exploration of the differences among members of any given ethnic group and of the similarities of persons across ethnic lines. Given that individuals can and normally do develop competencies in multiple cultures, the question for educators is how best to create learning environments which promote rather than inhibit the acquisition of multi-cultural competencies.[64]

4. Restructuring

Another approach to intercultural education is to critique and replace existing educational structures. Zilliacus and Holm criticize movements that do not "question the existing social structure or address issues related to structural inequalities and power."[65] Banks describes a social action level of multicultural education in which "students make decisions on important social issues and take actions to help solve them."[66] Banks sees social action as the goal of multi-cultural education, as he titles it, but recognizes that there can be a progression. He states, "It is not realistic to expect a teacher to move directly from a highly Mainstream-Centric curriculum to one that focuses on decision-making and social action. Rather, the move from the first to the higher levels of ethnic content integration into the curriculum is likely to be gradual and cumulative."[67]

Summary

In this chapter, we have sought to show some of the breadth of intercultural education. We first identified some of the categories of education that are common across cultures, though the approaches and expectations within these categories vary from culture to culture. We then explored some of the historical scope of intercultural education by

---

[63] Gibson, 7.
[64] Gibson, "Approaches to Multicultural Education in the United States," 16.
[65] Harriet Zilliacus and Gunilla Holm, "Multicultural Education and Intercultural Education," 4.
[66] James A. Banks, "Approaches to Multicultural Curriculum Reform," 19.
[67] Banks, "Approaches to Multicultural Curriculum Reform," 18.

highlighting some of the various terms and goals that educators have used over the years.

CHAPTER 3
Theories of ICE and Relational Intercultural Education

Introduction

In this chapter, an overview of theories of ICE will be provided, followed by the introduction and explanation of "relational intercultural education" (RICE).

Theories of Intercultural Education

Theory Feature	Positivist	Relativist	Constructivist	Critical Theory	Relational Interactionist
Epistemology	Absolute	Relative	Subjective & emerging	Objective + subjective	Divinely revealed & enabled human knowledge
Ontology	Objective reality	Relative reality	Subjective reality	Separate or embedded	Relationship & relational network created by interaction
Goal	Explanation & operation	Tentative	Reaching ideal goals	Description & change	To develop competencies in knowledge, attitudes, skills & behaviors.[68]
Research question	5 "Ws" - who, what, why......	How is culture communication?	How is reality constructed by the mind?	How to practice Critical pedagogy	Who & what happenings
Methodology	Objective & separate	Everything relative	Follow subjectively created reality	Contextual & system	Narrative of pattern of interaction

Figure 3-1. Summary of Five Theoretical Frameworks of ICE[69]

---

[68] Perry, Laura B. & Southwell, Leonie. "Developing intercultural understanding and skills: models and approaches." *Intercultural Education* (2011), 22:6, 453-466.

[69] Adapted from "Research Paradigms – Methodologies, Methods, and Practices," January 19, 2023, https://writeprofessionally.org/research-methods/2023/01/19/research-paradigms/.

The following charts will explore these five frameworks in more detail.

Feature Theory	Representative	Distinctive	Critique
Positivist	Cultural dimensions by Geer Hofstede and Fons Trompenaars, John Berry's cross-cultural psychology with his model of acculturation, and cultural assimilator methods.[70] Ruben advocated a behavioral approach of linking the gap between knowing and doing[71], that is, linking the gap between what individuals know to be intercultural competence and what they actually behave in its situations. C. E. Vontress's[72] and J. A. Banks's[73] cross-cultural counseling and intercultural education principles provide the framework for a new counselor education pedagogy	cultural dimensions, John Berry's cross-cultural psychology with acculturation, and cultural assimilator methods.[74]	Naïve reifications of culture. "Reification is the apprehension of human phenomena as if they were things, that is, non-human or possible suprahuman terms... (Berger and Luckmann, 1967)."[75] Cultural hierarchism: Western values of rationality are viewed as a revolutionary innovation in human history, which gives a legitimate reason for retaining authorities over other nations.

Figure 3-2. Five Theoretical Frameworks of ICE: Positivist

---

[70] Bennett, *Basic Concepts of Intercultural Communication*, 27-29.

[71] Ruben, B. D. Assessing communication competency for intercultural adaptation. *Group and Organization Studies*, 1, 334-354, 1976.

Ruben, B. D., & Kealey, D. Behavioral assessment of communication competency and the prediction of cross-cultural adaptation. *International Journal of Intercultural Relations*, 3, 15-48, 1979.

[72] Vontress, C. E. An existential approach to cross-cultural counseling. *Journal of Multicultural Counseling and Development*, 16(2), 73–83, 1988. https://doi.org/10.1002/j.2161-1912.1988.tb00643.x Also, references Vontress previous articles in 1979, 1985.

[73] James A. Banks. The Lives and Values of Researchers: Implications for Educating Citizens in a multicultural Society. *Educational Researcher*, Vol. 27, No. 7, pp. 4-17. published by American Educational Research Association, Oct 1998. http://www.jstor.org/stable/1176055 Also, See Banks 1981, 1993.

[74] Bennett, *Basic Concepts of Intercultural Communication*, 27-29.

[75] Bennett, *Basic Concepts of Intercultural Communication*, 26.

Feature Theory	Representative	Distinctive	Critique
Relativist	Ernest Gellner argues that "Relativism assumes or postulates asymmetrical world. Culture A has its own vision of itself and of culture B, and, likewise, B has its own vision of itself and of A... Each must learn to see the other in terms of the others' own notions (if at all), and this is, presumably, the task and achievement of the hermeneutic anthropologist (1992:56)." This idea of mutual causality and cultural relativism created a new intercultural theory. Edward T. Hall's contribution to intercultural education is the idea that culture is communication. Linguistics relativism was also developed from this perspective (Worf/Sapir Hypothesis, 1956).	Focuses on the systematic understanding of cultural observation and differences using data and analysis to objectify observation and formulate a universal hypothesis on cultures.	Bennett points out that the relativist theory of culture promotes comparative studies of different cultural contexts but does not necessarily enable people to communicate with competence. [76]

Figure 3-3. Five Theoretical Frameworks of ICE: Relativist

Feature Theory	Representative	Distinctive	Critique
Constructivist	J.R. Gellner: "culture is continuously in flux, never static and always contested, even within groups" [77] The observer interacts with reality via his or her perspective in such a way that reality is organized according to that perspective. [78]	Learners build knowledge; one's personal experience determines their reality	Assumes there is no objective reality and that learners have adequate frameworks to process new information [79]

Figure 3-4. Five Theoretical Frameworks of ICE: Constructivist

---

[76] Bennett, *Basic Concepts of Intercultural Communication*, 40.

[77] Geller, J. R. (2017). Terminology and intersections. In B. Kappler Mikk & I. E. Steglitz (Eds.), *Learning Across Cultures: Locally and Globally* (3rd edition). Stylus Publishing, 15.

[78] Bennett, M. J. (2013). *Basic concepts of Intercultural communication: Paradigms, principles, & practices* (2nd ed.). Nicholas Brealey, 99.

[79] Howard Lurie and Richard Garrett, "Deconstructing Competency-Based Education: An Assessment of Institutional Activity, Goals, and Challenges in Higher Education," *The Journal of Competency-Based Education* 2, no. 3 (2017): e01047, https://doi.org/10.1002/cbe2.1047.

Feature Theory	Representative	Distinctive	Critique
Critical Theory	C. E. Vontress's[80] and J. A. Banks's[81] cross-cultural counseling and intercultural education principles provide the framework for a new counselor education pedagogy	Both deductive and inductive studies of culture, which has the positivist element of using scientific methods and relativist idea of configuring subjective meanings from what individuals perceive	The complex elements in intercultural interactions include not only conceptual understanding of culture but also the psychological process of acculturation and practical skills for intercultural communication and competence

Figure 3-5. Five Theoretical Frameworks of ICE: Critical Theory

At its heart, most forms of contemporary intercultural education are political movements for social justice. In 1972, Paulo Freire suggested in *Pedagogy of the Oppressed* that education is at the forefront of combatting dehumanizing authorities.[82] Similarly, Banks has consistently seen intercultural education as a means of empowering social justice.[83] Christine Sleeter sees intercultural education as a means of "resisting oppression."[84]

---

[80] Vontress, C. E. An existential approach to cross-cultural counseling. *Journal of Multicultural Counseling and Development, 16*(2), 73–83, 1988. https://doi.org/10.1002/j.2161-1912.1988.tb00643.x Also, references Vontress previous articles in 1979, 1985.

[81] James A. Banks. The Lives and Values of Researchers: Implications for Educating Citizens in a multicultural Society. *Educational Researcher*, Vol. 27, No. 7, pp. 4-17. published by American Educational Research Association, Oct 1998. http://www.jstor.org/stable/1176055 Also, See Banks 1981, 1993.

[82] Paolo Freire, "Pedagogy of the Oppressed (Revised)," *New York: Continuum*, 1996.

[83] James A Banks, "Teaching for Social Justice, Diversity, and Citizenship in a Global World," vol. 68 (Taylor & Francis, 2004), 296–305.

[84] Christine E Sleeter, "Multicultural Education as a Form of Resistance to Oppression," *Journal of Education* 171, no. 3 (1989): 51–71.

Feature Theory	Representative	Distinctive	Critique
Relational Interactionist	Wan, et al., "Transformational Growth: Intercultural Leadership, Discipleship, Mentorship."	The very essence of Christian education philosophy is that "life is meaningless outside of Christ" and facilitators are to guide learners to the same conclusion.[85] Knight states that Christian education is a "redemptive act" and facilitators are "agents of reconciliation," pointing learners to the Savior is not confined to Christian institutions.	Knight describes teaching as the "art of loving God's children".[86]

Figure 3-6. Five Theoretical Frameworks of ICE: Relational Interactionist

Theoretical Framework of RICE

Theoretical Framework #1: Relational Interactionism

As Christian educators, we should seek a solid framework of intercultural education which involves these three aspects: knowledge (cognitive), attitudes and feelings (affection), skills and behaviors (psychomotor), since we are collaborating with individuals from different backgrounds and all hope for a better life.

Only with the power of God can a person be transformed from inside out. God must be involved in our culture in order for us to experience and undergo true behavioral change (i.e., transformation). From Hammer, Bennett, and Wiseman's perspective, intercultural sensitivity is "the ability to discriminate and experience relevant cultural differences" whereas intercultural competence is "the ability to think and act in interculturally appropriate ways."[87] Together they comprise the knowing and doing of intercultural education.

Gerhard Neuner offers a comprehensive view and description of the factors that need to be considered when introducing intercultural competence development into mainstream curricula. His work mainly focuses on the theoretical foundations with very pragmatic considerations. In his introduction for intercultural education, "It must inspire people's minds, stir their emotions and lend wings to their actions. Such a vision must be convincing in its theoretical foundation, appeal to practitioners, motivate

---

[85] George R. Knight, *Philosophy & Education: An Introduction in Christian Perspective*, Fourth (Berrien Springs, MI: Andrews University Press, 2006), 240–42.
[86] Knight, *Philosophy and Education,* 207–9.
[87] Hammer, Mitchell R., Milton J. Bennett, and Richard Wiseman. "Measuring intercultural sensitivity: The intercultural development inventory." *International journal of intercultural relations* 27, no. 4 (2003): 421-443.

them and support them in their daily work."[88] He focuses on the question of how people can assess whether intercultural competence is or has been developed through three dimensions:

- o The cognitive dimension (knowledge) is learning to know,
- o The affective dimension (emotions/attitudes/values) is learning to be,
- o The pragmatic dimension (skills) is learning to do.[89]

Wan's relational realism[90] emphasizes personal relationship on Beings/beings vertically and angelical and human beings horizontally that can impact an individual's life. From the relational interactionist perspective, we are created in God's image; with the foundation of relational realism, we have the capacity to be transformed and grow into the image of Christ individually and the status of Christ collectively (Eph 4:13). The Word[91] has the power to transform and conform us (the facilitator) into the image of God (Christ-likeness). Christians are to conform into the image of Christ (Rom 8:29; 1 Cor 15:49) by the transforming power of the Triune God and His Word (2 Cor 3:18). With the indwelling Holy Spirit, we can refuse to fit into the stereotype of secular values.[92] Self-awareness can only be actualized by our healthy reliance upon God and with consistent practice of self-reflection.

Spiritual renewal[93] must be intentional for the transformation of our heart and mind into God's likeness. The process of transformation in the context of relational realism not only brings out a dialogical process from ethnocentrism to ethno-relationalism through identity awareness, dialogical relationship, and narrative encounters; but also results in transformative relationships with God, facilitators, and the learners.[94]

Vicki Nishioka, a researcher with Education Northwest and frequent contributor to studies on teacher-student relationships, said, "sometimes teachers don't understand the importance that their relationship with each

---

[88] Gerhard Neuner, "The Dimensions of Intercultural Education," in *Intercultural Competence for All: Preparation for Living in a Heterogeneous World*, Council of Europe Pestalozzi Series, 2 (Council of Europe, 2012), 11.

[89] Neuner, "The Dimensions of Intercultural Education," 34.

[90] Enoch Wan "The Paradigm of Relational Realism", Occasional Bulletin 19, no. 2 (2006): 1, hhttp://www.westernseminary.edu/files/documents/faculty/wan/Relational%20realism-EMS-OBSpring2006.pdf.

[91] John 1:1-4

[92] Like those essentialists or positivists who hold the view that all people in a group show the same characteristics, an extreme stereotype of people.

[93] Romans 8. The Apostle Paul here talked about Christian life through the Holy Spirit, …for those who live in accordance with the Spirit have their minds set on what the Spirit desires. We have an obligation to live by the Spirit, no longer according to the sinful nature.

[94] Wan, Enoch & Siu Kuen Sonia Chan. Contextualization the Asian way: Relational Contextualization. *Asian Mission Advance*. Winter, 2023.

student has on that student's identity and sense of belonging."[95] The consistent marker of successful student relationships across several recent studies is simple: empathy.

A distinction needs to be made between internal positive change, which involves knowledge, skills, awareness, sensitivity, and attitude, and external positive change, which involves improved patterns of interaction.

According to the paradigm of "relational realism" proposed by Enoch Wan and his definition of "culture," an individual's lived experiences[96] with the immutable Triune God can enhance the reality of intercultural interactions and competence within the context of human society. Wan's concept of "culture" is dynamic and with convergence of the tri-systems of "theo-culture," "angel culture" and "human culture."[97] The interactions of personal Beings/beings are dynamic, rigorous, and progressing at three dimensions: cognitive, affective, and behavior aspects. The web of relationships formed by interaction of personal Beings/beings gradually form networks that are dynamic, fluid and complex. "Transformational change" initiated from the Triune God through the Kingdom of light ushers in "transformational change," in contrast to "transgressional change" stemming from the kingdom of darkness.[98] Transformational change impacts the whole person including character, personality, and temperament through the close-knit relationship of an individual with the Triune God (being = God working in me individually) and among fellow Christians (belonging = God working among us collectively). This holistic perspective will make assessment possible by observing the transformational change of the whole person.

The intercultural education framework that is based on relational interactionism[99] consists of important elements that Darla Deardorff suggested in her framework.[100]

> 1. *Attitudes*: Essential attitudes (such as respect, openness, curiosity, and discovery) are to be intentionally cultivated by RICE workers, since these are needed in the practice of RICE. The attitudes of openness

---

[95] Sarah D. Sparks, "Why Teacher-Student Relationships Matter," Education Week, March 12, 2019, https://www.edweek.org/ew/articles/2019/03/13/why-teacher-student-relationships-matter.html.

[96] Living among variations of "human culture" and "theo-culture" of the Triune God.

[97] Enoch Wan & Jon Raibley, *Transformational Change in Christian Ministry*, (Second Edition). Oregon: Western Academic Publishers. 2022: Figure 5.1 - p.41.

[98] See discussions in Wan, Hedinger and Raibley. *Transformational Growth: Intercultural Leadership Discipleship Mentorship. 2022:* Figure 2.7 (p.16).

[99] Enoch Wan "The Paradigm of Relational Realism", Occasional Bulletin 19, no. 2 (2006): 1, hhtp://www.westernseminary.edu/files/documents/faculty/wan/Relational%20realism-EMS-OB-Spring2006.pdf.

[100] Deardorff, Darla K. "The Identification and Assessment of Intercultural Competence as a Student Outcome of Internationalization at Institutions of Higher Education in the United States." *Journal of Studies in International Education* 10:241-266, 2006.

and curiosity imply a willingness and self-awareness to take risks when moving beyond one's comfort zone. Christians are to recognize the equality in dignity of all cultures[101], to realize its "Kingdom's identity"[102], to preserve its cultural identity and to ensure respect for it.[103] If one should desire to communicate "respect" to others, it is important to demonstrate that others are being valued.[104] These attitudes are foundational and essential for development of knowledge and skills needed for intercultural competence.

2. *Knowledge*: All cultures in the world are specific to themselves and not one culture in the world can claim to be universal. For the sake of developing intercultural competence and gaining a cultural knowledge of oneself and others, learning about other cultures is a necessary element for the practice of RICE. It is commonly recognized by researchers and scholars of intercultural studies that the following elements are essential: cultural self-awareness (meaning the ways in which one's culture has influenced one's identity and worldview), culture-specific knowledge and intercultural knowledge including understanding other worldviews, and sociolinguistic awareness. Of the items listed above, the importance of understanding the world from others' perspectives (perspective taking) is most foundational. Differences in cultural features do not break the unity of the universal values[105] that unite people, instead, it enriches people's life.[106]

3. *Skills*: Intercultural skills include ability in acquisition and processing of knowledge through observation, listening, evaluating, analyzing, interpreting, and relating. These skills are invaluable assets in extending the possibilities for comprehensive human cognitive development, mobilizing oneself to derive strength from one's personal past, to acquire elements of other cultures and thrive through this intercultural experience within cross-cultural contexts.

4. *Internal change in Outcomes*: These attitudes, knowledge, and skills ideally lead to an internal outcome that consists of flexibility, adaptability, an ethno-relational[107] perspective, and empathy. These are aspects that occur within the individual as a result of the open attitudes, acquired knowledge and skills necessary for intercultural competence. At this point, individuals are able to see from others'

---

[101] In reference to how God made all mankind equal, He does not show partiality.
[102] I define "Kingdom's identity" as the new identity that found in God's culture.
[103] UNESCO international document "Mexico City Declaration on Cultural Policies"
[104] Scripture tells us that we are all made in God's image.
[105] Universal values such as love, kindness, forgiveness, loyalty, honesty, and many more.
[106] Ivan S. Bakhov. Dialogue of Cultures in Multicultural Education. *World Applied Science Journal* 29 (1): 106-109, 2014. DOI: 10.5829/idosi.wasj.2014.29.01.13775
[107] See the discussion in Wan, Enoch & Siu Kuen Sonia Chan. Contextualization the Asian way: Relational Contextualization. *Asian Mission Advance*. Winter, 2023..

perspectives and to respond to them, not in an ethnocentric way but according to the way in which the other person desires to be treated. Individuals may reach this outcome in varying degrees of success.

5. *External Change in Outcomes*: The summation of the attitudes, knowledge, and skills, as well as the internal outcomes, are demonstrated through the behavior and communication of the individual, which become the visible outcomes of intercultural competence experienced by others. In other words, intercultural competence is the effective and appropriate behavior and successful communication in intercultural situations. It is also important to understand the implications of what is seen to be "effective" and "appropriate" behavior and communication: Effectiveness can be subjectively determined by the individual, whereas appropriateness can only be determined by the other person in such a context. The degree of appropriateness is directly related to cultural sensitivity and the adherence to cultural norms of the person involved.

The five elements described can easily be understood and analyzed in terms of the relational model of Intercultural Interactionism as proposed by Wan and Raibley (2022). The application of their theoretical framework can help in guiding efforts in improving intercultural competence in the practice of RICE.

Enoch Wan, director of the doctoral programs of Intercultural studies and intercultural education at Western Seminary in Portland, Oregon, developed a theological paradigm called "relational realism." This approach is intended to be an alternative to Paul Hiebert's missiological adaption of "critical realism." From the perspective of "relational realism," all existential reality, both its ontology and epistemology, can be viewed as uniformly contingent upon the creator God. More specifically, "relational realism" is "defined as the systematic understanding that 'reality' Is primarily based on the 'vertical relationship' between God and the created order and secondarily 'horizontal relationship' within the created order.[108]"

Wan highlights that just as God is existentially relational within Himself — existing as a single, ontologically uncreated being comprised of three persons (Father, Son and Holy Spirit)—so we too are designed to be in relationship. God calls us to be in vertical relationship with him and as a result, he calls us to impact humanity through horizontal relationship. Understanding our existential reality as being at its very core relational, it is hard to fall into the western traps of individualism and over-rationalism, or into the epistemological quagmire of post-modernity's relativism.

---

[108] Enoch Wan, "Relational Theology and Relational Missiology," *Occasional Bulletin* 21 (2007): 1–8.

Theoretical Framework #2: Educational Theory

Over the last several pages we have considered the relational interactionist theory, one of the foundational perspectives supporting RICE. Educational theory is the other foundation upon which RICE is built. We will briefly look at two elements of educational theory, namely Adult Education and Transformative Learning.

Adult Education
Andragogy, or adult education, is the foundational theory of education that considers education specifically designed for adult learners. Three key theorists for understanding and applying this approach are:
- Eduard Lindemann – one of the fathers of adult education (1926)
- Malcom Knowles – whose work with adult learners led to the widespread use of the word, "andragogy" to distinguish adult education from pedagogy (which deals with the education of children).
- Cranton and Taylor referred to transformative learning theory as "the New Andragogy"[109]

Transformative Learning
Transformative learning is another theoretical foundation for RICE. Several authors have explored the interaction between learning and changing; between education that "downloads" facts compared to education that affects thoughts, feelings, will, and priorities. Some of the major theoretical elements that serve as background for relational interactionist education include Jack Meizirow, Esther Meek, and Stephen Covey.

Jack Mezirow

Jack Meizirow introduced his ideas on transformative learning in 1978. His learning theory is one of the most important recent developments in adult education.

Mezirow's theory is built on the concept of Meaning Perspectives, also called "Frames of Reference." A Frame of Reference is a set of assumptions – broad, generalized, orienting predispositions that act as a filter for interpreting the meaning of experience. Those predispositions (frames of reference) are expressed through points of view, the expression of a habit of mind.

This concept of Meaning Perspectives has dimensions of thought, feeling and will. These perspectives are the "big picture" of a person's understanding of

---

[109] Edward W Taylor and Patricia Cranton, "A Content Analysis of Transformative Learning Theory," n.d.

life: they are wide-ranging in their impact: "They are proposals to experience one's life which involve a decision to take action."[110] "Perspectives are constitutive of experience. They determine how we see, think, feel and behave."[111]

A layer below "Meaning Perspectives" in Mezirow's theory is referred to as "Meaning Schemes." The "Meaning Scheme" layer is more concrete and deals with specific knowledge, beliefs, value judgments, and feelings that are articulated in an interpretation. Groupings of meaning schemes, when considered together, become the expression of a habit of mind.

Due to the key role of meaning perspectives and meaning schemes, the verbal expression of one's thoughts is seen as an important part in adult education. This is explained further by the concepts of:
   Reflective discourse, an important part in the theory of effective learning.
   Active dialog, which is the expression of Hebermas' ideals of rational discourse.[112]

Meaning perspectives are usually formed in childhood through the process of acculturation within one's culture. Three categories of meaning perspectives are recognized:
- Epistemic meaning perspectives - how we know and learn
- Sociolinguistic meaning perspectives (socio cultural meaning) – what we know by way of language and culture
- Psychological meaning perspective – how knowing relates to one's personality, self-concept, any anxieties or inhibitions

When we speak of transformation, it is the transformation of those varying levels of meaning perspectives that we have in mind. Theorists see ten phases in the transformation of meaning perspectives:

- A disorienting dilemma
- Self-examination with feelings of fear, anger, guilt, or shame
- A critical assessment of assumptions
- Recognition that one's discontent and the process of transformation are shared

---

[110] "The Psychology of What Motivates Us," Verywell Mind, accessed October 29, 2024, https://www.verywellmind.com/what-is-motivation-2795378.
[111] David Boud, "Experience and Learning: Reflection at Work. EAE600 Adults Learning in the Workplace: Part A," n.d., https://www.academia.edu/29435057/Experience_and_Learning_Reflection_at_Work_EAE600_Adults_Learning_in_the_Workplace_Part_A.
[112] *Robert J Cavalier, "Introduction to Habermas's Discourse Ethics,"* n.d.

- Exploration of options for new roles, relationships, and actions
- Planning a course of action
- Acquiring knowledge and skills for implementing one's plans
- Provisionally trying new roles
- Building competence and self-confidence in new roles and relationships
- A reintegration into one's life on the basis of conditions dictated by one's new perspective

Esther Meek

Esther Meek's Covenantal Epistemology is another of the foundational educational theories that supports RICE.

Meek's epistemological framework challenges the western epistemic default with the idea that all acts of knowing follow a pattern of covenant relationship. She developed and publicized her theory through a series of publications: *Longing to Know (2003), Loving to Know (2011), A Little Manual for Knowing (2014), and Contact with Reality (2017).* Her approach to education focuses more on the nature of learning and knowing, less on the actions of teaching. Along those lines, she holds that learning is the responsible human response to the struggles of life, and that we learn by focusing on coherent patterns to which we then willfully submit.

Some of her most relevant concepts include:
- The prime evidence of human learning is found in ordinary acts of knowing.
- Her critique of western paradigms of thinking that dichotomize between relativism and absolutism (based on western learnings' "epistemic default" on one hand, and modern, post-modern dichotomies of relativism or absolutism on the other).
- Knowing, as explained by Meek, is characterized not by correspondence, but instead by covenant relationship.
- Knowing is a process resulting in an "act of knowing" rather than knowledge as an entity which one obtains.
- She speaks of the problems of "a Daisy of dichotomies" through which knowledge becomes impersonal and boring (this as a critique of Mezirow's meaning perspective.)
  - Mezirow's approach, in Meek's opinion, overemphasized rational discourse and underemphasized the role of imagination and emotions.

- Theory is the real knowledge while application is secondary and derivative
- Creates division between the disciplines of theology and applied theology
- Meek argues that an act of integration is profoundly human and personal; we must be mindful not to conceive of meaning perspectives in a mechanical or deterministic sense.
- Finally, Meek's covenantal knowledge approach includes what she calls "Subsidiary-Focal Integration:"
  - An assertion regarding the fundamental structure of all acts of knowing
  - Consists of a focal pattern and numerous subsidiary clues
  - Influenced by Polanyi's "tacit knowing." This integration occurs as we "attend *from* the proximal *to* the distal term"[113]
    - In that way, then, acts of knowing always consist of a relation of "from-to."
    - Subsidiary-focal awareness explains the active, personal role of the knower, without necessitating anti-realism or subjectivism
    - Finally, Meek also speaks of the antithesis of learning: Destructive Analysis

Stephen Covey

The last of our theorists in education as transformation is Stephen R. Covey. He identified six paradigms of human interaction.[114] They are:

Win/Win	Lose/Lose
Win/Lose	Win
Lose/Win	Win/Win or No Deal

Theory of Relational Interactionism

Relational interactionism is a narrative approach describing interactions between personal Beings/beings that form relational networks between Triune God, angelic and human beings. It is an interdisciplinary framework developed from practical considerations of interaction of personal

---

[113] Kenneth J. Gergen, "Social Pragmatics and the Origins of Psychological Discourse (Chapter 6)," in *The Social Construction of the Person*, n.d., https://www.researchgate.net/publication/290002177_Social_Pragmatics_and_the_Origins_of_Psychological_Discourse#fullTextFileContent.

[114] https://www.leaderwholeads.com/paradigms-of-human-interaction.html (retrieved Oct. 28, 2024)

Beings/beings forming realistic relational networks, in multiple contexts (e.g. theo-culture, angel-culture, and human culture), at multiple levels. From this narrative framework, several key-terms can be defined as follows:

> "society" as the consequence of dynamic interactions of personal Beings/beings, leading to the formation of a social entity.[115]
> "culture" as the context and consequence of patterned interaction of personal Beings/beings.[116]
> "relational reality" as the complex of networks formed by the patterned interactions of personal beings at both micro and macro levels, in multiple contexts of socio-cultural variations.[117]

The simple study of Gen. 3 below illustratively describes socio-cultural reality being formed, preserved, and changed through repeated and complex relational interaction between personal Beings/beings. There are two kinds of interaction between Triune God, angelic-beings and human-beings in Gen. 3 as defined below:

- Justice-oriented interaction: interaction between personal Beings/being manifesting God's justice and righteousness.
- Grace-oriented interaction: interaction between personal Beings/being manifesting God's grace and mercies.

A narrative study of justice-oriented interaction in Gen. 3 between Jehovah, the snake, Adam and Eve:

- Calling for Adam after the Fall (broken relationship) and he was afraid because of his nakedness and shame 3:8-10 (contrast to "naked but not ashamed" when harmonious relationship was intact (2:25))
- Judgement & curse of the snake: 3:14-15
- Judgement of Eve: 3:16
- Judgement of Adam and the curse of the land: 3:17-19

However, within God's judgement, there are grace-oriented interactions:

- A prophetic pronouncement of "the seed of woman" and Satan (3:15; Gal 4:4-5)
- Instead of the use of fig leaves to cover their own shame (v.7), the Lord God made garments of skin to clothe them (v.21) – a symbolic and prophetic act of the shed blood of Jesus Christ for the remission of sin (Rom 13:11-14; Gal. 3:27; Heb 9:22)

---

[115] Wan and Raibley, *Transformational Change in Christian Ministry*, 9.
[116] Enoch Wan, "A Critique of Charles Kraft's Use/Misuse of Communication and Social Sciences in Biblical Interpretation and Missiological Formation," *Global Missiology, Research Methodology*, October 2004, 29.
[117] Wan and Raibley, *Transformational Change in Christian Ministry*, 9.

A narrative Study of 1Timothy 1: grace-oriented interaction between Jesus Christ and apostle Paul:[118]
- The unworthiness of pre-conversion Saul of Tarsus: 1Tim 1:13
- Grace-oriented interaction between Christ and Paul: 1:14-16

The theological foundation of relational interactionism as found within the Trinity is illustrated in Figure 3-6:

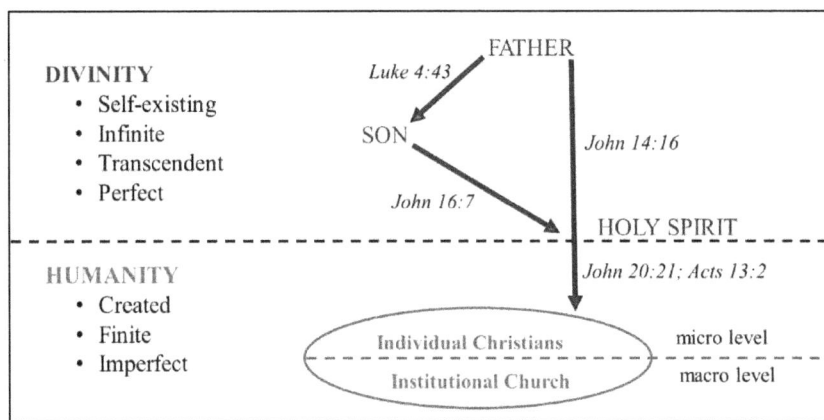

Figure 3-7. The interactive relationship within the Trinity and beyond[119]

The figure below shows "relational interaction model" diagrammatically in comparison to "relational realism" (in earlier publications)[120] and "relational transformation" (in recent publications)[121] by Enoch Wan.

---

[118] I thank Christ Jesus our Lord, who has given me strength, that he considered me trustworthy, appointing me to his service. 13 Even though I was once a blasphemer and a persecutor and a violent man, I was shown **mercy** because I acted in ignorance and unbelief. 14 The **grace of our Lord** was poured out on me abundantly, along with the **faith and love** that are in Christ Jesus.

[119] "Mission" and "Missio Dei": Response to Charles Van Engen's "Mission Defined and Described," In *Missionshift: Global Mission Issues in the Third Millennium,* Edited by David J. Hesselgrave and Ed Stetzer, 2010:44.

[120] Wan, Enoch. "Relational Theology and Relational Missiology." *Occasional Bulletin, Evangelical Missiological Society,* Vol. 21, No. 1 (2007).

—. "The Paradigm of "Relational Realism". *Occasional Bulletin, Evangelical Missiological Society,* Vol. 19, No. 2 (2006).

—. "Theology of Unmerited Favor: Interdisciplinary Study and Practice." (in Chinese), HK: Tien-Dao Publishing. eLibrary. 2016.

[121] Wan, Enoch. 2021. "Narrative Framework for Relational Transformational Change." EMS National Conference, Unpublished manuscript. Western Seminary.

Paradigm Number	Relational Realism	Relational Transformation	Relational Interactionism
Purpose: to show	vertical + horizontal	Transformational change	Dynamic interaction between Beings/beings
Packaging	Static	Dynamic, fluid and processual	
Presentation (audience)	In-house: Christian		Christian + non-Christian

Figure 3-8. Comparison of Three Paradigms

Summary

In this chapter, we contrasted five frameworks which can be thought of as the basis of intercultural education: positivism, relativism, constructivism, critical theory, and relational interaction. We then explored the theoretical bases of alternative approaches: relational interactionism and relational intercultural in education. Next, we will look at the biblical and thematic foundations of relational intercultural education.

Wan, Enoch. "Issues and Practice Related to Intercultural Education: IE701 Lecture PowerPoint Notes," March 2021.

Wan, Enoch. "Relational Transformation Leadership - An Asian Christian Perspective." *Asian Missions Advance* (April 2021). http://www.asiamissions.net/relational-transformational-leadership-an-asian-christian-perspective/.

Wan, Enoch and Howard Shauhau Chen. 2021. *Marketplace Transformation: Motivating and Mobilizing: Chinese Churches in the Silicon Valley for Gospel Transformation.* Western Academic Publishers.

Enoch Wan and Jon Raibley. *Transformational Change in Christian Ministry.* Second Edition Oregon: Western Academic Publishers, 2022.

Enoch Wan , Mark Hedinger, Jon Raibley. *Transformational Growth: Intercultural Leadership/Discipleship/Mentorship.* Oregon: Western Academic Publishers, 2023.

CHAPTER 4:
Biblical and Thematic Foundations

Soo Min (James) Park and Jon Raibley

Introduction

The premise of this book is that education takes place between people, not because of methods or techniques. From that perspective, we have looked at background foundations having to do with education, cross-cultural education, and relational education. In this chapter we move into the biblical and thematic foundations specific to relational interactionism.

We have described relational interactionism as a framework that considers how personal beings form relational networks (belonging) in multiple contexts, with various consequences (becoming). These consequences can be either positive or negative. We have used the term transformational growth to describe positive change which originates from God and impacts people and groups through their horizontal relationships in terms of positive spiritual, moral, social, and/or behavioral change. Transgressional change, on the other hand, is negative influence that results in increased separation from God and others.

James A. Smith discusses the concept of deformative influences in our lives. He states, "Pastors need to be ethnographers of the everyday, helping parishioners see their own environment as one that is formative, and all too often *de*formative."[122] This deformative impact, like transformational growth, can have spiritual, moral, social, and/or behavioral influence on our lives and the lives of those around us.

During a recent doctoral class on "Transformational Change and Intercultural Discipleship" which two of the authors co-taught, students were asked to work in groups to look at people in the Bible who experienced transformational growth or transgressional change. They also examined the theme of salvific grace – God's goodness that reconciles sinners to Himself. Their findings form the basis for the examples and discussion of these themes in this chapter, as we explore the process of 'becoming,' whether that is in positive or negative ways. We conclude by comparing our framework of transformational growth to Jack Mezirow's theory of transformational learning.

---

[122] James K. A. Smith, *You Are What You Love: The Spiritual Power of Habit* (Grand Rapids: Brazos Press, 2016), 40.

Transformational Growth

We will look first at examples of transformational growth in the Bible, which resulted in deeper vertical relationships, and other positive changes.

Naomi and Ruth

Being:

Naomi and Ruth were individual human beings with distinct personalities, values, experiences, and cultural backgrounds. In Ruth chapter 1, we see that Naomi was an Israelite woman who had raised two sons, experienced the difficulty of living in a foreign land for 10 years, and felt the grief of losing her husband and two grown sons. Ruth was a Moabitess, with a different cultural and religious background than Naomi. She was younger and was not a mother but had also suffered the loss of her husband.

Belonging:

Naomi and Ruth shared various connections and interactions that contributed to their shared sense of belonging. They both lived as foreigners in the other person's culture, they had lived together for ten years and had experienced bereavement together. Despite the negative attitude that Jews had toward Moabites (Deut. 23:3), Ruth chose to follow Naomi and stay in relationship with her (Ruth 1:16-17). She also expressed commitment to Naomi by her words and actions and learned Jewish culture and religious practices from her.

When we examine these narrative elements, we see that Ruth showed a willingness to learn, change, and adapt to a different culture as Joseph had in Egypt (Genesis 41:41 and 42:23). She developed trust and favor as Joseph (Gen. 39:21-22) and Daniel (Dan. 1:20, 2;48) did. And she faced uncertainty and hardships with Naomi, as Nehemiah did with the exiles returning to Jerusalem (Neh. 4)

Becoming;

Ruth and Naomi both showed evidence of change in the narrative. Ruth's change was positive and transformational, as she began to follow God (1:16), and became an ancestor of King David, and of Jesus (4:17). Naomi, however, initially shows transgressional change. The story tells us,

> So the two of them went on until they came to Bethlehem. And when they came to Bethlehem, the whole town was stirred because of them. And the women said, "Is this Naomi?" She said to them, "Do not call me Naomi [pleasant]; call me Mara [bitter], for the Almighty has dealt very bitterly with me. I went away full, and the Lord has brought me back empty. Why

call me Naomi, when the Lord has testified against me and the Almighty has brought calamity upon me?" (Ruth 1:19-21).

Naomi identified herself as bitter, afflicted by God, and as one who had suffered loss. By the end of the story, however, she recognized the blessing of the Lord:

Then the women said to Naomi, "Blessed be the Lord, who has not left you this day without a redeemer, and may his name be renowned in Israel! He shall be to you a restorer of life and a nourisher of your old age, for your daughter-in-law who loves you, who is more to you than seven sons, has given birth to him." Then Naomi took the child and laid him on her lap and became his nurse. And the women of the neighborhood gave him a name, saying, "A son has been born to Naomi." They named him Obed. He was the father of Jesse, the father of David. (Ruth 4:14-17).

Paul and Timothy

Paul and Timothy are another example of people who influenced each other for transformational growth.

Being:

Here again we see similarities and differences between them as distinct beings. Paul was a Jew who describes himself as "...advancing in Judaism beyond many of my own age among my people, so extremely zealous was I for the traditions of my fathers." (Gal. 1:14), while Timothy was multicultural, with a Jewish mother and Greek father (Acts 16:1). Paul came to faith in Christ as an adult, as a result of a personal encounter with Jesus (Acts 9:1-19); Timothy was taught to believe in Christ by his grandmother and mother (2 Tim. 1:5), probably when he was a child (2 Tim 3:15).

Belonging:

In terms of belonging, they traveled together on missionary journeys and had a relationship as close as a father and son (Phil. 2:22-23). By birth, Paul belonged to the nation of Israel and the tribe of Benjamin (Phil. 3:5), while Timothy was circumcised as a young adult to be accepted by Jewish believers (Acts 16:3). Together, they belonged to the family of God, and with other believers, were members of the body of Christ, and fellow heirs of God's promises (Eph. 3:6).

Becoming:

Through his teaching and example, Paul influenced Timothy to grow more in godliness (1 Tim. 4:7), discernment (2 Tim. 2:15), and purity (2 Tim. 2:15), to be ready to preach (2 Tim. 4:2), to be more alert (2 Tim. 4:3-4), to endure suffering (2 Tim. 4:5), and to fulfill the call of an evangelist and minister (2 Tim. 4:4). Timothy in turn encouraged Paul; Phil. 2:19-24 states,

> I hope in the Lord Jesus to send Timothy to you soon, so that I too may be cheered by news of you. For I have no one like him, who will be genuinely concerned for your welfare. For they all seek their own interests, not those of Jesus Christ. But you know Timothy's proven worth, how as a son with a father he has served with me in the gospel. I hope therefore to send him just as soon as I see how it will go with me, and I trust in the Lord that shortly I myself will come also.

Here we see that Timothy's service to the churches, as Paul's representative and messenger, not only encouraged the churches, but cheered Paul as well (v. 19), providing encouragement while he was in prison.

There are other examples of transformational change occurring through the interaction and influence that Paul and Timothy had on other believers. The figure below, for example, outlines some of the impact that Paul had in the lives of the Ephesian church.

Area	Reference	Influence
Being	Acts 19:1-12	Has limited understanding of the Gospel
	Acts 19:28-41	Lived in idolatry, unbelief (city riot as transgressional change)
	Eph. 4:13	Infants in the faith
Belonging	Eph. 4:17-24	Paul was an example of godly living
	Acts 20	Paul lived among them, teaching, testifying
Becoming	Eph. 2:1	From dead in sins to alive in Christ
	Eph. 2:10	Participants in good works God has planned for them
	Eph 2:19	Members of household of God; citizens

Figure 4-1. Examples of Paul's Influence on the Ephesian Church

Transgressional Change

We can also look at examples of transgressional change in Scripture, where the people involved become less obedient to God, more distanced from Him, and poorer reflections of His character. We see this process, of course, in the story of the temptation and sin of Adam and Eve.

Adam and Eve

Being:

The beings involved in the narrative of Genesis 3 are the serpent, Eve, Adam, and God. The serpent is a created being who is described as crafty (Gen. 3:1), who questions (3:1) and denies (3:4) God's statements. (3:4). Thomas Constable states, "Probably the tempter was actually Satan, who in this event possessed and controlled a literal snake. Satan came to Eve disguised, unexpected, and using a subordinate, as he still does today."[123] Satan was part of the angel culture[124], which includes both holy and fallen angels. Adam and Eve were both human beings, but not yet with a sin nature. They had the ability to choose to obey or disobey God's commandments.

Genesis 3:6 states, "So when the woman saw that the tree was good for food, and that it was a delight to the eyes, and that the tree was to be desired to make one wise, she took of its fruit and ate, and she also gave some to her husband who was with her, and he ate." Eve's reasons for disobeying God's command parallel the categories of temptation listed in 1 John 2:6, as shown in Figure 4-2.

Category of temptation 1 John 2:16	Temptation of Eve Genesis 3:6	Description of Temptation
Lust of the flesh	Good for food	The desire to *do* something contrary to God's will, i.e., eat the tasty fruit
Lust of the eyes	Delightful to look at	The desire to *have* something apart from God's will, i.e., possess the attractive fruit
Pride of life	Desirable for obtaining wisdom	The desire to *be* something apart from God's will, i.e., as wise as God, or gods)

Figure 4-2. Comparison of 1 John 2:16 and Genesis 3:6[125]

Belonging:

At the beginning of Genesis 3, Adam and Eve are members of a marriage without sin or shame (Gen. 2:25). They belonged to a community within Eden that included God, themselves, and the animals, within a setting without sin or shame. They also belonged to a relationship of direct interaction with God

---

[123] Thomas L. Constable, "Notes on Genesis," Edition 2024, 92, https://www.planobiblechapel.org/tcon/notes/html/ot/genesis/genesis.htm.
[124] Wan, "Rethinking Urban Mission in Terms of Spiritual and Social Transformational Change."
[125] Adapted from Constable, "Notes on Genesis."

(Gen. 2:16). After sinning, Adam and Eve joined the group of disobedient angels who had rejected God's authority. Because of Adam's rebellion, sin affects all humans, resulting in guilt, broken relationships, suffering, and death.[126]

Becoming:

In the process of disobeying God's command, Adam and Eve experienced many transgressional changes that separated them from God, including following lies instead of truth (3:4), broken relationship between God and human beings (Gen. 3:8), shame and fear (3:10), blaming others (3:12-13), pain (3:16-17), futility in work (3:17-19), and death (3:19). In addition, Romans 5 lists other consequences of this rebellion: sin entered the world (Rom. 5:12), death spread to all humans (5:12, 15), and God's judgement brought condemnation (5:16). The good news of Romans 5, of course, is the contrast of Jesus to Adam, who creates transformative change in those who believe in Him:

> But the free gift is not like the trespass. For if many died through one man's trespass, much more have the grace of God and the free gift by the grace of that one man Jesus Christ abounded for many. And the free gift is not like the result of that one man's sin. For the judgment following one trespass brought condemnation, but the free gift following many trespasses brought justification. For if, because of one man's trespass, death reigned through that one man, much more will those who receive the abundance of grace and the free gift of righteousness reign in life through the one man Jesus Christ.[127]

Sodom and Gomorrah

Another example of transgressional change is the story of Sodom and Gomorrah, as given in Genesis 19:1-28, with several New Testament passages that provide commentary on the story, including:

> If by turning the cities of Sodom and Gomorrah to ashes [God] condemned them to extinction, making them an example of what is going to happen to the ungodly; and if he rescued righteous Lot, greatly distressed by the sensual conduct of the wicked (for as that righteous man lived among them day after day, he was tormenting his righteous soul over their lawless deeds that he saw and heard); then the Lord knows how to rescue

---

[126] Christopher Morgan, "The Nature of Sin," The Gospel Coalition, accessed July 8, 2024, https://www.thegospelcoalition.org/essay/the-nature-of-sin/.
[127] Romans 5:15-17

the godly from trials, and to keep the unrighteous under punishment until the day of judgment, [2 Pet. 2:6-9].

Sodom and Gomorrah and the surrounding cities, which likewise indulged in sexual immorality and pursued unnatural desire, serve as an example by undergoing a punishment of eternal fire. [Jude 7]

Being

In these passages, Lot and the residents of Sodom are contrasted, as seen in Figure 4-3. The narrative shows a great clash here in terms of goals, communication styles, the demonstration (or lack of) mutual respect, and willingness to change.

Lot	Residents of Sodom
Hospitality (Gen. 19:3)	Sexual immorality (Gen. 19:5, Jude 7)
Attempted protection of guests (Gen. 19:6-8)	Attempted harm to Lot (Gen. 19:9)
Grateful for rescue (Gen. 19:19)	Destroyed by God (Gen. 19:13, 25; Jude 7)
Afraid of fleeing to the hill country (Gen. 19:19)	
Distressed by the conduct he saw (2 Pet. 4:7-8)	
Declared to be righteous (2 Pet. 4:7-8)	

Figure 4-3. Comparison of the actions and character of Lot with the residents of Sodom

Belonging:

Lot and his family were sojourners in Sodom, and had built relationships with some of the residents, to the point where his daughters were engaged to citizens of the city (Gen. 19:14). But they were still seen as outsiders, as shown in Genesis 19:9. "But they said, "Stand back!" And they said, "This fellow came to sojourn, and he has become the judge! Now we will deal worse with you than with them." Then they pressed hard against the man Lot, and drew near to break the door down." The relationship that Lot had with the residents of Sodom was not one of mutual respect, and the influence which the two groups had on each other was negative and transgressional, rather than transformative.

Becoming:

The transgressional change that Sodom and the neighboring cities experienced was judgement and destruction. Lot, though he escaped the destruction, also suffered negative consequences from his connection with

Sodom. He lost his wife, two potential sons-in-law, his house, and any property he had in the city. He also experienced moral compromise by offering to give his daughters to the residents for abuse and exploitation. It is likely that he also experienced negative physical and emotional suffering from these losses.

Textual Examples

Our class also spent time looking at portions of Paul's writings, to find examples of transformational growth and transgressional change. We color-coded chapters of the text to help identify the various elements. For example, below is I Thessalonians 4:4-18, showing the transformational growth of the believers.

Color key:
  Being   Belonging   Becoming

4 Finally, then, brothers, we ask and urge you in the Lord Jesus, that as you received from us how you ought to walk and to please God, just as you are doing, that you do so more and more. 2 For you know what instructions we gave you through the Lord Jesus. 3 For this is the will of God, your sanctification: that you abstain from sexual immorality; 4 that each one of you know how to control his own body in holiness and honor, 5 not in the passion of lust like the Gentiles who do not know God; 6 that no one transgress and wrong his brother in this matter, because the Lord is an avenger in all these things, as we told you beforehand and solemnly warned you. 7 For God has not called us for impurity, but in holiness. 8 Therefore whoever disregards this, disregards not man but God, who gives his Holy Spirit to you.
9 Now concerning brotherly love you have no need for anyone to write to you, for you yourselves have been taught by God to love one another, 10 for that indeed is what you are doing to all the brothers throughout Macedonia. But we urge you, brothers, to do this more and more, 11 and to aspire to live quietly, and to mind your own affairs, and to work with your hands, as we instructed you, 12 so that you may walk properly before outsiders and be dependent on no one.

13 But we do not want you to be uninformed, brothers, about those who are asleep, that you may not grieve as others do who have no hope. 14 For since we believe that Jesus died and rose again, even so, through Jesus, God will bring with him those who have fallen asleep. 15 For this we declare to you by a word from the Lord, that we who are alive, who are left until the coming of the Lord, will not precede those who have fallen asleep. 16 For the Lord himself will descend from heaven with a cry of command, with the voice of an archangel, and with the sound of the trumpet of God. And the dead in Christ

will rise first. 17 Then we who are alive, who are left, will be caught up together with them in the clouds to meet the Lord in the air, and so we will always be with the Lord. 18 Therefore encourage one another with these words.

   This chapter discusses the roles of God and believers, the vertical and horizontal connections between them, and the transformational growth that is taking place in the believers.

   We also looked at positive and negative change in the book of Galatians. Here are some of the things we found in Galatians chapter 1:1-24, which shows both transformational and transgressional changes;

Color key:
   Being   Belonging   Transformational   Transgressional

1 Paul, an apostle—not from men nor through man, but through Jesus Christ and God the Father, who raised him from the dead— 2 and all the brothers who are with me, To the churches of Galatia:
3 Grace to you and peace from God our Father and the Lord Jesus Christ, 4 who gave himself for our sins to deliver us from the present evil age, according to the will of our God and Father, 5 to whom be the glory forever and ever. Amen.
6 I am astonished that you are so quickly deserting him who called you in the grace of Christ and are turning to a different gospel— 7 not that there is another one, but there are some who trouble you and want to distort the gospel of Christ. 8 But even if we or an angel from heaven should preach to you a gospel contrary to the one we preached to you, let him be accursed. 9 As we have said before, so now I say again: If anyone is preaching to you a gospel contrary to the one you received, let him be accursed.
10 For am I now seeking the approval of man, or of God? Or am I trying to please man? If I were still trying to please man, I would not be a servant of Christ.
11 For I would have you know, brothers, that the gospel that was preached by me is not man's gospel. 12 For I did not receive it from any man, nor was I taught it, but I received it through a revelation of Jesus Christ. 13 For you have heard of my former life in Judaism, how I persecuted the church of God violently and tried to destroy it. 14 And I was advancing in Judaism beyond many of my own age among my people, so extremely zealous was I for the traditions of my fathers. 15 But when he who had set me apart before I was born, and who called me by his grace, 16 was pleased to reveal His Son to me, in order that I might preach him among the Gentiles, I did not immediately consult with anyone; 17 nor did I go up to Jerusalem to those who were

apostles before me, but I went away into Arabia, and returned again to Damascus. **18** Then after three years I went up to Jerusalem to visit Cephas and remained with him fifteen days. **19** But I saw none of the other apostles except James the Lord's brother. **20** (In what I am writing to you, before God, I do not lie!) **21** Then I went into the regions of Syria and Cilicia. **22** And I was still unknown in person to the churches of Judea that are in Christ. **23** They only were hearing it said, "He who used to persecute us is now preaching the faith he once tried to destroy." **24** And they glorified God because of me.

In this chapter we see both transformational growth and transgressional change as people responded in various ways to God's grace and the influence of others.

Theological Components

We've looked at various examples of positive and negative change in Scripture. In this section we will explore some of the theological components of transformational growth and transgressional change by looking at examples of principles of each that are given in scripture. We will divide these into the categories of being, belonging, and becoming, as shown in the figures below. In each category, we also look at how the two types of change can influence each other. Items under the black right-to-left arrow indicate some of the detrimental impact that transgressional change can have on the process of transformational growth. Likewise, statements under the red left-to-right arrow remind us that transformational growth can slow and influence transgressional change.

Transformational Growth	Influence of Changes	Transgressional Change
Image and likeness of God (Gen. 1:26-27) Image of Christ (Rom. 8:29) Chosen, adopted by God (Eph. 1:4) Redeemed, forgiven (Eph. 1:7), justified by faith (Rom. 5:1), sanctified in Christ Jesus (1 Cor. 1:2) Reconciled to God (Rom. 5:10-11, Col. 1:22) Alive with Christ (Eph. 2:4) Reconcilers (2 Cor. 5:18-19)	⬅————— Can affect without causing changes or removal of election, effectual call, adoption, regeneration, redemption, justification by faith, and reconciled vertical relationship with God —————➡ Can affect and alter all aspects of transgressional change	Image of God (Gen. 1:26-27) Alienated from God, hostile to Him (Col. 1:21) Dead in transgressions and sin (Eph. 2:1-2) Whole person affected by sin (Ps. 51:5), Enslaved to passions and pleasures (Titus 3:3), living in the futility of their minds (Eph. 4:17) Idolaters (Eph. 5:5) Attempt to establish own

		righteousness apart from God (Rom. 10:3-4)

Figure 4-4. Example Scriptural components of transformational growth and transgressional change with relation to Being

Transformational Growth	Influence of Changes	Transgressional Change
Heirs of God (Rom. 8:17, Eph. 1:11-14) Members of the kingdom of Christ (Col. 1:13) Members of the church, Christ's body (Col. 1:18) Citizens of heaven; members of God's household (Eph. 2:19) Dependence on God (John 15:4) Partakers of the divine nature (2 Pet. 1:4)	← Belonging: Essential and foundational belonging unaffected in the vertical Perception regarding vertical can be weakened followed by various forms of spiritual oppression and setbacks Horizontal relationships can weaken or deteriorate in the visible aspect of belonging → Can affect and alter all aspects of transgressional change	Belong to the domain of darkness (Col. 1:13, 1 John 5:19) Followers of the prince of the power of the air; children of wrath (Eph. 2:2-3) Separated from Christ (Eph. 2:12) Slaves of sin (Rom. 6:20-21) Self-centered, selfish ambition (Ja. 3:14) Under teaching and influence of demons (1 Tim. 4:1)

Figure 4-5. Example Scriptural components of transformational growth and transgressional change with relation to Belonging

Transformational Growth	Influence of Changes	Transgressional Change
Holy and blameless (Eph. 1:4) Mature in Christ (Eph. 4:13-15) Eternal demonstration of God's rich grace (Eph. 2:7) Sharers in God's eternal glory through Christ (1 Peter 5:10) Recipients of eternal life (John 5:24, Rom. 5:21) Greater display of fruit of the Spirit (Gal. 5:22-23) Spiritual resurrected bodies (1 Cor. 15:42-44) Reign with Christ (2 Tim. 2:12) Conformed to the image of His Son (Rom. 8:29)	← Becoming: temporal spiritual and moral weakening, but the ultimate trajectory unaltered → Can affect and alter all aspects of transgressional change	Trajectory of sin: evil people will go from bad to worse (2 Tim. 3:13) Deceiving and being deceived (2 Tim 3:13) Recipients of judgement and eternal destruction (2 Thes. 1:9, 2 Pet. 3:7) Greater display of fruit of the flesh (Gal. 5:19-21) Eternal separation from the favorable presence of God (Rev. 21:8) Accumulating wrath for the day of judgment (Rom. 2:5) Increasing in lawlessness (Matt. 24:12)

Growing in grace and knowledge of Christ (2 Pet. 3:18) Transformation through renewal of the mind (Rom. 12:2)	

Figure 4-6. Example Scriptural components of transformational growth and transgressional change with relation to Becoming

Transgressional affects can be prevented by the following mechanisms:
- Prayerfulness
- Spiritual warfare
- Discernment and wisdom
- Knowledge of the truth of God's word
- Reliance on the armor of God (Eph. 6: 10-20)
- Intentional awareness of the presence of God
- Dependence on the Spirit of God

Similarly, transformational affects can be prevented from having their effects in the following ways:
- Self-reliance
- Hardening of heart
- Lack of trust in God
- Persisting in a self-centered perspective
- Listening to lies rather than God's truth
- Lack of true repentance

Ephesians 5:15-17 and similar scriptures remind us of the importance of choosing to act in ways that bring about transformational growth: "Look carefully then how you walk, not as unwise but as wise, making the best use of the time, because the days are evil. Therefore do not be foolish, but understand what the will of the Lord is."

Theological Foundations for Transformational Growth

We will now look at some of the specific theological principles that Scripture discusses with respect to transgressional growth.

Rebirth, Reconciliation, Restoration

All transformational growth stems from the rebirth, reconciliation, and restorative (interactional) work of God. This growth is a natural and inevitable consequence of the new life that initiates at spiritual rebirth and is made possible only through faith in Christ, by applying His reconciling work through His righteous life and substitutionary atonement at the cross[128]. Growth is the process of restoring God's fullness in Christ. God intended to give the full restoration of the likeness of God to His elect from eternity.[129] The full restorative process of the likeness along with all sanctifying grace will culminate in the glorified state of the believer at the time of consummation.

Nature of Transformational Change

The nature of transformational growth is correlated and interconnected to the nature of sanctification and grace as the growth is the result and manifestation of the latter two. Although various, all forms of transformational growth result in greater relational connection with Triune God, obedience to God's laws and commands, greater transformational influence horizontally, and Christocentric cognitive, affective, and behavioral development and advancement. Transformational growth is holistic and includes being, knowing, and doing.[130]

Directionality and Mechanism

Transformational growth always results in further restoration and reflection of *Imago Dei* in a redeemed individual. Furthermore, such restoration and reflection cause greater glory to God, greater closeness to God, and greater holiness and purity (blamelessness) within and for the redeemed individual spiritually.[131] Although transformational growth can be taxonomized into more specific types and categories, these are caused through involvement, teaching and learning, reminder, repetition, and application of the Word, prayer, fellowship and interaction within the body, the presence of God, and the practice of spiritual disciplines described in the Scriptures.

Trajectory of Transformational Growth

All transformational growth in individuals stems from the inception of regeneration by the Holy Spirit. From then on, a redeemed individual goes

---

[128] Belgic Confession Article 20, 24; Westminster Larger Catechism Question and Answer 30; Westminster Shorter Catechism Question and Answer 25.

[129] Belgic Confession Article 37; Heidelberg Catechism Question and Answer 86.

[130] Enoch Wan and Jon Raibley, *Transformational Change in Christian Ministry* (Portland, OR: Western Academic, 2022) 62; Belgic Confession Article 24; Westminster Confession of Faith Chapter 13; Westminster Larger Catechism Question and Answer 75; Westminster Shorter Catechism Question and Answer 35.

[131] Belgic Confession Article 24; Westminster Confession of Faith Chapter 13; Westminster Larger Catechism Question and Answer 30, 75; Westminster Shorter Catechism Question and Answer 35, 38.

through various stages of growth toward full maturity in Christ and glorification in the eschaton.[132]

Transformational Interactions

Transformational growth is contingent upon transformational interactions. This is because human beings are dependent beings through relational matrices we are immersed in; no human being can bring ontological changes to himself on his own. Interactions leading to transformations are majorly confined to interactions with Triune God, Christian-to-Christian interactions through the body and communities, and interactions with angelic beings.[133] Although human agents are involved (e.g. Acts 10; 15:1-35), transformational growth is characterized by taking place in the presence of God, and no transformational growth is possible outside God's involvement in the process.

Perichoresis

The harmony and unity found in loving interactions within the Trinity provides the model and guideline for interactions for transformational growth. As such, transformational growth is facilitated by reciprocity, love, peace, mutuality, dialogue, understanding, agreement, and togetherness.

Theological Foundation for Transgressional Change

Establishing a robust theological foundation on transgressional change is important for both theoretical and practical purposes. With a well-grounded theological understanding, Christian scholars and educators can more effectively diagnose, analyze, and evaluate human changes in various cultures and scenarios, and can devise scriptural strategies and educational praxis to prevent, minimize, or alter the course of transgressional changes by the grace of God. The following paragraphs highlight some of the fundamental themes that are essential in this theological foundation.

Total Depravity

Total depravity provides the reasons and explanations for the transgressional behaviors of unregenerated human individuals. Inherited from the fall, unregenerate human beings are separated from God, spiritually dead, and ontologically unable to do good on their own.[134] This condition

---

[132] John Murray, *Redemption Accomplished and Applied* (Grand Rapids, MI: Wm. B. Eerdmans Publishing, 1955), 177-183; Belgic Confession Article 24.
[133] Wan and Raibley, *Transformational Change in Christian Ministry*, 41-43.
[134] Total depravity does not indicate the attainment of the utmost degree of deformation and transgressional change, but rather, describes the effect of sin's utter pervasiveness to all areas of life in an unregenerate individual.

affects all faculties of a fallen man (cognitively, affectively, behaviorally) and all aspects and areas of his life.[135]

Original Sin

After Adam and Eve's fall, their rebellion against God's command resulted in the transmission of a sinful nature to all their posterity.[136] The result is that all human beings, born under natural human relationships, are born under sin, which in turn implies that all human beings' thoughts, attitudes, and actions flow in connection to the original sin and results inevitably in actual sins, unless intervened by Divine grace.[137]

Nature of Transgressional Change and the Nature of Sin

The nature of transgressional change is correlated to the nature of sin as the former is the result and manifestation of the latter. Consequently, the nature of transgressional change is also influenced by the degree and kinds of sin the change is related to. There are various forms of transgressional change, but they are all rooted in rebellion against God, separation and alienation from God, disobedience to His laws and commands, and a humanistic and man-centered focus. Since transgressional change is dependent on the kind and participation in sin as its cause, the degree of change or deformation is correlational to the degree and amount of involvement with a sin.[138]

Directionality and Mechanism

Transgressional changes always result in the suppression and distortion of *imago Dei* (image of God) in human individuals. Although transgressional changes can be taxonomized into more specific types and categories, these are caused in the progression of the pursuit or indulgence in desire of the flesh, desires of the eyes, and the pride of life (1 John 2:16). Such progression, apart from God's intervening grace, results in further distance from God, hardening of one's heart, and further futility that accompanies negative fruit.[139]

---

[135] Louis Berkhof, *Systematic Theology* (New Combined Edition; Grand Rapids: Eerdmans, 1996), 184. Heidelberg Catechism Question and Answer 8; Westminster Confession of Faith 6:2-4.

[136] Louis Berkhof, *Systematic Theology*, 184; Belgic Confession Article 15.

[137] Westminster Larger Catechism Question and Answer 25; Westminster Shorter Catechism Question and Answer 18.

[138] Westminster Larger Catechism Questions and Answers 150-151; Westminster Shorter Catechism Question and Answer 83.

[139] Heidelberg Catechism Question and Answer 8.

The Trajectory of Transgressional Change

All transgressional change stems from original sin and the sinful nature inherited from the fall, and if unimpeded, results in eternal judgment, torment, and punishment[140]. While transgressional change can occur in a redeemed Christian's life for a period of time, it differs from that of the non-elect in that the elect's transgressional change is always overcome and overwhelmed by the intervening work of the Triune God through the imparting and bestowing of transformational grace.[141] Although redeemed individuals may struggle with the sinful nature that resides within them, with regeneration, with no excuse for persisting in sin, and with the abundance of grace available in Christ, the redeemed can overcome sin. They are able to experience a different terminus for the trajectory of change than the non-elect based on the merit of Christ through faith.[142]

Transgressional Interactions

Transgressional changes occur through transgressional interactions. These interactions can be influenced by demonic entities in the spiritual realm, individual human beings belonging to the kingdom of darkness, indulgence in or inclinations toward sinful desires, and sometimes by redeemed Christians speaking and behaving in misalignment with spiritual truths or by not pursuing and following the leading and counsel of the Holy Spirit.[143] These influences collectively contribute to a progressive deviation from God's will and further entrenchment in sin. This highlights the need for divine intervention and the transforming power of Christ given through the Holy Spirit.

Natural Law

Although values, beliefs, and customs differ across cultures, a moral norm is given to all for their awareness of their transgressional state unaided by the salvific grace available through the Son (Rom. 1:18-20). Despite this awareness, fallen man is unable to change the transgressional trajectory apart from the intervention and aid of someone on a different ontological trajectory.[144]

---

[140] Belgic Confession Article 37; Westminster Confession of Faith 6.6, 33.2; Westminster Larger Catechism Question and Answer 89; Westminster Shorter Catechism Question and Answer 19; Gal. 5:19-21.

[141] Westminster Confession of Faith 13.3.

[142] Westminster Confession of Faith 5.7.

[143] Westminster Confession of Faith Chapter 13.

[144] Stephen J. Grabill, *Rediscovering the Natural Law in Reformed Theological Ethics* (Grand Rapids, MI: Wm. B. Eerdmans, 2006); Heidelberg Catechism Question and Answer 8; Westminster Confession of Faith Chapter 9. Westminster Larger Catechism Question and Answer 27; Westminster Shorter Catechism Question and Answer 19.

Salvific Grace Leading to Transformation

Introduction

Transformation is only possible for humanity through the saving grace of God. Therefore, establishing scriptural and theological foundations for salvific grace is essential to deepen our understanding of transformational processes, operational dynamics, transformation-inducing elements, transformation-favoring relationships, and the nature of transformation itself. The following section examines various graces in an individual's journey of salvation with an emphasis on gospel-centered transformation focused on two essential foundations.

Scriptural Foundations

Numerous salvific graces contribute to the transformation of a redeemed individual throughout the person's journey of salvation. Although these salvific graces were planned and conceived by the Triune God before the foundation of the world through *pactum salutis* (the covenant of redemption), the various graces which pertain to a redeemed individual can be portrayed to take significant roles in different ontological stages of the relational transformational paradigm of being, belonging, and becoming. The following outlines these in three stages characteristic of relational transformation.

Being. Types of salvific grace given by Triune God to an individual being for salvation include:

- election (Eph.1:4), predestination (Rom. 8:29), effectual call (Rom. 8:28), impartation of salvific faith (Eph. 2:8-9),
- rendering of repentance (Ezek. 36:26-27, Acts 11:18), forgiveness of sin (Eph. 1:7, Col. 1:13-14), regeneration (John 3:3-7, Titus 3:5), conversion (John 3:3)
- Adoption into the household of God (Rom. 8:15-17, Eph. 1:5) and new identity (i.e. child of God-Gal. 3:26, redeemed-Col. 1:13-14, citizen of heaven-Phil. 3:20-21, coheir with Christ-2 Tim. 2:12, ambassador of Christ- 2 Cor. 5:20, priest like king-1 Pet. 2:9, new creation-2 Cor. 5:17, etc.)
- Crucifixion of sinful desires, denial of self, and submission to Christ and to His words (Rom. 6:6-7, Gal. 2:20)
- Restoration of vertical relationship with Triune God and true worship (1 Cor. 6:17, John 4:23-24, 2 Cor. 5:18-19)
- Participation in Christlike character (2 Pet. 1:3-4)

- *duplex beneficium* which is the imputation of Christ's righteousness (Rom. 3:21-22, Phil. 3:8-9) and the imputation of the person's sin onto Christ (Isa. 53:5-6, 2 Cor. 5:21)) and union with Christ (Rom. 5:1-2,1 Cor. 6:17, 2 Cor. 5:18-19,21)
- Knowledge of the Son and the Father, and eternal life (John 17:7)

Belonging. Salvific grace given by Triune God to a redeemed individual's belonging for salvation include:

- Sacraments (Acts 2:38, Matt. 28:19-1 Cor. 11:23-26)
- Preached words and inscripturated words (Eph. 3:7-8, Col. 1:28-29, 1 Thess. 2:13)
- Fellowship within the body (Acts 2:42, 1 Thess. 5:11, 14, Heb. 3:13, 1 John1:7)
- Exercising of different spiritual gifts in the body for strengthening and edification (Rom. 12:4-6, 1 Cor. 12:12-14, 1 Pet. 4:10-11)
- Carrying one another's burden and complementarity through diverse perspectives and experiences within the body (Gal. 6:2,1 Cor. 12:12-27)
- Communal worship, corporate identity, communal narrative making (Ps. 113:1-3, Matt. 18:20, Acts 2:42-47, Rom. 15:5-6, 1 Pet. 2:9)
- Connection within the body for edification and reciprocal learning and teaching (Rom. 12:4-5, Col. 3:16, 1 Thess. 5:11)
- Shared vision, goal, and destination (Ps. 113:1-3, Rom. 12:4-6, Phil. 2:2, 1 Cor. 1:10, 1 Pet. 4:10-11, Heb. 10:24-25)
- Reciprocity and mutuality with one another in the body (Rom. 12:10, 1 Cor. 12:25-26)
- Love, faith, and hope in the faith community (John 13:34-35, Rom. 15:13, 1 Cor. 8:1b, Gal. 5:6, Heb.10:23)
- Christ's special presence for gathered believers (Matt. 18:20)
- Inclusivity and horizontal relationships (Matt. 11:28-30, Gal. 3:28, Col. 3:15)
- Opportunities to receive mentorship, discipleship, coaching, counseling, training, and teaching (Matt. 28:19-20, Heb. 10:24-25, 1 Thess, 5:11)
- Developing deep roots in the gospel through iteration and reverberation through interactions and reflective discourse within the body (Rom. 10:17, Col. 3:16, Phil. 3:1, 2 Pet. 1:12-13)
- Hermeneutical community to deepen one's understanding and learning in the inscripturated words and relationships primarily with Triune God and secondarily with others (Col. 3:16).
- Bearing fruit in the kingdom and glorifying God (John 15:8, Rom. 15:5-6, Col. 1:9-10, Phil. 1:9-11)

Becoming. Salvific grace given by Triune God to a redeemed individual's becoming include:

- Inner renewal and perspective transformation (2 Cor. 2:14)
- Progressive sanctification (1 Thess. 4:3, Phil. 2:12)
- Perseverance until eschaton (Phil. 1:6)
- The Holy Spirit drawing the individual closer to the Triune God (John 14:26, Rom. 8:14-16, 1 Cor. 2:12)
- Transformational growth cognitively, affectively, and behaviorally through the Holy Spirit's teaching, counseling, conviction, illumination, and guidance (John 14:26; 16:13, 16:17, 1 Cor. 2:12, Gal. 5:16)
- Greater intimacy with Triune God (John 15:4-5, Eph. 3:17-19)
- Greater love for Triune God and for others (Gal. 5:22, Phil.1:9, Heb.10:24)
- Fulfilling the callings and mission of God (Matt. 28:19-20, Rev. 7:9-10)
- Growth in knowledge and understanding of Triune God and concerning His words (John 14:26, Col. 1:10, 3:9, 2 Pet. 3:18)
- Bearing more fruit in the kingdom (John 15:8, Col.1:10, Phil. 1:11)
- Greater horizontal transformational influence (2 Cor. 3:18)
- Increased volitional strength and self-control for refusing false, wrong, and evil, and in seeking good, true, right, excellent, and noble (Phil. 4:8, 2 Pet. 1:5-7)
- Perfect unity within the body and attaining the measure of the fullness of Christ (Eph. 4:13)

Theological Foundations

While there are many theological foundational layers for the salvific grace leading to transformation, certain essential theological underpinnings must be addressed. These layers are critical for advancing discussions and research on the transformational paradigm, ensuring theological coherence, guarding against heretical assertions, and faithfully representing the scriptural paradigmatic aspects of transformation inherent in relational paradigms for relational education. The following paragraphs briefly address some of these essential and foundational theological underpinnings.

Pactum Salutis and the Eternal Decree of Triune God

All grace for an individual after the fall is contingent upon the Sovereign decree of Triune God onto salvation, not based on any merit of mere human beings and derived from any firsthand choice of mere human beings, but based on the mysterious intra-Trinitarian covenant of redemption (*pactum salutis*) in eternity.[145] All transformational grace which begins with election and that extends to glorification in the *ordo salutis* (order of salvation) is therefore an unfolding of the divinely initiated intra-Trinitarian covenant and is carried and accomplished by the Three Persons of the Trinity (Rom. 8:30).

Covenant Theology

The nature and the kind of relationship, interactions, and grace involved between Triune God and human beings are characterized by the kind of covenant an individual being is in with God. The scripture provides two overarching paradigms of covenants: covenants of works (Adamic/Covenant of Creation (Gen. 2:16-17)) and covenants of grace (Abrahamic (Genesis 12:1-3; 15:1-21; 17:1-27), Davidic Covenant (2 Samuel 7:8-16), New Covenant (Hebrews 8:6-13; Luke 22:20), etc.). Although common grace is bestowed upon all of humanity, salvific grace is exclusively confined to participants of covenants of grace through salvific faith in Christ as personal Lord and Savior.

Missio Dei

Salvific grace is anchored in the missional nature of God. Transformation, driven by the Divine character, involves active participation of all three Persons of the Trinity in man's salvation and in his ongoing sanctification, and this work of the three Persons is characterized by unity and harmony of *perichoresis*.[146] Therefore, each stage of transformational progression aligns with God's redemptive metanarrative and is characterized by its doxological intent, purpose, result, and unfolding (Eph. 1:5-6).[147]

Two-Age Eschatology

A regenerated human being undergoes transformational changes characterized by the eschatological tensions of the 'already' and 'not yet.' However, this transformational process culminates definitively with the manifestation of grace leading to glorification. At this final stage, transformation ceases with the arrival of perfect freedom from sin, a resurrected spiritual body, and complete knowledge perfectly suited for the glorified state of the believer. With glorification, the two-age eschatology marked by the 'already' and 'not yet' aspects of transformation comes to an

---

[145] Belgic Confession Article 16; Westminster Confessions Chapter 3; Westminster Larger Catechism Question and Answer 12; Westminter Shorter Catechism Question and Answer 7.

[146] Westminster Confession Chapter 2; Westminster Larger Catechism Question and Answer 9; Westminster Shorter Catechism Question and Answer 6; Stephen Seamands, Ministry in the Image of God: The Trinitarian Shape of Christian Service (Downers Grove, IL: IVP Books, 2009),142.

[147] Ralph D. Winter, "The Future of Evangelicals in Mission, in *Missionshift: Global Mission Issues in the Third Millenium*, ed. David Hesselgrave and Stetzer (Nashville, TN: B&H Academic, 2010).

end, as the believer enters into the fullness of God's presence and glory where there is no longer a 'not yet' in the *ordo salutis*.[148]

Creator and Creature Distinctions

Salvific grace for transformation is instilled in individual elect human beings within circumscribed trajectories of transformations permitted for them as creatures. This implies that there is no transfer of Divine essence into the creature before or after the glorification, and that grace is given to a man to bring about transformational changes within circumscribed trajectories particular to the nature of man. Such distinction preserves the essence and the nature of human transformation against pantheism and panentheism where Divine transcendence is overlooked.[149]

Monergism

Some salvific graces that lead to transformation are monergistic in their ontological nature (requiring no involvement of human will nor human response and carried solely by Divine initiatives and actions; election, predestination, regeneration, adoption, etc.).[150] While many salvific graces remain monergistic, certain transformations and transformational processes within individuals have both monergistic as well as synergistic components in the operations of various salvific grace.

Synergism (Individual and Corporate)

Some forms of salvific grace leading to transformation are characterized as individually synergistic whereby human beings cooperate and partake in the transformational events or steps volitionally at individual levels (sanctification, perseverance, responding with faith, etc.).[151] Moreover, some salvific grace to transformation is characterized as communally synergistic whereby human beings cooperate and partake volitionally under the more direct horizontal influence of other human beings through communal (corporate) settings.

---

[148] Richard Baxter, cited in *A Puritan Golden Treasury*, compiled by I.D.E. Thomas (Carlisle, PA: Banner of Truth, 2000), 24; Wayne Grudem, *Systematic Theology: An Introduction to Biblical Doctrine* (Zondervan Publishing and InterVarsity Press, 1994), 828; John Murray, *Redemption Accomplished and Applied* (Grand Rapids, MI: Wm. B. Eerdmans Publishing, 1955), 166-173.

[149] Westminster Confessions 7.1.

[150] Westminster Confession 9.3-9.4; Westminster Larger Catechism Question and Answer 67, Westminster Shorter Catechism Question and Answer 31.

[151] Heidelberg Catechism Question and Answer 86-129.

Concursus Divinus (Divine Concurrence)

God is sovereign over all transformations whether they are monergistic or synergistic. Through *concursus*, God accomplishes everything according to His Divine will even in synergistic participation and cooperation.[152] Consequently, grace remains truly grace and is not ultimately dependent on man's intrinsic effort or intrinsic merit; even man's endeavor and volitional participation toward transforming direction and good, is a result of grace (1Cor 15:10, Phil 2:12-13).[153]

Exclusivism and Union with Christ

Exclusivism and union with Christ are at the core of all true ontological transformations of man. Since transformation, in a scriptural sense, is viewed as requiring a fundamental and ontological change in one's nature and orientation to God from spiritual deadness through union with Christ, transformation not only encompasses psychological and sociological aspects, but is also spiritual.[154]

Duplex Beneficium and Substitutionary Atonement

All human transformation hinges upon Christ's sinless incarnation and His meritorious works of righteous living and Divine sacrifice. This is because the transformation of fallen human beings and the restoration of the imago Dei are only possible through the only God-man, through whom a human being's sin can be done away with via *duplex beneficium* of Christ.[155] Christ Jesus, as revealed in the gospel, is not only the absolute and necessary foundation for a transforming process, but is the reason and place where all transformations themselves exist and take place.

Divine Accommodation and Contextualization

Transformational change is not independent on the culture in which an individual is embedded. While grace is sovereignly determined and administered by the Triune God and its essence remains unchanged, it is manifestly contextual and can vary based on an individual's culture, situation,

---

[152] Westminster Confession 5.1; Belgic Confession Article 13.

[153] Refer to the following for more discussions and elaborations on concursus: Michael Horton, *The Christian Faith: A Systematic Theology for Pilgrims on the Way* (Grand Rapids: Zondervan, 2011), 544-552.

[154] Heidelberg Catechism Question and Answer 20; Belgic Confession Article 22; Westminster Confession 8.5; Westminster Larger Catechism Question and Answer 39, Westminster Shorter Catechism Question and Answer 21.

[155] Belgic Confession Article 20, 22; Heidelberg Catechism Questions and Answers 37, 60; Westminster Confession 8; Westminster Larger Catechism Question and Answer 49, Westminster Shorter Catechism Question and Answer 25.

narrative and historical background, and needs. Consequently, although transformations may be evident, they must be evaluated through their fruits and their alignments with scriptural norms.

Comparisons of Relational Transformational Change Paradigm and Jack Mezirow's Transformational Learning Theory

The relational transformational change paradigm, based on relational realism and interactionism, has many commonalities as well as many distinctive theoretical and mechanistic features compared to Jack Mezirow's transformational learning theory. Delineating these commonalities and distinctions is crucial because Mezirow's transformational learning is insufficient to describe and prescribe the epistemological mechanisms that underline transformational learning in relational interactionism. Furthermore, the failure to delineate the commonalities and distinctions can lead to inaccurate and incorrect educational prescriptions, inappropriate teaching techniques, erroneous teaching strategies, mistaken educational methods, and incorrect theoretical formulations and applications. Although relational transformational change has many similarities with Mezirow's transformational learning theory, there are many conspicuous differences that cannot be reconciled between the two. The following paragraphs briefly sketch some of the major commonalities and distinctions of the two in terms of their focus, approach (transforming mechanisms), transformational logic, domains of learning, ontological boundaries and progression, epistemic norms, core elements, conducive conditions for transformation, and phases of change.

Focus of Transformation

Although both paradigms offer perspectives on transformational change and the processes involved, the relational transformational change paradigm differs in its Christocentric and holistic focus from Mezirow's transformational learning theory's self-centric and cognitive focus. Relational transformational change emphasizes the Person of Christ, orientation to Christ, the will and activity of Christ, the glory of Christ, and the covenant and sovereign lordship of Christ. In contrast, Mezirow's transformational learning theory emphasizes self-awareness, self-discovery, self-agency, and self-autonomy in the process. Additionally, relational transformational change spans spiritual, relational dynamics, cognitive, affective, and behavioral processes, whereas Mezirow's theory is predominantly focused on the cognitive process in the overall change[156].

Transforming Mechanism (Approach)

Both paradigms embrace human reasoning, but relational transformational change is more relational and covenantal, while Mezirow's theory is more individualistic and critically self-focused. Relational transformational change views all transformational change as interpersonal, contingent upon one's vertical relational interactions with God and horizontal interactions with others. It posits that the foundational meaning perspective is an individual's orientation towards Christ.[157] In contrast, Mezirow's theory reduces the relational aspect, emphasizing individual autonomy and critical self-outlook.[158]

Since relational transformational change is covenantal, it holds that transformational change cannot occur in the absence of vertical interaction with God, even with horizontal interactions present.[159] Mezirow's theory, neglecting this covenantal approach, anchors the act of knowing primarily on individualism and self-autonomy.

Transformational Logic

Both paradigms incorporate James E. Loder's five steps of transformational logic: conflict, interlude for scanning, constructive act of imagination, release and openness, and interpretation.[160] However, they differ in integrating Loder's four human dimensions: "the lived world," "self," "the void," and "the Holy."[161] Relational transformational change considers all

---

[156] Although Mezirow 's theory involves dialogical and some social aspects, the theory heavily relies on the cognitive process of an individual while others serve to aid or facilitate this. Mezirow states, "I believe an act of learning can be called transformative only if it involves a fundamental questioning and reordering of how one thinks or acts." Stephen D. Brookfield, "Transformative Learning as Ideology Critique," in *Learning as Transformation: Critical Perspectives on a Theory in Progress* (San Francisco: Jossey-Bass, 2000), 139.

[157] Ryan Gimple and Enoch Wan, *Covenant Transformative Learning: Theory and Practice for Mission* (Portland, OR: Western Academic Publishers, 2021), 68.

[158] Susan Collard and Michael Law, "The Limits of Perspective Transformation: Critique of Mezirow's Theory," *Adult Education Quarterly* 39.2 (1989): 99-107; Tom Inglis, "Empowerment and Emancipation," *Adult Education Quarterly* 48.1 (1997): 3-17.

[159] Even in the case of the first transformational change of non-believers' conversions, it is the vertical interaction that ultimately draws, regenerates, imparts faith, causes the person to repent, adopts, and establishes salvific relationship with Triune God.

[160] James E. Loder, *The Transforming Moment* (Colorado Springs: Helmers & Howard Pub, 1989), 35.

[161] The four components which each connect to human dimensions are labeled by James Loder as "a four-fold knowing event"; James E. Loder, *The Transforming Moment* (Colorado Springs: Helmers & Howard Pub, 1989), 64-91.

four dimensions, while Mezirow's theory focuses mainly on the self and context.[162]

Domains of Learning

Relational transformational change views instrumental and communicative learning on a continuum, whereas Mezirow's theory dichotomizes them. This continuum is essential for relational transformational change, as knowing in every sense is considered interpersonal and a result of relational interactions.[163] Additionally, while both paradigms accept dialogical roles, relational transformational change expands the ideals of rational discourse within the transformation causative process.[164]

Ontological Boundaries and Progression

Although both paradigms accept general revelation for human interactions and in epistemic domains, the relational transformational change paradigm goes beyond the general and embraces both general and special revelation. Such stances on revelation have several essential implications and distinctions regarding their ontological boundaries and progressions of transformation in their respective spheres of learning.

Due to the lack of special revelation in guiding of the epistemic process, Mezirow's transformational learning is circular (impenetrable to another ontological state), bounded in the ontological state of *non posse non pecarre* (not able to not sin), and is relativistic in defining the ontological nature of transformational change. Nevertheless, with both general and special revelation guiding the epistemic process within the relational matrix with proper relational vertical connection, relational transformational change is ontologically progressional either from *non posse non peccare* into *posse non peccare* (able not to sin) or progressional in the state of regenerated state (*posse non peccare*) toward *non posse peccare* (unable to sin) in glorification with Being(s) Who is capable of bringing changes beyond human self. Furthermore, the nature of transformational change in relational transformational change is concrete and non-relativized since transformational change is not determined and defined by subjectivities and the subjective self but is ultimately dependent on the immutable Triune God and His immutable words that both penetrate and transcend situations and self.

---

[162] Gimple and Wan, *Covenant Transformative Learning*, 47.
[163] Gimple and Wan, *Covenant Transformative Learning*, 41.
[164] Gimple and Wan, *Covenant Transformative Learning*, 66.

Epistemic Norms

While both paradigms incorporate normative dimensions in learning and change, they differ in providing epistemic standards. Mezirow's theory relies on community consensus to validate meaning perspectives.[165] In contrast, relational transformational change sees validation as an epistemic activity provided in Christ (John 14:6), through the Holy Spirit (John 16:13), and from the Father (Matt 16:17), intertwined with the existential and situational aspects of knowing.[166]

Core Elements (Epistemic Stages)

Both paradigms embrace experience, dialogue, and critical reflection as core elements for transformational learning. However, relational transformational change adds vertical confirmation, acknowledging Christ's lordship and submission to Triune God for all acts of knowing and learning. This vertical confirmation includes direct scriptural confirmation, conviction, assurance, peace, joy, comfort, God's presence, illumination, discerning God's will, hearing the Holy Spirit, and following His leading.

Conducive Conditions for Transformational Learning

Even though the two paradigms differ in how they define the conditions necessary for transformative learning, they are compatible in their assertions and elaborations of such conditions.[167] Mezirow asserts "ideal conditions for transformational learning" by stating that "one's posture towards learning, towards others, and towards the yet-to-be-known" affects one's ability to engage in reflective discourse and that it consequently affects the outcome of the transformational change. While relational transformational learning uses another terminology called "epistemological etiquette," relational transformational learning is compatible with Mezirow's ideal learning condition and it further expands from his ideal conditions.[168]

Phases of Change

Relational transformational learning shares the ten phases of transformational change with Mezirow's theory but expands them to account for a wider range of epistemic experiences.[169] Added phases include exposure to awe-inspiring experiences, encountering a bigger and more appealing metanarrative, quest for more insight, cognitive experiment, conviction,

---

[165] Gimple and Wan, *Covenant Transformative Learning*, 53.
[166] Gimple and Wan, *Covenant Transformative Learning*, 52-53.
[167] Gimple and Wan, *Covenant Transformative Learning*, 41.
[168] Gimple and Wan, *Covenant Transformative Learning*, 67.
[169] Refer to Chapter 3 for the full list of Jack Mezirow's ten phases of change.

illumination, interactional confirmation and affirmation, discernment, wisdom and understanding from Triune God, hearing from God (through scripture, prayer, fasting, etc.), and seeking God's glory and faithful covenant response.

Summary

In this chapter, we have explored some of the Biblical and thematic foundations of relational interactionism, which we will build upon as we discuss relational intercultural education. We have looked at Biblical examples of transformational growth and transgressional change, and discussed the theme of salvific grace, in terms of being, belonging, and becoming. We have also compared transformational growth to Mezirow's transformational learning theory, to help clarify the similarities and differences between these two frameworks. We will next take a look at the defining characteristics of relational intercultural education based on these foundational understandings.

CHAPTER 5
Understanding Intercultural Education

Introduction

In this chapter, we will build a model for Intercultural Education. The model will grow progressively through a number of stages:
- Understanding ministry
- Understanding relational ministry
- Understanding relational intercultural ministry
- Understanding education as a form of ministry
- Understanding relational intercultural education – RICE

Understanding Ministry in Biblical/theological perspective

In 2 Corinthians, Paul's most autobiographical epistle, he compares the ministry of "the letter" with the ministry of "The Spirit." The ministry of the letter grew from Moses' experiences with the Decalogue. Moses, a man who knew God face-to-face (Exodus 33:11), had a personal interactive relationship with God. In that relationship, after 40 days of intense interaction, God gave him the Ten Commandments (Exodus 34 – 35). The relationship began with deep Spiritual and interactive relationship that led to the establishment of the written Law.

However, some of those who heard that law, both contemporaries of Moses and later generations, focused on fulfilling the written law without knowing the living God who gave that Law. To use the ministry phrases we have previously introduced, praxis (which is mechanical at its core) took priority over theology (which is relational at its core). Or in even more powerful words, the mechanical took precedence over the relational. A methodological perspective led eventually to the Pharisees' approach that Jesus condemned.

In 2 Corinthians chapter 3, Paul demonstrates the proper interaction between the invisible world of Spiritual life and the outer world of practice and form. There is a reality that is personal interaction with the Living God. Moses' ministry was based his living relationship with God. Some other people grew in their relationship with God through that Law – based first on a healthy relationship and then also on being careful to keep the Ten Commandments as best they could. Such was the intent. But others relied on simply copying the structures without pursuing the reality of the relationship.

Ministry must have structure. There have to be methods, plans, approaches to teaching, to preaching, to leading. But ministry done in God's way will be built on a heart that seeks the Lord and that walks in relationship with Him. It is not enough to follow the methods of those who came before; in fact, following the methods without a relationship is "dead works." God calls us first to know Him, and then to serve Him and humanity in the bonds of that personal relationship.

On the other hand, a relationship that has no outward form is also weak. We are not called to withdraw from the world, but to engage the world. This calls us to develop methods and strategies. Praxis is important but must grow from theology. Action and methods are important but must grow from relational interactions. The written law was valuable, but only when it grew from a relationship with the living God.

In this chapter, we propose that ministry, including education, be understood to be the outworking of a dynamic, healthy and growing relationship with the Triune God and the outworking of healthy appropriate growing relationships with people. Vertical relationship comes first; horizontal activities come second. Faithfulness to God is priority; fruitfulness in outcomes is secondary. Being precedes doing.

Relational Ministry

When we speak of relationship (or any of its cognates), we are describing the interaction between two or more Creator Beings and/or created beings. This relational concept can be considered in various ways:

<u>Descriptively</u>: using descriptive adjectives, we can describe the sort of interaction that exists between two or more Beings/beings. So, for instance, we could speak of a harmonious relationship, a romantic relationship, or a competitive relationship. This way of thinking about relationship is grounded in real world descriptions of actual relationships. To use the language of the previous section, this is discussing relational praxis.

<u>Theoretically/theologically</u>: relationality can also be a lens for understanding the world. Theologically, relationality sheds light on the vertical relationship between Creator and creation. Theoretically, relationality identifies the elements that can be used to <u>analyze</u> a relationship. Relationality as a theoretical framework also allows for the <u>creation of models</u> to better understand and engage in vertical and horizontal life interactions.

Seen in this light, we again see that relational interaction has primary essence as the "heart" of interaction long before the actual pragmatics of a given relationship come into focus.

To further advance the connection between relationship and ministry, we will use three different terms to discuss the paradigm of relational realism: relational realism, relational transformation, and relational interaction.[170]

---

[170] Enoch Wan and Jon Raibley, *Transformational Change in Christian Ministry Second Edition* (Western Academic Publishers, 2022), 6–7.

All three of those terms have been used in recent literature to speak to horizontal interactions between people and other created beings. All three terms are also valuable to describe elements of God working in us, among us, and through us.

However there are differences between these three theoretical perspectives on relationality. Much like the same four ingredients (bread, cheese, vegetable and meat) can be combined in different ways to produce a hamburger, a sub sandwich, a cheese sandwich or a taco, in that same way by varying the purpose, packaging and presentation relationality can also take different shapes.

Model / Number	Relational Realism	Relational Transformation Paradigm	Relational Interactionism Paradigm
1. Purpose: to show	Vertical + horizontal	Transformational change	Dynamic interaction between Being/being
2. Packaging	Static	Dynamic, fluid and processual	
3. Presentation	In-house: Christian		Christian + non-Christian

Figure 5-1. Comparison of Three Paradigms[171]

The Components of Relationship

Looking at relationships from both theological and practical terms, then, we also find it is important to have an analytical framework by which to better understand a given specific relationship as well as the general concept of relationship. We find that analytical framework in the work of Enoch Wan and Natalie Kim.[172]

They proposed that relationship be described and analyzed through the lens of five factors that shape relationship:

1. *BEINGS/beings*

The **nature of the Beings/beings** involved. This relational factor speaks to the horizontal and vertical relationships between Creator and created

---

[171] Wan and Raibley, *Transformational Change in Christian Ministry*, 16.
[172] Enoch Wan and Natalie Kim, *Relational Intercultural Training for Practitioners of Business As Mission: Theory and Practice* (Western Academic Publishers, 2022).

beings (including angel and demon beings). In both the Divine and the created the Bible speaks of personal traits and characteristics of each Being/being. These traits can include spiritual gifts, personal strengths or abilities, maturity in spiritual and physical terms, physical attributes, mental and emotional formation, etc.

2. Closeness

The **closeness** level of the relationship refers to relative levels of appropriate and actual closeness. This refers, for example, to the feelings of friendship or enmity (which is also a form of relational interaction).

Siu Kuen Sonia Chan integrates the concept of Transactional Analysis (TA) into the discussion of relational education and relational communication.[173] Based on the counseling classic, *Games People Play* by Eric Berne [174] we understand that relationships by nature involve reciprocal interaction, but the members of any given dyad do not necessarily act or respond in the same way. Berne speaks of "Parent/Child/Adult" ego states in this regard. Using this language, then, one person in a Parent ego state might speak and act to others who are in the "child" ego state. The "parent" may be directive, even controlling. The "child" may be rebellious or obedient. In such pairings, people may understand their relationship in many ways[175].

Building on that "ego states" idea, we propose that intercultural ministry involves discernable postures of the people involved. Rather than Bernes' "ego states" we can envision the posture of one person in relationship to the other. Figure 5-2 visualizes these different postures that parties in an intercultural setting could assume.

Action/Stimulus Posture	Expected Response Posture
Dialog	
Control	Obey
Influence	Engage/Be Curious
Manipulate	"Get my way"

Figure 5-2. Possible Postures of Stimulus and Response

---

[173] Siu Kuen Sonia Chan, "A Relational Model of Intercultural Learning and Interactions" (Dissertation, Portland, OR, Western Seminary, 2023), 145–62.

[174] Eric Berne, *Games People Play: The Psychology Of Human Relationships*, 2010, Chap. 16-17.

[175] Eric Berne, *Games People Play*. New York: Ballentine Books, 1964. pp 28 – 30.

3. *Context*

The geographical and social **context** in which a relationship exists has an impact on the way that a relationship is manifest. A workplace relationship will be different than the relationship found in homes or neighborhoods. Church interactions in a small rural church are in a different context than the relationships we find in urban megachurches.

4. *Culture*

Patterns of life, including patterns of relationship, that are normal and accepted within one **culture** can vary greatly from what is accepted in another culture. Issues like how men and women interact, the sort of relationship between bosses and workers, and the appropriate and accepted patterns for relationship between a child and an elder, for example, are likely to vary widely from one culture to another.

Relationships affect people in at least three ways: through emotional interaction, content-driven interaction, and social meaning that is part of an interaction. It is important to keep in mind that across cultures, all three of these relational aspects can vary. In other words, in a relationship between people from culture A and culture B, it is very possible that their patterns of life will not simply differ due to "culture." They will differ in terms of how to understand emotional interactions, understanding of concrete, content-laden issues, and in terms of expected social interactions.

5. Influence

Influence speaks of the desired outcomes and the actual impact that one person has on the others. The relationship between a teacher and student involves the desired influence of teaching well, gaining new knowledge, and perhaps graduating from a formal school. That relationship will be quite different from, for example, the relationship between a grandmother and her grandchild. Both the classroom and the grandmother bring relational elements to teaching a new topic and/or skill. From an educational point of view, informal education, non-formal education and formal education all have different levels of expected influence, yet all are clearly forms of education.

Siu Kuen Sonia Chan again integrates an important element at this level of "influence."[176] Referring to essays by educator and communicologist Gregory Bateson, Chan shows how his categories of learning and categories of communication are relevant to relational interactionism. There is education that truly intends to pass on new information in an emotionally/relationally passive way. As an example, I am not much of a sports fan but I can tell you how local professional teams are ranked much of the time. It is not that it is

---

[176] Chan, "A Relational Model of Intercultural Learning and Interactions," 87–92.

very important to me, but it is simply because the news sources that I watch include that information. I receive it passively.

A more emotionally engaged level of learning and communication has to do with incremental changes in things that a learner already knows and uses. Learning the newest upgrades to the digital tools that I use would be a personal example. I am engaged – this is important information because it helps me to do my work better. It is built on what I already know. But it is not emotionally or relationally profound.

A third level In Bateson's approach Is where learning begins to challenge assumptions. Values, choices, frameworks of understanding are compared and contrasted with other ideas. This level of learning and communicating engages not only cognitively but in other ways, too, depending on the topic being considered.

Bateson's fourth level of potential influence promotes evolutionary change. This is not the "epiphany" stage, but it is where education influences a shift from one existing worldview to a different worldview.

The last of Bateson's categories calls for transformative change. This, in Bateson's model, is fueled by a source outside of oneself. This is the epiphany that requires some type of revelation from outside.

These five categories correspond to the discussion of influences by Natalie Kim. There could easily be other categories suggested, and yet the important insight in Bateson's work is that within education and ministry and communication we face a wide variety of depth of involvement. Some of our educational processes are aimed at superficial, basic knowledge. Learning the books of the Bible in canonical order is a simple memory matter. It is important but not particularly transformative.

Growing in grace and knowledge, on the other hand, is a life-on-life influence – it would be closer to the transformative level of Bateson's work. Considering the depth of influence that we seek in a ministry setting is an important part of the educational ministry.

This analysis of relational ministry shows the fallacy of aiming at curriculum or content development solely as the object of Christian education (or other ministry). When Paul wrote about the ministry of the Spirit (2 Cor 3) he described a relationship that leads to actions and forms. Unfortunately it is part of human nature to look at the actions and miss the personal interactions: to simply copy the ways of thinking, the words, and the actions that others have used successfully and ignore the underlying personal interactions. That copying of the forms is what Paul condemns as the "ministry of death." The copying of forms was the defining trait of the Pharisees of the New Testament. They focused on cold mechanical fulfilment of ordinances and commands, but they had no living relationship with the Giver of Biblical truth. A real relationship will take a healthy heart attitude and will create a form. But simply following the form without the relationship is a sort of false ministry; a ministry of death.

Ministry is a set of activities and structures that grow from a living relationship. Mechanical ministry tries to copy the actions without paying attention to the underlying relationships (vertical and horizontal). We draw support for this definition from Jesudason Baskar Jeyaraj who writes, "Christian ministry can be defined as the ministry done by the church believing, worshipping and following the message and the model of the Father, Son and Holy Spirit, the Triune God."[177]

Ministry that follows only the form is theoretical. Ministry that follows only the model will sooner or later leave its moorings of sound doctrine and will take the pragmatic steps that seem humanly most effective. Christian ministry in appropriate relational terms follows the message AND the model of Triune God to serve with both theory and practice, shaping the head, the heart and the hands in relational interaction[178].

Relationality in both theological and pragmatic terms has one further element, made clear by Enoch Wan and Jon Raibley [179]: it is progressive rather than static. While it is true that relationality can be discussed as a theoretical topic, it is developed in dynamic, changing real-world relationships. For that reason, we speak of relationality in terms of "being/belonging/becoming."

Transformation takes place as people with their own unique personalities (beings) come into relationship with other people and with Creator Beings (belonging), leading to change; "becoming." That Being/Belonging/Becoming triad is the growth pattern for relational interactionism. Based on the nature of the created beings/Creator Beings involved, and as relational patterns develop (belonging) that are appropriate to the closeness/friendship of the people, the expected patterns in their cultural setting and the sort of environment where they interact, we see transformation in terms of the influence that one part of the relationship brings to the other/others.

IV. Understanding Intercultural Ministry

Ministry is not essentially the actions, but it is actions that grow from healthy and biblically appropriate vertical (primarily) and horizontal (secondarily) relationships.

Ministry actions can include worship, offering/sacrifice, using one's spiritual gifts for the building up of others, growing in grace and knowledge through prayer, Scripture, psalms and hymns and spiritual songs. Ministry

---

[177] Jesudason Baskar Jeyaraj, *Christian Ministry: Models of Ministry and Training* p 23
[178] Enoch Wan, "Global People and Diaspora Missiology" (Presentation at Plenary session, Tokyo 2010—Global Mission Consultation, Tokyo, Japan, May 13, 2010).
[179] Wan and Raibley, *Transformational Change in Christian Ministry Second Edition*, 2022, 87.

can include evangelistic efforts at bringing people into a healthy relationship with the Redeemer. Ministry can include teaching and counseling and making disciples. These actions done with appropriate vertical relationship are "ministry of life." These actions done without regard to a healthy vertical relationship are "dead works;" like a skeleton that has mechanical shape but no life.

When this sort of living, vertical ministry crosses from one culture to another, it often calls for changes and shifts – what we call contextualization. That contextualization will adapt thought patterns, words, times of day, relationship patterns, communication patterns, etc. so that both the host and the expat culture feel comfortable and able to understand both the outward actions and the inward attitudes and relationships.

Intercultural ministry speaks of the action that grows from healthy and biblically appropriate relationships that cross cultural boundaries. This means that the being/belonging/becoming growth is shaped by patterns of thought, action, relationship, communication, education, and leadership that are acceptable for all of the cultures involved in the ministry.

Stating this description of intercultural ministry is deceptively simple for the reason that people around the globe suffer from what sociologists call "The False Consensus Effect".[180] This is the error of so normalizing one's own patterns of life that it is simply taken for granted that others also follow those patterns – or at least aspire to those patterns. This is the thinking that is shocked to learn that people in one part of the world eat with forks when the life experiences of the other person uses chopsticks or fingers.

Of course, eating utensils is an overly simplistic illustration. Legal patterns, writing patterns, and concepts of what makes for good social manners are also examples. The person whose form of greeting is a hug and kiss on the cheek may well find a handshake to feel cold, aloof and uncaring. The form carries the meaning, even though the handshaking-greeter may well have a tender heart attitude toward the person being greeted.

---

[180] Charlotte Nickerson, "False Consensus Effect: Definition and Examples," November 3, 2022, https://www.simplypsychology.org/false-consensus-effect.html.

Heart of Ministry	Actions to demonstrate that ministry	Cultural variation #1 (as illustration)	Cultural Variation #2 (as illustration)
Worship Triune God	Music	Hymns played on the organ	Contemporary guitars
Learn Bible content	Teaching	Formal school with print material as foundation	Informal understanding through oral methods
Care for widows and orphans	Provide meals	Daily lunches taken to the homes of widows and orphans	Invitation for elderly to live in homes with younger families
Evangelism	Telling the Good News to those who haven't yet heard	Home Bible study	Street corner preaching and giving out tracts
Congregational life	Gather together for encouragement and growth	Meet in a dedicated church building that is cared for by professional building maintenance staff	Meet in homes of believers

Figure 5-3. Christian Ministry Elements

Going back to Wan and Kim's model of what is included in relationship, we can begin to make small adjustments to the practice of ministry from one place so that it better fits the patterns of life of another people group:

Element / Example	Examples of what could be included	Cultural variation #1 (as illustration)	Cultural variation #2 (as illustration)
Being Being/being	Gender, age, gifting, aptitudes for certain kinds of work Experiences and life history	Ministry leadership reserved for older men	Ministry leadership open to women and across ages
Belonging Culture	Eg. 1: Cultural patterns of oral/literate communication, building preferences, time use Eg. 2 The form that a given ministry takes – how it is done, when, where, etc.	Eg 1: Early morning prayer meetings every day Eg. 2 Very punctual to start every event at the agreed upon time; use of published material prepared by experts from other places	Very informal, with conversation in the group leading the teaching. The leader responds to questions or situations that arise in the lives of the congregation.
Context	Ministry is shaped by the physical context, level of acceptance of Christianity; and urban v rural setting	Worship in a hostile context might not involve singing out loud	Worship in a social situation that includes acceptance of Christianity could include open-air worship in the park.
Closeness	The affection that people have for one another and how that is demonstrated. Friendliness, personal sharing of needs or concerns in the congregation	Very private people who share with very few others: perhaps the pastor serves as a kind of counselor for the congregation	A culture of openness where people are willing to share their problems and failures. Church prays for one another freely and openly.
Becoming Influence	The impact or influence that people have on one another	Ministry that focuses on relational situations, so people gain from lots of conversational input from others	Ministry focuses on curricula that allows specific themes to be studied and learned academically but in a relational/social environment.

Figure 5-4. Illustrations of cultural outworking of 5 relational elements

Summary: Ministry is understood to be the actions that grow from an internal "heart" desire to jointly worship and serve the Lord and people. The forms of that service might change from one place to another, and so intercultural ministry is the adjustment of outside forms to match the customary patterns of a group of people, and yet at the core those ministry activities all demonstrate the same heart of relational service to the Lord and His people.

V. Opportunities for Intercultural ministry

Given our definition of ministry as not essentially the actions, but actions that grow from healthy and biblically appropriate vertical (primarily) and horizontal (secondarily) relationships, we can see that the teaching/learning interaction within a teacher/student relationship can easily be seen as potentially a form of Christian ministry.

We say "potentially" because a teacher or a learner who focuses on the outer elements and does not consider the heart may show outward activities consistent with teaching but without the relationship; this is not Relational Intercultural Education (RICE).

At the same time, a teacher in a cross-cultural setting may use outward forms that are appropriate and common in his/her homeland and completely miss the fact that the learners' patterns of thought and communication are quite different. To use a phrase that the author has used through a lifetime of teaching, "if the students didn't learn, then the teacher didn't teach." There is a two-way relationship in teacher/learner relationship. A teacher who leans on patterns of thought, expression, or classroom management that are foreign and unfamiliar to the learners will most likely not find a successful teaching relationship.

Summary

1. Education is a type of ministry
2. Education, like other forms of ministry, is not essentially the outward actions but rather is the inward attitudes and relationships. There always is some sort of method for educators, but that method must reflect and grow from the heartfelt relational attitudes underlying it.
3. Education that crosses intercultural barriers must use patterns of thought and action that are familiar to the learners, not necessarily comfortable to the teachers. If the teacher demands that the learning patterns of his/her homeland be followed, there is essentially a lack of relational continuity between learner and teacher.
4. Relational intercultural education (RICE) will contain both content and methods, shared in both vertical and horizontal relationships. The key

to intercultural education is a heart that seeks to be faithful in a healthy vertical relationship as well as fruitful in a horizontal relationship.

Ministry Type	Faithfulness in home culture	Fruitfulness in home culture	Faithfulness in a host culture (cross cultural)	Fruitfulness in a host culture (cross cultural)
Education – formal	Seek first the Kingdom of God; wanting to know God through His Word through any means possible	Bible school degree	Seek first the Kingdom of God; wanting to know God through His Word through any means possible	Correspondence or online options. Christian school or Bible College
nonformal	Seek first the Kingdom of God	Daily Bible study with online resources	Seek first the Kingdom of God	Daily Bible study at local church with other believers
informal	Seek first the Kingdom of God	Dinner table talks and Bible readings	Seek first the Kingdom of God	Chatting with grandchild about answers to prayer.
Evangelism	Be ready to give the reason for the hope within you	Hand out tracts at a grocery store	Be ready to give the reason for the hope within you	Invite family members to a church service
Witness	That our community would glorify God for the good works we do	Take flowers and plants to shut-ins at Christmas time	That our community would glorify God for the good works we do	Live with the elderly, caring for all of their physical needs.
Life of the Congregation	Be at peace with all men, especially the household of faith	"agree to disagree" on points of church life	Be at peace with all men, especially the household of faith	Allow the pastor/leaders to make all decisions so there is no disagreement.

Figure 5-5. Illustrations of Ministry areas in relational intercultural perspective

At this point, we have taken on the concept of ministry, added to it "relational ministry," and then "intercultural relational ministry." It is now time to briefly consider how RICE – Relational Intercultural Education, fits into this discussion of Relational Intercultural Ministry.

The simple fact is that education can be done as ministry. It can also be approached in secular terms, of course, but for our purposes that is not a point we need to belabor. We simply want to affirm that when a Christian seeks to influence another Christian toward a deeper understanding of God, His Word, and His ministry, we are effectively considering a form of ministry that we call education. Figure 5-6 shows how the form of ministry we call "education" can be seen in relational and intercultural terms. In this table, we are able to understand relational intercultural education.

Ministry is serving God and others for the glory of God	Education is one kind of service to people that can glorify God (Mt 28:20: *teaching* them to obey all things I have commanded you)	Note: Not all education is Christian ministry, but education that is truly Christian is a form of ministry that is seen in the Bible.
Education can be relational	Relational education recognizes God's presence in the teaching/learning relationship; it also recognizes being/belonging/becoming process of horizontal growth.	Christian education can be approached mechanistically and methodologically. A deliberate focus on the characteristics, context, closeness, cultural expectations and desired influence will point toward relational education.
Relational Education can be Intercultural	Education in an intercultural context led by relational teacher who shapes educational plans to fit learner's cultural patterns is relational intercultural education (RICE)	Not all Christian relational ministry is intercultural, even if it is in an intercultural or multicultural context. To be intercultural, it must be understandable from the perspective of the learners' cultural patterns.

Figure 5-6. Education as relational and as intercultural ministry

CHAPTER 6
Characteristics of RICE

Introduction

Relational Intercultural Education is being applied by various practitioners around the world. We move now to a description of some of the current trends that are helping to advance this approach.

Current Trend #1; RICE is relational at its core

Since the modern era began, Western educators and Western interculturalists have understood there to be a sort of preferred or best methodology for teaching/learning (a methodology we might call "best practices"). Praxis became the foundational evidence of educational methods as educators shared stories of "success" or "failure" and built those experiences into theories of education. We are left with models of adult education and education for children that largely focus on the content, the context, the delivery style, and occasionally on intercultural variables. These models of education, though, rarely take on a cohesive, comprehensive relational focus that speaks to the "heart" of the Beings/beings, closeness, context, culture, and influence. What is to be taught and how it is to be taught become the "methods" that show up in the curriculum of our teacher-training.

The first complexity about RICE, then, is that it is fundamentally different than methodological or curriculum-focused approaches. RICE is relational at its core. That complexity turns out to be a strong advantage in practice, but it is a complex task to develop that new way of thinking.

The first priority for RICE is that the educator(s) involved develop a faithful relationship with Triune God and with people. Of secondary importance is any question of methods and structures used to advance education. This complexity exists in response to the thought patterns of modernity which have shaped much of the last centuries' educational theory.

Current Trend #2: RICE is process-oriented

A second complexity is that western educational structures have largely been designed with an "outcomes" approach that suggests certain methods which should lead to particular outcomes. Finish lines are essential.

The relational interactionism approach, summarized as Being/Belonging/Becoming, is quite different. Rather than defining ends, it focuses on a relational process. The use of gerunds in Wan and Raibley's "Being/Belonging/Becoming" model is no accident: relational education is an ongoing process by which the interaction of Beings/beings (each with their own characteristics and relational patterns), are in dynamic interactive relationship (belonging) with one another which leads to transformational change and growth (becoming).

The author of this chapter works in medical interpretation and has been to many physical therapy appointments. Often when there are hand injuries, the therapists will use ordinary clothes pins, clipped in a row around the lip of a box or bucket. The patient in those cases is to pinch each of the clothes pins, take it off the surface to which it is clipped, and set it onto a tabletop.

Imagine someone who misunderstood the reason for this exercise and thought that the aim or outcome was only to get all the clothes pins off of the box and onto the table. There are many faster and more efficient ways to remove the clips than to pinch them one at a time!

But the desired impact is happening internally, not externally. In the physical therapy appointment, the clothes pins are not the outcome: movement of the tendons and muscles of the patients' arms is the aim.

Relational Interactionism focuses on the "tendons and arm muscles." It is using an educational task, done in a relational way and with relational emphasis, for the goal of glorifying God. God never calls us to go into all the world and teach language acquisition or mission strategy. Those are the clothes pins. The goal that He has is that His people would relationally love Triune God and relationally love one another. The "pinching" of a class in mathematics or languages or hermeneutics is part of God's educational plan: relationally belonging to Him and to one another and growing in that relationship. That is how He can make all things work together for good to those who love Him and are called according to His purpose.

RICE is more interested in the process of belonging and holistically becoming, and less interested in the curriculum issues that a given formal, nonformal or informal educational situation may use. RICE understands education to be a process.

Current Trend #3: RICE deliberately adjusts to complex human interactions

The third complexity of RICE is that it deliberately identifies numerous variables that, by affecting the relationships involved, may also affect the educational patterns involved. We all recognize the apparent power in standardization. That power is seen when a given curriculum or method is understood to be effective across a very wide range of learners. RICE forfeits that apparent power of standardization, though, by recognizing the wide range of variables with which both the teacher and learners will deliberately engage:

- Divine Beings are present and active
- Created beings are present and active

- Created beings have varying characteristics, giftings, strengths and weaknesses.
- Some people are naturally "close" to others and seem approachable.
- Any given person will have a friendly feeling toward some people, and not be so attracted to others.
- The context in which a relationship is found is part of the learning/teaching relationship.
- The context in which a relationship is found is not static: there are many times when people in a family context also work in the same business together or are part of the same church community.
- Cultural patterns shape relationships: the appropriate interactions for men/women, young/old, professional/laborer etc. all have social rules – usually unwritten and very powerful.
- The influences that are sought from a relationship create another variable. Those seeking to learn a new trade will have a different relationship with their apprenticeship program leaders than those who want to interact with those same people as neighbors.

The relational educator will be aware of many more variables than his/her counterpart in traditional educational settings. Those variables, though, allow for relational interaction toward influences that go far beyond simply mastering a given knowledge, skill, or emotional topic.

RICE does not so much seek to create standardized approaches to teaching, but rather adjusts and adapts to the complex realities of human interactions. This can create a less "effective" and yet more profound educational setting.

Summary

In this chapter, we have examined some of the key characteristics of Relational Intercultural Education as being relational at its core, process-oriented, and deliberately responsive to complex human interactions. We also explored some ways in which these trends can help increase the amount of change-producing positive influence that educational participants can have on each other. We will next look at some of the challenges that we can face when using a RICE approach.

CHAPTER 7.
Challenges of RICE

Introduction

We have looked at some of the current trends that are helping to advance a relational approach to intercultural education. In this chapter, we will explore some of the challenges that RICE needs to address in order to be effective.

Challenge number 1: Ethnocentrism

Based on the concepts presented in this book, there are some obvious challenges for those who would promote RICE as an educational approach. Perhaps first on this list is the False Consensus Effect[181]. People tend to imagine that their own behaviors and attitudes are common and appropriate. We expect that what motivates "me" will motivate "you." We expect that we share the same values and beliefs. We believe that in a perfect world, most people would adapt the way of life that "I" already have. [182] If one assumes that their own behaviors and attitudes are normative, then interaction in another culture, with clearly different behavioral and attitudinal norms, will obviously create a challenge.

The antidote for that fallacy of thinking is cultural humility. The ability to think that people who come from different intercultural contexts are equally intelligent, equally moral, equally skilled, and equally as able as we are is the single best way to overcome the challenge of the False Consensus Effect.[183]

In close second place, the practice of being involved in an interactive relationship itself becomes part of the solution to this challenge. When people interact with one another in recreation, worship, over a plate of food, or in work situations (among many other examples), we learn to see deeper into the thoughts, beliefs, and values of the other person. Being deliberate about interactive relationships has the potential for helping us overcome this complexity.

---

[181] Choi, Incheol and Oona Cha, "Cross Cultural Examination of the False Consensus Effect." *Frontiers in Psychology.* Fpsyg-10-02747 accessed Jan 7, 2024.

[182] Interestingly, recent research shows that this fallacy is more pronounced in Individualistic cultures such as the United States and Western Europe. Asian studies show a tendency to lower levels of the False Consensus Effect.

[183] Nickerson, "False Consensus Effect."

Challenge number 2: Intercultural (Mis)communications

In the realm of intercultural communication, there are many ways that RICE practitioners can be misunderstood. For instance, not recognizing nuances that accompany different verbal and non-verbal communication prompts. In the United States, a "smile says friendship to everyone."[184] In other cultural contexts, it may be that a smile has other, less winsome meanings. Verbal and non-verbal communication patterns are shaped by cultural practice. One of the challenges of RICE is to understand and communicate well across a wide range of cultural communication patterns.

Similarly, thought patterns are shaped by cultural practice. Some cultures tend to begin thinking with universal observations and then derive implications to the particular example in their context. Others look at the immediate situation and then generalize their thoughts to the larger universe outside. Some thought patterns focus first on the individual; others shape their thinking from the collective, plural group and see the individual in secondary importance.

Considering these (and many other) intercultural communication issues, the practice of RICE is complicated by the need for intercultural (and often interlinguistic) adaptation.

Challenge number 3: Emphasis on Attitudes

Another challenge that the RICE approach faces is that it is sensitive to the attitude of the people involved in the different relationships. Cultural researcher and trainer Milton Bennett's DMIS model points to this attitude issue. In Bennett's model[185], the attitudes of all people involved in an intercultural situation are divided into ethno-centric and ethno-relative levels. Ethno-centric attitudes range from being unaware of cultural differences to being dismissive of those differences. On the ethno-relative side of the spectrum, attitudes range from awareness of the significance of cultural patterns all the way to an active seeking to engage in a diversity of cultural patterns.

Bennett's model helps us to appreciate the importance of attitude toward intercultural training. A trainer or trainee in a RICE program who is largely ethno-centric or, worse, who enters with prejudice against "other" cultures will not likely be satisfied by the education. Methodological teaching approaches can avoid this problem by positing some kind of objective reason for the training program. RICE, on the other hand, sees relationship as both the method and one of the outcomes. A negative attitude about other beings

---

[184] Walt Disney Company theme song from the 1960s when this author was a young viewer of the Walt Disney show.

[185] "DMIS Model," *IDRInstitute* (blog), accessed April 8, 2024, https://www.idrinstitute.org/dmis/.

involved, about the process of belonging, or about the outcomes of becoming will short-circuit the good that RICE seeks to do.

With appreciation for the attitudinal issues that Bennett raises, though, we also recognize that Christian education has a foundational epistemology that recognizes *a priori* truth claims of the Bible. This foundation is at odds with the fundamental teaching of the DMIS constructionist approach.

Ethno-relationality as proposed by Wan and Chan becomes the Scriptural answer to this problem[186]. This model allows for a firm foundation of biblical ethics and yet also creates a model for growth within vertical and horizontal relationships. Ethno-relationality permits us to think in terms of relational growth toward God. Ethno-relationality also allows for horizontal relationships. When those relationships include people whose life patterns were shaped in one culture AND people whose life patterns come from another culture, we face the challenge of attitudes. Within the Kingdom of God, the fact is that this attitude has been dealt with scripturally since the very beginning of the Christian Church: Jews and Greeks had to change their attitudes and their relationships so that they could cooperate within the one house that is the household of God. In our day, ethno-relationality likewise calls on us to form the attitudes, skills and knowledge necessary to cooperate well across cultures.

We have a strong advantage in that quest: the Spirit of God. A fascinating narrative in how the Spirit of God shapes attitudes in the context of cross cultural ministry is found in Acts 16. Paul and Silas, Jewish by birth and practice, are joined by Timothy (half Greek) and Luke (Gentile) as the Spirit sends them to Philippi. In that city, the Spirit opens the heart of Lydia, an immigrant businesswoman from Thyatira. The Spirit also opens the heart of a jailer who was touched by Paul and Silas' response to hardship. God's Spirit brought fruit; the people came from diverse cultural backgrounds and all were faithful in their service to God.

Challenge number 4: Inviting God into a teaching/learning relationship

The RICE approach to education, growing as it does from the Relational Paradigm, begins with the assumption that God is present and involved. This is challenging to Western educators who have embraced modernity over the past centuries. Even Christian educators can work with the tacit assumption that God is at best an observer in work that is ours to do. Learning to see God as actively involved even in the roles and responsibilities that He has given to us is a challenging part of the RICE approach. The Acts 16:14 illustration of the Lord opening Lydia's heart to the things taught by Paul reminds us that

---

[186] Chan, "A Relational Model of Intercultural Learning and Interactions."

human involvement is important, but not sufficient. We cannot open hearts. God is actively involved, and we humans are to be faithful in our stewardship and responsible in our efforts. Learning to re-think our "either God does this, or I do this" mental categories is a challenge.

In some educational situations, this recognition of both vertical and horizontal relationships in a teaching situation becomes even more complicated. There are some teaching/learning contexts that include government prohibitions against explicit recognition of God's involvement. We trust the Spirit of God to give wisdom, strength, and faith in those situations. In some cases, the RICE practitioner will obey God instead of man (following the example of Acts 5:27 – 29). In other cases, the RICE practitioner may instead be salt and light without explicit public recognition of God's presence in the relationships. Our faith is in a God who understands much better than we do when it is time to speak and when to refrain from speaking (Ecclesiastes 3).

Challenge number 5: Teaching and Training Oral Learners and Digital Oral Learners.

Oral Learners.

Tom Steffen and William Bjoraker, in their volume *The Return of Oral Hermeneutics* speak of oral communication's "concreteness, comprehensiveness, and communal learning"[187] and discuss components of communication that are inherent in oral media[188]:

- Orality concentrates on the concrete.
- Orality concentrates on conflict, changes and clashes.
- Orality calls for communal, face-to-face dialog.
- Orality prefers discussion from the whole to the parts.
- Orality is nonlinear in its processing of a story.
- Orality favors apprenticeship learning.
- Orality favors learning in small steps taken over a period of time.
- Orality is based on experience.
- Orality is based on communal relationships.
- Orality requires participation.
- Orality focuses on stories, symbols and ritual.
- Orality engages the emotions and imagination.
- Orality highlights conversations and actions.
- Orality unveils meaning through demonstration.
- Orality describes rather than defines.

---

[187] Steffen and Bjoraker, *The Return of Oral Hermeneutics*, p 67.
[188] Steffen and Bjoraker, *The Return of Oral Hermeneutics*, 68 – 72.

- Orality is by nature responsive to a moral code of honor/shame.
- Orality demonstrates the art of rhetoric.
- Orality assumes ambiguity within limits.
- Orality is tied to the collective memory of a people.

In a word, oral teachers present truth through the narrative form of stories, recounting either actual events or fictious fables. In contrast, text-based teachers prefer propositional statements and tight definitions upon which to base their lessons.

For the intercultural educator, there are two important questions to consider related to media use: which is the medium preferred within the group of students, and which medium best conveys the content to be taught. There are times when a list of propositions is entirely appropriate for both audience and content (consider the Ten Commandments). On the other hand, narrative forms of teaching and learning can convey a deeper sense of the ethos and context that surrounds a lesson and calls on learners to engage emotionally as well as cognitively with the lesson.

Digital Oral Learners.

Intercultural education in the 21st century has a new challenge, the reality of Digital Oral Learners. Traditional oral learners had no (or practically no) access to written materials. Their education into the ways of their people was based on the verbal, oral stories that they received from previous generations.

Some educators would hold that oral learning is superior to text-based learning, as seen in this quote:

> Digital Orality is about combining modern technological resources with the most ancient forms of communicating and learning. Orality-based methods and strategies are the most effective ways people have learned and communicated from the beginning of time. We now know that the principles and concepts of orality are also the most effective ways of changing behavior.[189]

Traditional text-based literate learners formed a new set of thinking patterns by their heavy use of printed materials. The written messages, lessons, novels, notes, essays etc. all shaped the way that these cultures thought and communicated. "Without writing, the literate mind would not and could not think as it does, not only when engaged in writing but normally

---

[189] Jerry Wiles, "Digital Orality: New Signs of Spiritual Opportunities," *International Orality Network* (blog), accessed January 6, 2024, https://orality.net/content/digital-orality-new-signs-of-spiritual-opportunities/.

even when it is composing its thoughts in oral form. More than any other single invention, writing has transformed human consciousness."[190] Clearly, both oral and text-based education have significant impact on those trained by them.

In our digital, computer-generated world, orality and text-preference education are no longer the only options. Technology has now provided computerized access to videos, memes, podcasts, and a wide variety of other communication forms that are used for educational purposes. These digital forms of communication have created new thought patterns for their users. The phrase, "digital oral learners" is used to describe communication preferences and educational approaches that use computer-generated forms to communicate rather than printed words on the one hand, or purely oral communication on the other.

These digital options have advantages. "With digital orality strategies and online training resources, we can equip leaders and disciple makers to reach and disciple those who are without access to print and technology-based resources."[191]

The digital orality options have also given rise to doubts. For example, can character issues be successfully addressed in digital formats? Similarly, many question whether community interaction can be facilitated by digital means. It seems, to some anyway, that digital interactions tend to isolate people from each other rather than develop a sense of community.

Yet, those same issues of community and character development have been referenced as strong advantages for developing digital education by proponents. The quotes below will show some of the alternative views about character and community formation in a digital-oral communication environment.

"There is skepticism among educators about character formation in online education. Many cannot imagine that real transformation can be achieved in any format other than in the traditional model of residential education with in-class face time. Profound spiritual formation, however, can and has happened through quality and effective learning in online education."[192]

"The goal is character formation, and educators can provide opportunities for students to change something about themselves and grow as persons. This is best accomplished in a community that values knowing and being known. Learning together influences a deeper level of engagement."[193]

---

[190] Ong, *Orality and Literacy*, 77.
[191] Wiles, *Digital Orality*.
[192] Joanne J. Jung, *Character Formation in Online Education: A Guide for Instructors, Administrators, and Accrediting Agencies* (Grand Rapids: Zondervan Publishing House, 2015), 15.
[193] Jung, *Character Formation in Online Education*, 60.

The Holy Spirit can transcend time and space to create connections that would otherwise not exist. Lowe and Lowe comment, "As the Spirit of God works in and through the connections and interactions that comprise the spiritual ecology of the church, the holiness that characterizes individual believers and the body of Christ as a whole spreads as contagious spiritual influence from one member to another."[194]

Lowe and Lowe acknowledge that the effectiveness of spiritual formation in a (digitally) mediated environment is debated. They state, "While there are many who reject the possibility of fellowship, community, and spiritual growth apart from the physical gathering of believers in a face-to-face encounter, we are not among them." [195] They go on to affirm that the work of the Holy Spirit is not limited by proximity: "Our study of the ecology of spiritual formation has led us to recognize that God's Spirit can perform his miraculous work of transformation when Christians are gathered and when they are scattered."[196]

> Writing and reading, as has been seen, are solo activities (though reading at first was often enough done communally). They engage the psyche in strenuous, interiorized, individualized thought of a sort inaccessible to oral folk. In the private worlds that they generate, the feeling for the 'round' human character is born— deeply interiorized in motivation, powered mysteriously, but consistently, from within.[197]

> Christians who study together at a distance have a common bond of connection that transcends physical time and space. The Holy Spirit is purposely unconstrained by physical proximity and freely operates in and through space to accomplish redemptive transformation. Thus, through our union with Christ and our common indwelling by the Holy Spirit, we are endowed with the capacity to be connected to the Trinity and to one another without being constrained by time and space.[198]

> All Seminary education must overcome some kind of distance -- either distance from faculty and fellow students (online education) or distance from one's community (residential education). The online student has the disadvantage of distance from a faculty member and fellow students, while having the tremendous advantage of proximity to his or her community.[199]

> ... students are able to stay *in situ* so that learning and transformation occurs – or is able to occur – in community. For this reason, we are

---

[194] Lowe and Lowe, *Ecologies of Faith in a Digital Age*, 195.
[195] Lowe and Lowe, 220.
[196] Lowe and Lowe, *Ecologies of Faith in a Digital Age*, 220.
[197] Ong, *Orality and Literacy*, 150.
[198] John Cartwright *et al.*, *Teaching the World: Foundations for Online Theological Education* (Nashville: B&H Academic, 2017), 166.
[199] Cartwright et al., 171.

encouraging others to reorient their thinking from "a community of learners" to "learners in community," a direct reference to our desire to partner more fully with ministries to promote authentic, life-changing spiritual transformation."[200]

Summary

RICE places priority on a heart of faithfulness instead of focusing solely on cognitive "head-knowledge."

RICE also sees the importance (in secondary position) of fruitfulness: intercultural relational education needs some kind of structure- a program, a school, a church, perhaps online, perhaps residential. It may be formal, or it may be nonformal. The people involved may include informal interactions as part of the training that takes place.

---

[200] James E. Stewart, "A Snapshot of the Student Experience - Pre-Interview Questionnaire," October 25, 2011.

CHAPTER 8
The Practice of Relational Intercultural Education for Intercultural Ministry

Introduction

The following discussion is limited to transformative andragogy within a Christian context. Before the explanation of "how" in the practice of relational intercultural education, we will compare two approaches: functional and relational approaches.

Functional and Relational Educational Approaches

Functional Perspective of Cultural Brokers and Bridging Cultural Gaps

In the discussion of missional theology and the communication of the Gospel, "culture gap" is a concept of Paul Hiebert whose assumption is that communication is an integral part for building relationships and transferring information. If we apply Hiebert's approach to intercultural education, then an intercultural teacher/trainer must overcome the chasm between them and a student/trainee who is from another culture. The evangelical intercultural teacher/trainer, according to Hiebert, is to engage in exegeting both Scripture and the culture of those being taught/trained. The reason is "to meaningfully communicate the gospel in human contexts."[201] Based on Hiebert's understanding, the role of the intercultural teacher/trainer is to be a "culture broker" who is tasked to "build bridges" across this figurative gap[202] within the intercultural approach he proposed.

With this functionalist emphasis, Hiebert is perceived to effectively have stripped multicultural individuals of some of their greatest potential.[203]

In this book, we propose a relational interactionist framework as an alternative with the emphasis on "relational education," "interculturally," and "interculturality" as expressions of transformational change.

Relational Intercultural Education as an Alternative

Intercultural education is a process by which mono-cultural individuals are to be influenced by the intercultural teacher/trainer who has been

---

[201] Paul G. Hiebert, *The Gospel in Human Contexts: Anthropological Explorations for Contemporary Missions* (Grand Rapids, Mich: Baker Academic, 2009), 12.
[202] Paul G. Hiebert, *Anthropological Insights for Missionaries* (Grand Rapids, Mich: Baker Book House, 1985), 229.
[203] Alfred C. Krass, "Contextualization for Today," *Gospel in Context* 2, no. 3 (July 1979): 29.

transformed by his/her dynamic interaction with the Triune God who is actively involved with believers in multiple dimensions leading to the transformational change in them ("being") and through them ("doing") "that they should seek God...and find Him." (Acts 17:24-31)

The intercultural educator as a "multicultural individual"[204] with "interculturality"

According to Benet-Martinez and Hong, a "multicultural individual" is "a person who positions himself between two (or more cultures) and incorporates this experience into their sense of who they are."[205]

In this book, we take for granted that an "intercultural educator" is an individual who operates between two or more cultures with an intercultural orientation and self-perception interculturally.

"**Interculturality**" includes multiple dimensions of self-identity (psychological), multiculturality (ideational), intentionality (attitudinal) and practicality (operational). Thus, the intercultural teacher/trainer is somebody whose "interculturality" includes:

- a subjective construction of identity (psychological),
- embracing "multiculturality" as an ideal characteristic of himself/herself (ideational) and a desirable goal for growth,
- with the ability to navigate among different cultural spaces.
- competence in two or more languages,
- able to relate and interact harmoniously with those who are culturally diverse.[206]

The above narrative of **"interculturality"** provides objective and measurable indicators for relational interaction among those who are culturally diverse within a cross-cultural context of operation.

"Relational interactionism" is a both/and framework, placing priority on "relationship being formed by interaction of personal Beings/beings, but with the inclusion of functional roles of "cultural broker" (personal interaction) and "bridge builder" (in the case of chasm of cultural gap). Within the framework of "relational interactionism," priority is placed on "relationship" (being) over "function" (doing). Before we shift the discussion on relational

---

[204] Benet-Martinez and Hong's definition of a "multicultural individual" is helpful because of the recognition of key elements such as knowledge, identification, and internalization.

[205] Verónica Benet-Martínez and Ying-yi Hong, eds., *The Oxford Handbook of Multicultural Identity* (Oxford University Press, 2014), 11–12, https://doi.org/10.1093/oxfordhb/9780199796694.001.0001.

[206] Luna, Ringberg, and Peracchio, "One Individual, Two Identities: Frame Switching among Biculturals," 283.

intercultural education, let us briefly discuss the useful functional elements in Hiebert's approach.

In Hiebert's model, cross-cultural workers are "culture brokers" [207] for they serve as intermediaries (who are to mediate and facilitate interactions) among people from different cultural backgrounds.[208] They are not merely cold-hearted observers, but active participants in shaping intercultural dynamics by interpreting, translating, and mediating cultural meanings and practices, they perform crucial roles in "bridging cultural gaps," and fostering mutual understanding. They are expected to broker/negotiate relationships, reduce relational conflict, and aid in mutual understanding.[209] As "cultural bridges," cross-cultural workers are able to connect different cultures: catalyzing positive exchanges and enhanced intercultural understanding and creativity.[210] They form a bridge that enables the flow of cultural exchange and mutual learning by bringing together participants' multiple cultural identities and leveraging this dual capacity to positively influence dialogue, interactions, and relation-building among culturally diverse groups, playing pivotal roles in promoting intercultural understanding and cohesion. When they navigate between cultures, they can challenge entrenched and embedded cultural assumptions and foster broader perspectives of people involved in the intercultural interaction. Their unique positioning allows them to navigate between two groups, fostering communication, exchanging ideas, mediating, and in some ways, serving as an ambassador from one culture to another.[211] They can also introduce alternative ways of thinking and behaving, enriching the multicultural environment with varied intercultural ideas and practices. In short, their role as "cultural bridges" can easily aid in managing diversity and promoting inclusivity, fostering a harmonious and enriched collective society.

---

[207] As "culture broker," they are multiculturally capable to operate even outside of the cultures that they most personally familiar with, see Sujin Jang, "Cultural Brokerage and Creative Performance in Multicultural Teams," *SSRN Electronic Journal*, 2017, 3, https://doi.org/10.2139/ssrn.3056274.

[208] Joan Weibel-Orlando, Frances E. Karttunen, and Margaret Connell Szasz, "Between Worlds: Interpreters, Guides, and Survivors," *Ethnohistory* 42, no. 4 (1995): 662, https://doi.org/10.2307/483151.

[209] Shu-Sha Angie Guan, Afaf Nash, and Marjorie Faulstich Orellana, "Cultural and Social Processes of Language Brokering among Arab, Asian, and Latin Immigrants," *Journal of Multilingual and Multicultural Development* 37, no. 2 (February 17, 2016): 151, https://doi.org/10.1080/01434632.2015.1044997.

[210] Jang, "Cultural Brokerage and Creative Performance in Multicultural Teams," 6.

[211] Hiebert, *Anthropological Insights for Missionaries*, 229.

Relational Intercultural Education

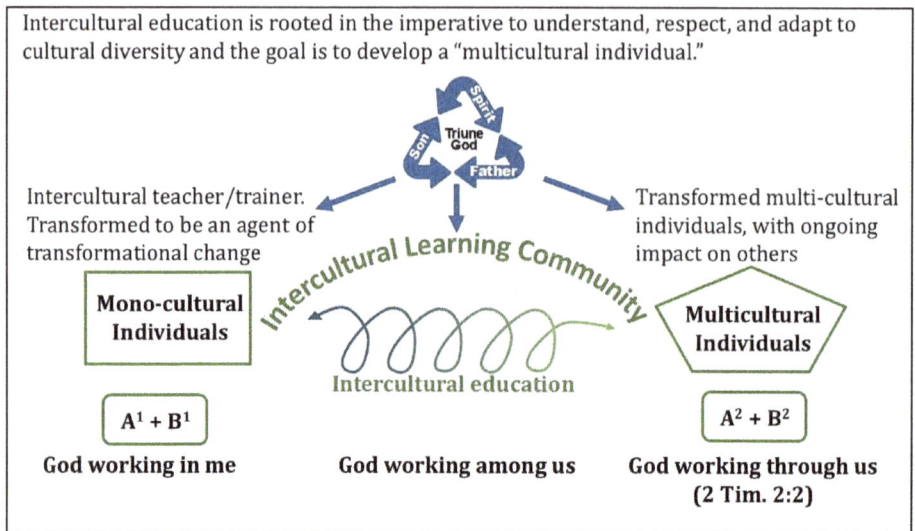

Figure 8-1 Relational Intercultural Education

The significant influence of the multicultural teacher/trainer on monocultural individuals is through the intercultural learning community as agents of Gospel-centered transformation, leading to transformational change of "A¹ & B¹" to become "A² & B²"

The Operations of Relational Intercultural Educator

Hiebert's "critical realism" (i.e. the epistemological and ontological stance) is an attempt to strike a balance between positivism and instrumentalism. He acknowledges objective truth that is subjectively comprehended.[212] Based on "critical realism," he proposed "critical contextualization" to be carried out by the "cultural brokers" in the context of cross-cultural mission/ministry (as compared to "relational contextualization" proposed by Wan & Chan).[213] They are expected to perform the role of breaking down and interpreting the Gospel's message within different cultural contexts in order to allow it to become meaningful and relevant within the local cultural framework.[214]

---

[212] Paul G. Hiebert, *The Missiological Implications of Epistemological Shifts: Affirming Truth in a Modern/Postmodern World,* Christian Mission and Modern Culture (Harrisburg, Pa: Trinity Press International, 1999), 69, https://search.ebscohost.com/login.aspx?direct=true&db=e000xna&AN=242967&site=ehost-live&scope=site.

[213] Enoch Wan and Siu Kuen Sonia Chan, "Contextualization the Asian Way: Relational Contextualization," *Asian Missions Advance,* no. 78 (Winter 2023), https://www.asiamissions.net/asian-missions-advances/amadvance-52-60/asian-missions-advance-78/.

[214] Hiebert, *The Gospel in Human Contexts,* 27–28.

Hiebert's expectation of mission workers (being multicultural individuals) as "brokers" and "bridges," end up reducing them to the role of performing such functions, as did Grunlan and Mayers and Charles Kraft. His position on missionary anthropology takes a functionalist approach.[215]

At a surface level, Hiebert's conceptualization of being "bi-culture" as "a new culture that arises in the interaction of people from two different cultural backgrounds," seems to be beyond functionalism because of its focus on relationships.[216] The "biculture" role is middle ground, such as "3rd culture kid," as individuals communicate and navigate two different cultures.[217] However, unlike the "3rd culture kid," concept, the biculture of Hiebert is limited in scope as it only exists between two specific given cultures and is still a functional construct with the "purpose" to communicate for relational outcome.[218]

In contrast to the functionalist orientation of "cultural brokers and bridges," in relational interactionism, multicultural individuals become integrated as part of the "dynamic nature of interaction that takes place within cultures and between cultures."[219] Relational interactionism posits that understanding is constructed through relational interactions. Multicultural individuals, therefore, through their relational interactions, can impact the formation, preservation, and changing of socio-cultural reality and influence understanding across cultures.[220] Though these interactions may appear as bridging or brokering between cultures, the depth of these interactions is much greater than simply the functions performed. In essence, multicultural individuals relationally interact in appropriate ways across a diversity of cultures.

The grafting of a branch of an apple tree or a grape vine is an apt analogy of the organic relationship that occurs with multicultural people who are well integrated into two or more cultural settings. A bridge is mechanical and carries discrete pieces of traffic across a chasm. A grafted branch, on the other hand, becomes organically related to the host plant as well as carrying inherent parts of its "parent" source. Rather than carrying traffic, people who live out a relational interactionist life are truly carrying part of each (or all) cultures in them. They are more than simply "couriers" of cultural units. They share life across multiple cultural contexts.

---

[215] Enoch Wan, "Critique of Functional Missionary Anthropology," *His Dominion* 8, no. 3 (April 1982): 2.

[216] *Paul G. Hiebert, Anthropological Reflections on Missiological Issues* (Grand Rapids, Mich: Baker Books, 1994), 147–49.

[217] David C. Pollock and Ruth E. Van Reken, *Third Culture Kids: Growing up among Worlds*, Revised edition (Boston: Nicholas Brealey Publishing Boston, 2009), 17.

[218] Hiebert, *Anthropological Reflections on Missiological Issues,* 149–58.

[219] Wan and Raibley, *Transformational Change in Christian Ministry*, 58–59.

[220] Wan and Raibley, *Transformational Change in Christian Ministry*,19.

Relational Intercultural Educator Navigating Cultures

Relational intercultural educators can provide key insights into culture through their relational interactions[221] (similar to Hiebert's concept of "exegeting humans.")[222] "Culture learning is people learning" in relational interactionism.[223] An intercultural educator may provide practical aid in reducing cultural offense, either through their knowledge of the culture, or through their ability to interact with greater cultural sensitivity.

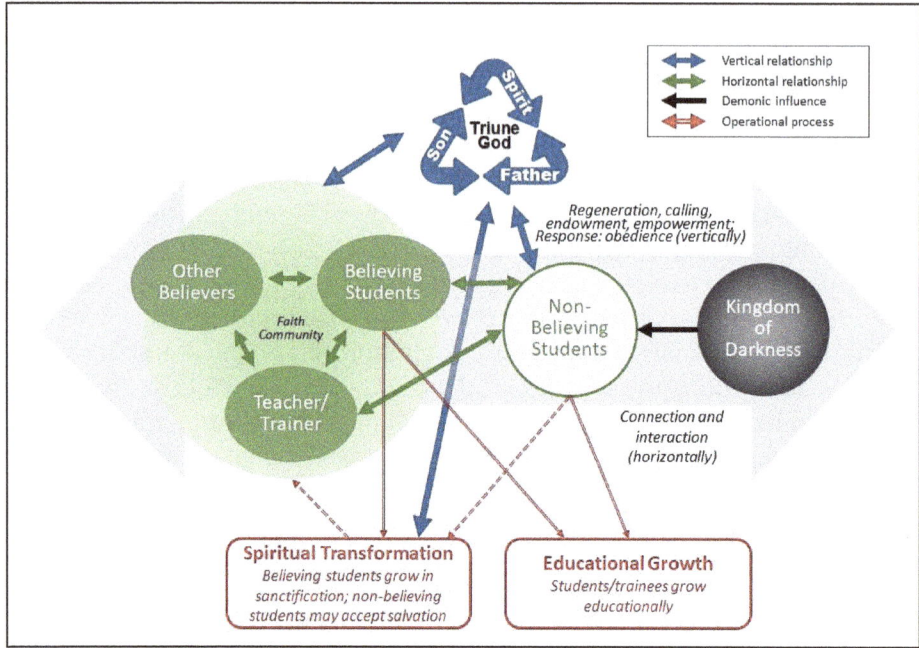

Figure 8-2. Complexities: possible transgressional change

Relational intercultural education (RICE) is a process in which the transformed multicultural teacher/trainer impacts monocultural individuals ("being = God working in us individually") through "intercultural learning community" (belonging = God working among us collectively"), leading to transformational change towards "multiculturality." Narratively speaking, a "relational intercultural educator" (RICE-R) is a multicultural individual who is an agent of transformative Gospel-centered change within intercultural

---

[221] Hargrave notes: (a) the process of "doing anthropology" and the preparation, observation, and data required for this, and (b) barriers to culture learning including offending the culture of observation, see Susan Hargrave, *Doing Anthropology* (Kangaroo Ground, Vic.: South Pacific Summer Institute of Linguistics, 1993), 29.
[222] Hiebert, *The Gospel in Human Contexts,* 59.
[223] Hargrave, *Doing Anthropology,* 39.

learning communities in *koinonia* with Kingdom-orientation in which they can grow together to become God-honoring multicultural individuals.

The theological assumption of RICE is that "the heart of God's mission is relational."[224] As such, RICE is not solely oriented towards the transmission of intercultural knowledge, transferring of intercultural skills, behavioral modification of "intercultural know-how," in the learning environment.[225] There is also the theoretical assumption of "relational interactionism." That is, the vertical dynamic interaction beginning with the Triune God, is foundational in impacting the horizontal dynamic interaction between RICE-R and students/trainees.[226] RICE-R can relate and provide insight to monocultural students/trainees through faith in God's active involvement to open hearts, through anthropological observation and through human exegesis.[227]

Intercultural Learning Communities

A learning community is "an instructor's attempt to create a safe and relationally interactive environment which could include being openly welcoming, participatory, interactive, collaborative, and intercultural."[228] This collectivist approach allows students/trainees to engage in meaningful interactions, not just with intercultural knowledge, but also with each other.[229] It acknowledges the diverse cultural backgrounds of students and seeks to create an environment conducive to growth, both in knowledge, skills, and more importantly, relationships. "God working among us" is a description of participants interacting and growing together with the intercultural learning communities. The functional approach places the onus of "teaching" on the teacher/trainer and the expectation on students/trainees "to learn." "Such divisions do not take seriously the reality that each individual needs to be a teacher in order to be a learner, and a learner in order to become and continue to be a teacher"[230] within an intercultural learning community. It is worth mentioning that Everist acknowledges the roles of teacher and learner remain within learning communities; she also champions the importance of a cyclical or mutual exchange of learning and teaching between members of learning communities.[231]

---

[224] Wan and Raibley, *Transformational Change in Christian Ministry*, 177.
[225] Wan and Raibley, *Transformational Change in Christian Ministry*, 181.
[226] Wan and Raibley, *Transformational Change in Christian Ministry*, 172–73.
[227] Paul Hiebert, *Gospel in Human Contexts*, 59.
[228] Wan and Raibley, *Transformational Change in Christian Ministry*, 140.
[229] K. Patricia Cross, "Why Learning Communities? Why Now?," *About Campus 3*, no. 3 (July 1, 1998): 4, https://doi.org/10.1177/108648229800300303.
[230] Norma Cook Everist, *The Church as Learning Community: A Comprehensive Guide to Christian Education* (Nashville, TN: Abingdon Press, 2002), 23.
[231] Everist, *The Church as Learning Community*, 23.

Within the relationships of a learning community, we also learn to see God through others' eyes. In the experience of one of the authors, for example, living in Latin America gave me insight into the collective nature of Christianity that I had not experienced in my highly individualistic homeland. Through Latino communities, I came to understand God in new ways, and I came to understand the Church in new ways. The interculturalist, in essence, is both learning and teaching within intercultural relationships.

In the RICE approach, culture is deemed to be paramount to building relationships in learning communities. Tim Hatcher rightly explains that the impact of a culture upon educational approaches cannot be underestimated since "the purpose of education determines the choice of the educational delivery system, and culture influences the process."[232] In light of Everist's position above, a practical outworking of the impact of culture can be seen in learning communities with high power distance, which could be easily found in many Asian cultures. In such settings, teachers hold respected positions and are considered the expert on matters. She insightfully does not erase the roles of teacher and learner; however, she notes that individuals must relate as both learners and teachers. Within intercultural learning communities, RICE-R is a teacher/trainer within the distinct cultural backgrounds serving as conduits for transformative intercultural interaction. He/she plays a critical role in enhancing the diversity of perspectives and experiences, thereby fostering a richer learning environment for growth together. He/she possesses invaluable knowledge and insights from his/her experiences of navigating multiple cultures and potentially multilingual competencies, enriching the collective learning experiences within the intercultural learning community.[233]

RICE-Rs often are able to connect members from different cultures within the community and exert a significant influence on dialogues, interactions, and relations-building among culturally diverse groups, driving intercultural understanding and cultivating cohesion.[234] Within such a context, they also transmit and interpret cultural meanings, crucially mediating and facilitating intercultural interactions among members from diverse cultural backgrounds. Their engagement is not merely transactional nor transmissional, but transformational.[235]

---

[232] Tim Hatcher, "Towards Culturally Appropriate Adult Education Methodologies for Bible Translators: Comparing Central Asian and Western Educational Practices," n.d., 3.

[233] Geneva Gay, "Preparing for Culturally Responsive Teaching," *Journal of Teacher Education* 53, no. 2 (March 2002): 106, https://doi.org/10.1177/0022487102053002003.

[234] Ci-Rong Li et al., "A Multilevel Model of Team Cultural Diversity and Creativity: The Role of Climate for Inclusion," *The Journal of Creative Behavior* 51, no. 2 (June 2017): 178–79, https://doi.org/10.1002/jocb.93.

[235] Jim Cummins, Joanne Tompkins, and Sonia Nieto, "The Light in Their Eyes: Creating Multicultural Learning Communities," *TESOL Quarterly* 35, no. 1 (2001): 200–201, https://doi.org/10.2307/3587870.

Within relational interactionism, the interactions of participants within intercultural learning communities are grounded in multiple cultural realities, they bring a level of cultural fluency that allows them to mediate and interpret divergent cultural assumptions and behaviors. As learners, both RICE-R and students/trainees can engage in rich class discussions and challenge assumptions. RICE-R can introduce multiple ways of knowing and foster inclusive pedagogies relationally.[236] All participants within the intercultural learning communities can easily gain from their participation in such collective interaction within culturally diverse contexts, and can:

- facilitate the development of greater intercultural competencies,
- enhance their ability to interact effectively with people from various cultural backgrounds,
- add significant value to intercultural learning communities, enriching the learning experiences for all participants,
- enabling them to manage these complexities and even transform them into opportunities for learning and growth.[237]

Through the interactions within intercultural learning communities, multicultural individuals bring depth and diversity to relationships and learning, regardless of whether they are a teacher or a learner, i.e. "God working among us."

Missiological and Educational Implications of Intercultural Learning Communities

From a missiological perspective, the gospel is multi-faceted, including individual, collective, and Kingdom-orientation.[238] The concept of intercultural learning communities is a fertile place for RICE-R to interact as gospel ministers and engage with the three facets mentioned above:

> Individual: RICE-Rs can cultivate spirituality and pursue sanctification within the intercultural learning community.
> Collectively: They are expected to nurture the development of vertical relationship with God among all participants.[239]

---

[236] Dawa Sherpa, "Socio Cultural Diversity Interplays on Motivational and Learning," Sotang, *Yearly Peer Reviewed Journal* 1, no. 1 (August 1, 2019): 68, https://doi.org/10.3126/sotang.v1i1.45743.

[237] Andre A Pekerti et al., "*N*-Culturals, the next Cross-Cultural Challenge: Introducing a Multicultural Mentoring Model Program," *International Journal of Cross Cultural Management* 15, no. 1 (April 2015): 9–13, https://doi.org/10.1177/1470595814559532.

[238] Wan and Raibley, *Transformational Change in Christian Ministry*, 46.

[239] Wan and Raibley, *Transformational Change in Christian Ministry*, 49.

Kingdom-orientation: They are strategic facilitators to usher in the reality of "communities of grace" with Kingdom-orientation.[240]

In general, with vertical dynamic interaction with the Triune God, we can expect that RICE-Rs are to be a relational conduit, horizontally overcoming cultural barriers and bridging cultural gaps. By way of relational interactions both vertically and horizontally, all participants within the intercultural learning communities can have missional impact for change in terms of the transformation of lives within their learning communities. If all members of a given intercultural learning community are already committed believers, this opportunity for growth and transformative change is even more meaningful and powerful. All brothers and sisters in Christ within the intercultural learning communities from various cultures can learn, work, love, serve and grow together ("God working among us"). Serving together beyond the intercultural learning communities, RICE-Rs and all participants, can reach outward towards other intercultural communities (i.e. "focus on engaging their neighbors by doing evangelism and justice") as co-participants in mission.[241] Together they can be instrumental cyclically in training other learning communities and preparing many to engage in mission with those from diverse cultural backgrounds and contexts (i.e. "God working through us"). As explained above, from these multi-facets of Gospel-centered transformation, RICE-R and all members within the intercultural learning communities can become pivotal relation-building Kingdom-workers in pursuit of transformational change beyond them.

The relational interculturalist is more than a static bridge that carries knowledge between cultures. They are gifted to flex between multiple cultural contexts to bring the Gospel presence (being) into both of the cultures present. That level of mutual involvement within given communities (belonging) facilitates the possibility of spiritual and cultural transformation (becoming).

---

[240] Wan and Raibley, *Transformational Change in Christian Ministry*, 49.
[241] Wan and Raibley, *Transformational Change in Christian Ministry*, 50.

Program Outcomes

Knowledge	Attitudes	Skills
Comprehension of the Gospel	Desire to follow Christ (disciple)	Utilize helpful tools to study the Bible
Gain understanding of major themes, genres, and teachings of the Bible	Godly attitude leading to piety & wisdom in obedience to God & nurtured by the family of God	Appropriately share testimony and Gospel message
Recognize the importance of Christian community & mutuality: "one and other"	Desire for the fruit of the Spirit (Gal 4)	Successfully attend and participate in church and its ministries
Understand the importance of the local church for learning & growth (church as body & reciprocity)	Receptive to God's molding & ready to help (the family of God locally towards growth and maturity)	Help others in need using his/her strengths.
Comprehension of common cultural dynamics.	The attitude of seeing cultural dynamics within the back-and-forth between humanity created in God's image on one side, and the effects of the Fall so that "all have come short of the glory of God."	The ability to recognize common cultural traits and adjust teaching accordingly.

Figure 8-3. Relational Andragogy & Transformative Change: three dimensions

Level	Knowledge	Attitude	Skills
Personal	✓	✓	✓
Group	✓		✓

Figure 8-4. Program outcomes in cross-cultural training

Goals, Objectives, and Activities

In the training curriculum design process, an entry and exit profile (program outcomes in knowledge, attitudes & skills) are established, followed by specifying program goals, writing learning objectives, and designing learning activities. For each of the three dimensions of program outcomes, goals will be specified. In addition, sample learning objectives and activities will be suggested. The goals pertain to the entire program and its outcomes, whereas the objectives and learning activities are narrower in focus and pertain directly to a particular lesson plan or unit that may be present within the overall curriculum.

Cross-cultural ministry readiness

The specific program outcomes related to Christian formation have already been established in knowledge, skills, and abilities. However, it is also important to ask *why* "cross-cultural ministry readiness" is considered an integral part of the training program. What are the overarching goals or purposes of this curricular component?

First and foremost, the goal of "cross-cultural ministry readiness" is to introduce the Person and message of Jesus Christ to the learners so that, through the work of the Holy Spirit, they might believe and receive Him as Savior and Lord.

Secondarily, the goal of "cross-cultural ministry readiness" is to teach learners the basic relational and behavioral patterns of following Jesus. As can be seen in the program outcomes, these are: specific bases of *knowledge*, such as knowing basic Christian doctrine; *skills*, such as being able to use Bible study tools effectively; and *attitudes*, such as cultural adaptability for Christian mission.

These overarching goals work together with the program outcomes to form specific learning objectives and activities within a particular lesson or unit. For example,………

Each of these lessons would have its own learning objectives, often termed with language such as "learners will be able to…" The lesson, for example, might have the following learning objectives:

1 Learners will be able to identify the multiple factors of …
2 Learners will be able to name three ways for cross-cultural communication….
3 Learners will be able to …

The *manner* in which these lesson objectives are achieved are considered to be the learning activities. For example, for the first objective above, residents might listen to a brief teaching segment about _____, or they might watch a video clip or read about the context of the story from their own textbook. As they do, they might be asked to take notes and list why ___. Or, for the third objective, students might be asked to imagine that they are the victims of prejudice and write a personal letter responding to Jesus. The learning activities directly accomplish the learning objectives for the lesson. The lesson is part of an overall unit that directly supports the program goals related to Christian formation. The learning outcomes, expressed in terms of knowledge, skills, and abilities, become the criteria that enable us to know whether or not the program is accomplishing what it set out to do.

Summary of Relationship between Outcomes, Goals, Objectives, and Activities

Each of the categories of program outcomes have been further developed by identifying the program goals related to each area. Additionally, potential lessons have been suggested so that specific objectives and learning activities can been seen. A summary of these relationships can be seen in Figure 8-5.

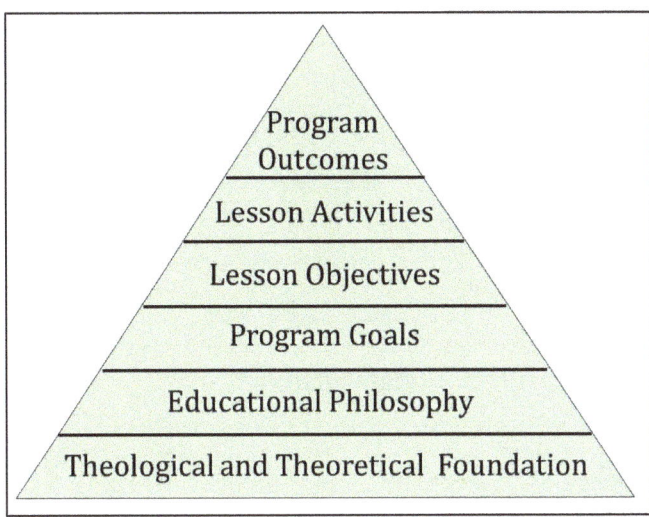

Figure 8-5. Pyramid of Educational Design: from Foundation to Outcomes

Notes:[242]
- TTF (Theological & theoretical foundation): Trinitarian paradigm & relational realism paradigm.
- Educational philosophy: transformative andragogy, outcome-based education.
- Program Goals: transformative change in belief and behavior.
- Lesson Objectives: dual focus: being + doing.

---

[242] Key references for this section are listed below:
- Lewis, Jonathan and Ferris, Robert. "Developing an Outcomes Profile." In *Establishing Ministry Training: A Model for Programme Developers*. Pasadena, CA: William Carey Library, 1995.
- Mezirow, Jack. *Learning as Transformation: Critical Perspectives on a Theory in Progress*. San Francisco: Jossey-Bass, 2000.
- Rogers, Alan. *Non-Formal Education: Flexible Schooling or Participatory Education?* CERC Studies in Comparative Education 15. Hong Kong: Kluwer Academic Publishers, 2005.

- Holistic Perspective: multiple dimensions of cognition, volition, affection, and action.
- Learning Activities: case specifics.
- Program Outcomes: situation specifics

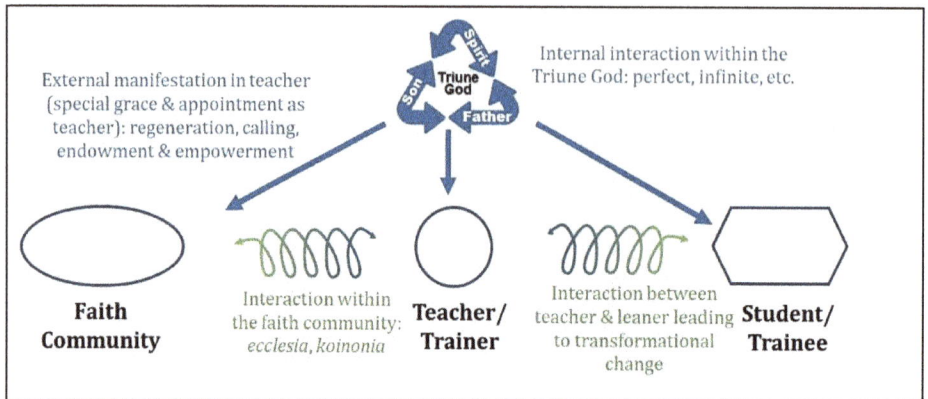

Figure 8-6. Christian adult transformational learning

Transformation involves:
  a. Ontological convergence of spheres (interplay and overlapping)
  b. Pedagogical confluence in dynamic interaction
  c. Integrative change: being + doing; belief + behavior.
  d. Multi-dimensional change: cognition + volition + affection + action within a relational context
  e. Transformative change: divine aid + godly teacher's input + Christian learner's response. Adults, willing to grow and change by entering a relational community, can experience positive change through interactive learning vertically and horizontally.

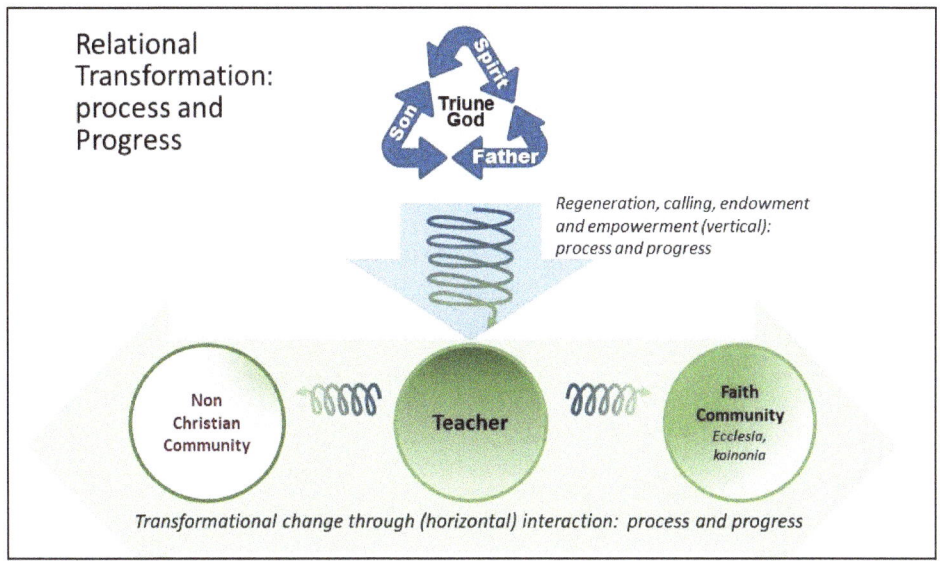

Figure 8-7. Relational transformation: process & progress

Notes:
- Interaction between teacher, learner and learning community (horizontal) leads to transformational change.
- Transformative change = divine aid + godly teacher's input + Christian learner's response (adult receptive to growth and change)

Summary

We began this chapter by contrasting functional and relational approaches to intercultural education. However, an effective educational approach also needs to be functional. The latter part of the chapter, therefore, focused on the practical elements that need to be considered in a relational approach to intercultural education. In Chapters 9 through 14, we will look at case studies of how RICE is being applied in actual ministry settings.

CHAPTER 9
Case Study #1 – Relational Language Acquisition.

Karen Hedinger

Introduction

Second Language Acquisition (SLA) is a discipline that goes back millennia. Ever since the Tower of Babel, people have had to learn other languages to be able to live and work with those from different language and cultural backgrounds.

Before His ascension, Jesus told His disciples to be His witnesses to the ends of the earth and make disciples of all nations. (Acts 1:8; Matt. 28:19-20) Since that day, Jesus' disciples have been His witnesses and have made disciples of the nations for over 2000 years. This has required countless global Kingdom workers to learn a new language.

Language learning has been taught using many methods over the centuries. Jack Richards and Theodore Rodgers have presented many of these approaches in their book, *Approaches and Methods in Language Teaching*.[243] Most of the approaches they presented as well as the curriculum and instruction I first taught were heavily skill and knowledge-based and better suited for a classroom setting. As would be expected, none of the approaches considered relationship with God as paramount to language learning or to building relationships with people in the target language.

For this reason, during my studies in the Doctor of Education in Intercultural Education program, by God's grace, I developed a relational approach to language acquisition which I named "Relational Language Acquisition (RLA)." In June 2020, RLA became the language acquisition training approach for the non-formal training branch of our ministry called CultureBound.

In this chapter, I will present one relational aspect of RLA, the Language Learning Community (LLC), showing how RICE is an integral part of language learning. It is through this LLC that God leads language learners (LL) to people with whom they can develop relationships and learn language.

---

[243] Jack C Richards and Theodore S Rodgers, *Approaches and Methods in Language Teaching* (Cambridge: Cambridge University Press, 2017).

Definitions

A few definitions need to be presented or repeated before discussing the LLC.

Relational intercultural education (RICE)
The formal/informal/non-formal process whereby the educator interacts relationally with the learner towards development/enrichment in "being" and "doing" (i.e. multidimensional elements such as cognitive, affective, volitional...etc.) within a cross-cultural context.[244]

Relational Language Acquisition (RLA)
RLA is an approach to create a language acquisition environment designed for global Kingdom workers that has relational interactionism as its basis. The primary relationship is the relationship between the Triune God (Beings) and people (beings). The secondary relationship is the relationship between people (beings). The characteristics of RLA are these two relationships, attitude and motivation, knowledge, and skills. We identify it as an ecology because it does not presuppose any particular approach or method to language learning. Rather, it posits that language learning by nature is relational.[245]

Relational interactionism
An interdisciplinary narrative framework that develops from practical considerations of dynamic interaction of personal Beings/beings, forming realistic relational networks in multiple contexts (i.e., theo-culture, angel-culture and human-culture) and with various consequences.[246]

Language Learning Community
The strategic use of social ecosystem relationships within a framework of experiential learning to provide a contextualized opportunity for LLs to facilitate language learning, relationship, and relational mission in themselves and others.[247]

Goals of the Language Learner

The goals of the LL are established in relational interactionism and include a dynamic vertical relationship with God and horizontal relationships with others.

---

[244] See Chapter 1.
[245] Karen Hedinger, "A Relational Language Acquisition Approach for Global Kingdom Workers" (Dissertation, Portland, OR, Western Seminary, 2020), 7.
[246] See Chapter 1.
[247] Based on work by Jon Raibley, unpublished IE709 power point presentation at Western Seminary (Portland, OR), Feb. 12, 2019.

Vertical Relationship

The first and foremost goal of the global Kingdom LL is to continually grow in relationship and dependence on God. It is in God that we live and move and have our being (Acts 17:28). Jesus told His disciples that, "Whoever abides in me and I in him, he it is that bears much fruit, for apart from me you can do nothing" (John 15:5).

We can see from John 15 that God is intimately involved in His followers' beings and lives. It is in this relationship that LL receive their call, their ability, and the motivation to learn. It is in this relationship that God equips Kingdom workers with everything good that we may do his will, (including providing knowledge, tools, and skills in language learning) working in us that which is pleasing in his sight, (for apart from him, we can do nothing) (Heb. 13:20-21 ESV).[248]

LLs also realize that God is working in the people to whom they have been sent. Acts 17:28 (see above) was stated to unbelievers. In Romans 5 we read, "But God demonstrates his own love for us in this: While we were still sinners, Christ died for us." Peter also told us, "The Lord is not slow to fulfill his promise as some count slowness, but is patient toward you, not wishing that any should perish, but that all should reach repentance" (2 Pet. 3:9).

Horizontal Relationships

When we consider relationship between humans, we realize that as believers in Jesus, we are to love others as He has loved us (John 13:34). Jesus demonstrated healthy relationship while He lived on earth. Healthy relationships are genuine and mutual, not one-directional or goal-oriented. The chart below summarizes characteristics of genuine relationship.[249]

Level	Knowledge	Attitude	Skills
Personal (individual)	Knowing cultural differences, barriers and bridges	Free from self-centeredness & ethnocentrism	Competence in communication and interaction
Group (institutional)	Appreciative understanding of one & another	Mutuality with respect & reciprocity	Intercultural interaction, godly partnership and God-glorifying reciprocity

Figure 9-1. Characteristics of Genuine Relationship

---

[248] K. Hedinger, "Relational Language Acquisition," 121.
[249] Enoch Wan and Mark Hedinger, "Transformative Ministry for the Majority World Context: Applying Relational Approaches," *EMS Occasional Bulletin*, Spring 2018, 10, https://www.emsweb.org/images/occasional-bulletin/volume-31/OB_Spring_2018.pdf.

LLs experience special challenges in building relationships because they are developing them across cultural and linguistic divides. We can say that the goal of LLs is to practice interculturality as defined earlier in this book.

Instead of being monocultural, interculturality is both the commitment and competence of someone venturing beyond his/her cultural background and boundary with multidimensional qualities, such as self-identity (psychological), multiculturality (ideational), intentionality (attitudinal) and practicality (operational). Thus, "interculturality" is the quality of an ideal intercultural teacher/trainer, including:

- a subjective construction of identity (psychological),
- a desire to embrace "multiculturality" as a goal for growth,
- the ability to navigate among different cultural spaces,
- the competence in two or more languages,
- the ability to relate and interact harmoniously with those who are culturally diverse.[250]

Global kingdom LLs have a higher goal than just becoming bilingual. They also are willing to change, to be sensitive to the target language speakers' behaviors and patterns. That receptiveness also opens the door for relationship.

How can LLs move towards greater interculturality, thus paving the way towards developing the ability to relate and interact harmoniously with those who are culturally diverse?

Language Learning Community (LLC)

In CultureBound's Language Course, participants are encouraged to develop a Language Learning Community (LLC) as a way to build genuine relationships while learning language.

The LLC is comprised of people who can assist LLs in learning the language, even if they only offer a word or phrase or small correction. More important than the language help, though, is that these are people with whom LLs have regular contact, thus opening the door to close enough relationships that Jesus can be seen in the LLs. LLs are encouraged to ask God to help build their LLC. It could happen that LLs might develop deeper relationships with some people in the LLC, sharing life on a deeper level. As language ability grows, LLs can verbally share the reason for the hope in them (1 Pet. 3:15).[251]

Below is an excerpt about the LLC from CultureBound's language training notebook.

---

[250] Luna, Ringberg, and Peracchio, "One Individual, Two Identities: Frame Switching among Biculturals," 283.
[251] K. Hedinger, "Relational Language Acquisition," 110.

Language Learning Community

We will be teaching you how to learn language from the speakers of that language, from people in the various contexts in which you live and function, even if you are attending a formal language school and/or have a trained tutor.

The most important member of your language learning community is God. He is the One who has directed you to build relationships with people by learning to communicate with them in their language and culture. He is also the One who will direct you to members of this community and superintend each relationship. Finally, He will work in the hearts and lives of you and your community members, as you live and show them love as Jesus has loved you.

Different people in your daily contexts will be willing to help you with your language. You might hire a language helper as we describe that role in our course. You might also find a local shopkeeper who is willing to listen to your beginner-level language and even offer suggestions. Some people at church, or work, or the market, or the park might also be willing to engage with you in the new language, even if it is only to listen and respond.

These people might know each other, or they might not. You might interact with some of these people more frequently than others, and your relationship with each person might look different from the others. They might not even realize that you consider them part of your language learning community.[252]

---

[252] Karen Hedinger, Mark Hedinger, and Lauren Wells, *LanguageCourse* (Portland, OR: CultureBound, 2020), 6.

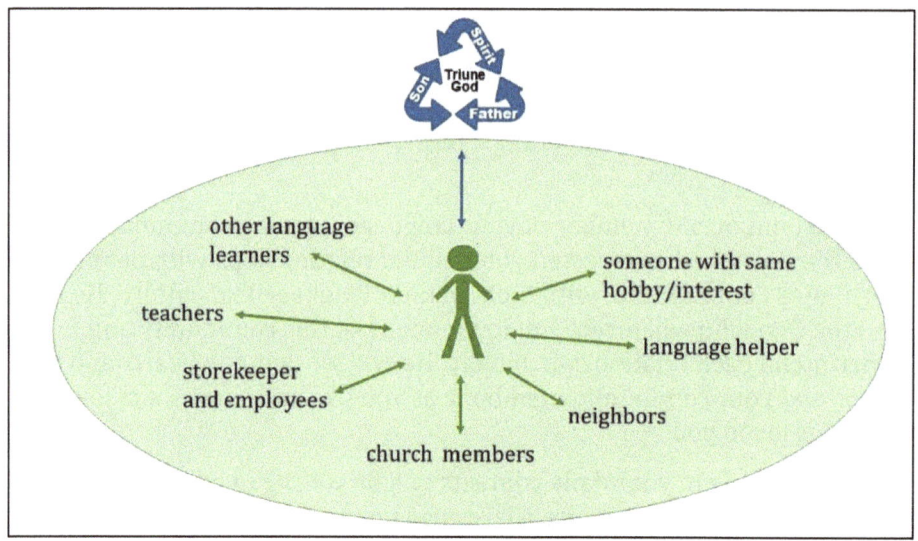

Figure 9-2. Language Learning Community

As LLs build relationships in the new cultural context, God's relational values should be the motivator and means by which LLs build relationship. As they are guided by the Spirit and intentionally observe and learn the various aspects of culture, they will more and more be able to live out God's relational values in an understandable way. As their language ability increases, LLs can talk with their brothers and sisters and unbelievers about God. Living life on life, being involved with people, and being able to talk about God and Scriptural truths should motivate LLs to never stop advancing in their study of the language. They should endeavor to learn how to communicate on deeper and deeper levels with those who are part of their community and networks.

At this point, it is important to stress that LLs are not building relationships with people to use them or to make them a project of evangelism. Genuine relationships are reciprocal with mutual respect. Jesus built genuine relationships with sinners without forcing them to believe in Him and without His condoning their sin or sinning Himself. (See Matt. 9:10, Mark 2:15, and Luke 15:2.)[253]

Language Trainer's Role in LLC

Even though language trainers do not usually know who will be in the LLs' LLC, trainers can pray for that community from a distance. As trainers prepare and teach, they are praying for the trainees and the people with whom they will build relationships, realizing that God already knows those

---

[253] K. Hedinger, "Relational Language Acquisition," 127.

people. The same prayers are lifted up during the training period. It is such an encouragement to know that God is leading and working in trainers, trainees, and target language speakers in the LLC, all at the same time. This is nothing that purely human endeavors could ever accomplish. It is part of the language learning ecology[254] and God's ecology.[255]

RLA is More Than LLC

Relational Language Acquisition has many more elements than just the development of an LLC. Instruction and experiential learning that includes attitudes, skills, and knowledge are also part of the structure of RLA. Some of these elements include:

God's relational values
Self-directed adult learning
Language learning skills and techniques
Working with language helpers
Articulatory phonetics

LLs need to have tools to effectively learn how to communicate in their target language. This was stated earlier in this book:

Ministry must have structure. There have to be methods, plans, approaches to teaching, to preaching, to leading. But ministry done in God's way will be built on a heart that seeks the Lord and that walks in relationship with Him. It is not enough to follow the methods of those who came before; in fact, following the methods without a relationship is "dead works." God calls us first to know Him, and then to serve Him and humanity in the bonds of that personal relationship... Praxis is important but must grow from theology. Action and methods are important but must grow from relational interactions.

Conclusion

RICE is the theoretical foundation of RLA and the LLC. It involves much more than learning a language which can be done without relationship.

The goal of RLA for global Kingdom workers is to encourage a growing relationship between God, LLs, and those who are in the learner's LLC. In relationship, through life and words, they can show God's love and be Jesus' ambassadors among the people to whom the Lord has sent them. This goal should motivate LLs to excel in their language competence, always striving to

---

[254] Ecology is part of the definition of RLA: We identify it [RLA]as an ecology because it does not presuppose any particular approach or method to language learning. Rather, it posits that language learning by nature is relational.
[255] K. Hedinger, "Relational Language Acquisition," 127.

learn more and communicate better and more deeply with the target language speakers that God has sent them to.

Works Cited

Hedinger, Karen. "A Relational Language Acquisition Approach for Global Kingdom Workers." Dissertation, Western Seminary, 2020.

Hedinger, Karen, Mark Hedinger, and Lauren Wells. *LanguageCourse*. Portland, OR: CultureBound, 2020.

Luna, David, Torsten Ringberg, and Laura A. Peracchio. "One Individual, Two Identities: Frame Switching among Biculturals." *Journal of Consumer Research* 35, no. 2 (August 1, 2008): 279–293.

Richards, Jack C, and Theodore S Rodgers. *Approaches and Methods in Language Teaching*. Cambridge: Cambridge University Press, 2017.

Wan, Enoch, and Mark Hedinger. "Transformative Ministry for the Majority World Context: Applying Relational Approaches." *EMS Occasional Bulletin* (Spring 2018). https://www.emsweb.org/images/occasional-bulletin/volume-31/OB_Spring_2018.pdf.

CHAPTER 10
Case Study #2- Relational Teaching Methods (RTMs).

Soo Min (James) Park

Introduction

An intercultural education theory has its own epistemological proposition, an ontological projection, educational procedures, goals, focus, and various pedagogies and teaching techniques. Although there are many aspects and components to the whole subject of intercultural education heuristically, each part is derived or connected within the whole based on the characteristic confines of its educational theoretical framework in significant ways. Therefore, in order to examine, address, and prescribe a proper educational pedagogy or a teaching method for learning, it is necessary to address and lay an appropriate and a justifiable educational foundation at the level of educational framework. Such a foundation is not only essential for furthering and developing education at the theoretical level but is also vital and has implications for the execution of education in all practical aspects.

Since Malcom Knowles' publication of "Andragogy, not Pedagogy" in 1968, and following many of his subsequent publications, there have been many educators' attempts and endeavors to investigate and ascertain various andragogical theories and teaching methods to suit various adult learning needs.[256] Since Christ commanded the disciplers to teach the disciplees to observe heuristically all that He commanded (cognitively, affectively, behaviorally, volitionally), as Christ's kingdom workers, Christian ministers involved in various intercultural teachings are also invited and called to study and reflect upon various teaching methods based on the characteristics of the learners to fulfill the Great Commission (Matt 29:19-20). As an intercultural minister and educator, I had years of teaching experience in cross cultural teaching, but the realization of the necessity to investigate and question the suitable teaching methods more critically occurred to me when I was pastoring and teaching a congregation in Lacey Washington; due to many intermarriages in the congregation with complex congregational characteristics in parts such as the lack of English literacy and limited English reading proficiency by some, restricted English vocabulary, and practical difficulty to teach the non-literate to read due to high propensity to save face yet having English as the only *lingua franca* for the congregation, I was pressed to search and investigate all available teaching methods.

---

[256] Malcolm Knowles, "Andragogy- not Pedagogy," *Adult Leadership 16* no.10 (April 1968): 350-352, 386.

In this chapter, firstly, I analyze five ICE frameworks at their epistemological level for their scriptural validation (positivism, relativism, constructivism, critical theory, and RI). Secondly, after the scriptural validation process of each framework, significant elements with implications for teaching and teaching methods are either deduced or noted from the recognizable description within the validated framework (RI markers). Lastly, I consider twenty-one teaching methods and assess them according to the essential elements of the framework. The goal of the assessment is to delineate suitable teaching methods for various Christian RICE ministries, including the development of hybridized relational teaching methods. The selection of the five RICE frameworks as well as the twenty-one teaching methods in this chapter are personal and are not meant to be comprehensive nor exhaustive.

Definitions

A few definitions are listed here before proceeding further with the pertinent discussions.

Educational Framework
Educational structure and philosophical foundation that supports, prescribes, and defines educational methods, techniques, strategies, curriculum design, learning assessment, and research.

Elements of Relational Interactionism (RI Markers)
Relational elements that play roles in affecting relational dynamisms and the quality, nature, and the extent of one's relational network and matrix.

Intercultural Education (ICE)
The formal/informal/non-formal process whereby the educator interacts relationally with the learner towards development/enrichment in "being" and "doing" (i.e. multidimensional such as cognitive, affective, volitional...etc.) within a cross-cultural context.[257]

Relational Interactionism (RI)
An interdisciplinary narrative framework that develops from practical considerations of dynamic interaction of personal Beings/beings, forming realistic relational networks in multiple contexts (i.e., theo-culture, angel-culture and human-culture) and with various consequences.[258]

Relational Intercultural Education (RICE)
An educator participating in God's *missio Dei* to nurture unity (with cultural diversity), mutuality (in communion and sharing), harmony (shalom - in spite of ethnic diversity), reciprocity (overcoming barriers,

---

[257] See Chapter 1.
[258] See Chapter 1.

e.g. intercultural communication) amidst interaction of personal Beings/beings within an intercultural context.[259]

· In the context of education, RICE is "the formal/informal/non-formal process whereby the educator interacts relationally with the learner towards development/enrichment in 'being' and 'doing' (i.e. multidimensional such as cognitive, affective, volitional... etc.) within an intercultural context.[260]

Relational Teaching Method (RTM)

An educational approach rooted in RI that prioritizes the primal vertical relationship with God and, secondarily, the horizontal relationships within the created order for relationally interactive transformative teaching and learning between teacher and students.

·In the context of education, relational teaching method is an educational approach which emphasizes horizontal relationships and relational aspects between teacher and students for the teaching and the learning process.

Teaching Method

A set of principles, procedures, strategies, and management techniques used by educators to enable student learning and to achieve the desired learning outcomes in the contexts of andragogy or pedagogy.

Scriptural Validation

The process of confirming the validity or alignment of a belief, concept, or theory with the teachings, principles, and messages of the sacred scripture (Bible).

Scriptural Validation and Invalidation of the Five Educational Frameworks

Since an education framework prescribes and determines various teaching methods at both their theoretical and practical levels, it is inevitable to address ICE at its theoretical foundation layer in order to ascertain the suitable teaching methods for practical applications at various Christian ministries. While there are various aspects of ICE as discussed and outlined in Chapters 1-8 such as epistemology, ontology, focus, goals, and different questions being asked, it would be sufficient to address the frameworks at the level of their epistemology. This is because education and its teaching methods are directly linked and related to the epistemology of their frameworks since epistemology deals directly with a major educational question, "How do people learn?"

---

[259] See Chapter 1.
[260] See Chapter 1.

Positivism

Positivism's epistemic stance, which emphasizes empirical observation while excluding introspection, intuition, and belief, is refuted by scripture, which acknowledges the validity of introspection, intuition, and the necessity of belief for knowledge acquisition. Scriptural examples, such as Adam and Eve's knowledge of their nakedness and Christ's teaching on knowing the truth through abiding in His Word, demonstrate that not all knowledge is derived solely from empirical methods (Genesis 3:7; John 8:31b-32a; John 5:24).

Relativism

Relativism's claim that all truths are relative and equally valid is decisively refuted by the scripture as the scripture clearly demarcates truth from lies and condemns falsehoods in ultimate promotion of truth. Numerous biblical passages condemn lying and assert the truthfulness of God's words and pointedly refutes relativism's assertion that all beliefs are equally valid (Proverbs 6:16-17b; Proverbs 12:22; Proverbs 19:5; Revelation 21:8h-j). Furthermore, the scripture attests to the intercultural transferability of knowledge, as seen in Christ's commission to make disciples of *all nations* which invalidates relativism's claim that true knowledge cannot be transferred across cultures (Matt. 28:19-20).

Constructivism

Constructivism's premise that knowledge is constructed from individual experiences and is not directly transferable is invalidated by the scripture, which declares that all knowledge ultimately comes from God and emphasizes the importance of transmitting knowledge from generation to generation. Various biblical passages command the teaching of God's words (Deut. 6:7; 11:19, Matt. 28:20). This assumes transferability of knowledge through relational means and refutes constructivism's denial of direct knowledge transfer. Additionally, scripture asserts that Christ is the ultimate source of truth and knowledge and thereby it invalidates constructivism's emphasis on individual construction of knowledge apart from divine revelation (John 3:27; Proverbs 2:6).[261]

Critical Theory

Critical Theory's focus on societal power imbalances and oppression is repudiated by the scripture, which teaches that Christ is Truth and the

---

[261] Divine revelation is usually used more in a narrow sense by many theologians. Here, it is used to refer the necessary agency of the Son for the enabling of an individual to perceive and know even in the sense of the general revelation and general knowing (John 3:27).

Creator of all things, and that societal injustices are a consequence of sin rather than the primary focus of epistemic endeavor. The scripture emphasizes Christ as the source of all knowledge and declares that societal oppression stems from human sinfulness. This redirects the focus of epistemic inquiry towards Christ rather than societal power dynamics (Job 39:17; John 14:5-6; Deuteronomy 28:34).

Relational Interactionism (RI)

Relational Interactionism on the other hand, in contrast to Positivism, Relativism, Constructivism, and Critical Theory, aligns with the teachings of the scripture, affirming that human knowledge is divinely revealed and enabled (Psalm 19:1-2; John 1:1; 1:14; 3:3; Romans 1:20; Hebrews 1:1-2) through Divine and human dynamisms. The scripture underscores the centrality of relational dynamics in human understanding, emphasizing both primal vertical and secondary horizontal relationships as foundational to perceiving reality and acquiring knowledge (Genesis 21:19; 2 Kings 6:18; Proverbs 1:7; 2:6; Matthew 28:19; John 1:17; 4:28-42; 6:44; 6:65). Epistemic endeavors are depicted in the scripture as intricately connected to relational interactions which unfold across multiple dimensions and contexts (Joshua 2:8-14; 1 Kings 10:1-9; Matthew 16:15-16; 16:18-19; 24:1-8; Mark 8:27-29; Luke 1:5-38; 2:8-20; 9:18-20; 17:11-19; John 1:43-49; 4:42; 6:1-15; 9:1-7; 9:35-38; 21:1-18; 2 Timothy 2:25). Although the scripture doesn't use the phrase "relational interactionism," the scripture indeed both prescribes and describes relational interactionism educational framework for human epistemic knowing through explicit command, through prescription or through various narratives that are portrayed in the scripture.

Markers of Relational Interactionist Educational Framework

Relational interactionism has dialogicality (D), collaboration (C), reciprocity (R), multi-domain and multi-dimensions of teaching and learning (i.e. cognitive, affective, behavioral, spiritual, social, moral, etc.) (M), relationship nurturing and relational network building (B), contextual adaptability (A), relationship orientation (over against task orientation, instrumentalization, and functionalism) (O), relational evaluability (over against lineal and measurable outcomes based evaluability) (E), Christo-centricity (X), and transformative learning inclusivity (T) as its major and essential educational components (markers).[262] Although this list is not an

---

[262] Enoch Wan and Jon Raibley, *Transformational Change in Christian Ministry*, 2d ed. (Portland, OR: Western Academic, 2022), 72; Relational interactionism shares a number of

exhaustive description of relational interactionism's characteristics, these descriptions can be utilized to assess compatibility and suitability of various teaching methods which take place in RICE paradigm via relational interactionism (RI) for various intercultural Christian ministry contexts.

Assessment and Delineation of Teaching Methods Based on RI Markers

The following paragraphs summarize the assessment (RI Assessment Score) of the twenty-one andragogical teaching methods based on the ten relational interactionism characteristics outlined earlier (D,C,R,M,B,A,O,E, X, and T), each accompanied by a description or characteristic. The methods were evaluated as possessing each of the ten characteristics based on either explicit possession of the characteristic or by possession of the potential for its actualization contingent upon their mode of implementation. After evaluating each of the teaching methods in ten categories, the number of qualifying characteristics were added to delineate compatible and the most suitable teaching methods in the context of RI.

Socratic Method. RI Assessment Score: 9/10 (D, C, R, M, B, O, E, X, and T)
- The method of inquiry and instruction employed by Socrates especially as represented in the dialogues of Plato and consisting of a series of questioning the object of which is to elicit a clear and consistent expression of something supposed to be implicitly known by all rational beings[263]

Problem-Based Learning. RI Assessment Score: 10/10 (All)
- Problem-based learning requires students to attempt to resolve problems rather than learn how to solve [264]

---

common components with Jack Mezirow's transformational learning theory in its theoretical framework for education such as the 10 phases of transformative learning, the 4 components of transformative learning, etc. Please refer to the following for more details on the commonalities, the differences, and the adjustments for Mezirow's transformative learning theory's incorporation into the relational interactionism framework: Enoch Wan and Ryan Gimple, *Covenant Transformative Learning: Theory and Practice for Mission* (Portland, OR: Western Academic, 2021). These components are not strictly confined to these ten and are subject for modifications as more research in relational interactionism unfolds.

[263] Merriam-Webster Online, s.v. "Socratic method," accessed November 21, 2023, https://www.merriam-webster.com/dictionary/Socratic%20method; George Polya, "On Learning, Teaching, and Learning Teaching," *The American Mathematical* Monthly 70, no. 6 (June - July 1963): 605-619, https://doi.org/10.2307/2311629; Jennifer L. Rosato, "The Socratic Method and Women Law Students: Humanize Don't Feminize," 7 *S. Cal. Rev. L. & Women's Stud.* 37, 40 (1997); Orin S. Kerr, "The Decline of the Socratic Method at Harvard," 78 *Neb. L. Rev.* 113, 116-118 (1999).

[264] Jill D. Burruss, "Problem-Based Learning," *Science Scope* 22, no. 6 (March 1999): 46-49, https://www.jstor.org/stable/43179798.

Debate. RI Assessment Score: 9/10 (D, C, R, M, B, O, E, X, and T)
- A regulated discussion of a proposition[265]

Group Discussion. RI Assessment Score: 10/10 (All)
- Emphasis on participants' ideas and experiences. Participants' comments on a particular subject are guided by the discussion leader to sharpen and deepen their understanding on the discussion subject matter[266]

Mentorship. RI Assessment Score: 10/10 (All)
- Promotes increase in ability to perceive, to see oneself and others in the broader context, to hold more complexities and ambiguities, and to make wholehearted commitment in the world[267]

Case Study. RI Assessment Score: 10/10 (All)
- Instruction based on real life examples
- Typically includes the following three interrelated components: a case report, a case analysis, and a case discussion [268]

Brainstorming. RI Assessment Score: 10/10 (All)
- A group creativity technique in which efforts are made geared toward a specific problem to find a conclusion by gathering a list of ideas contributed by the group members spontaneously.
- Comprised of an open discussion about a given problem among all the team members with equal participation from all[269]

---

[265] Merriam-Webster Online, s.v. "debate," accessed November 21, 2023, https://www.merriam-webster.com/dictionary/debate.

[266] Marjorie B. Rachlin, "Discussion Method," in *Labor Education for Women Workers* (Philadelphia: Temple University Press, 1981), chap. 9, pp. 111-119, https://doi.org/10.2307/j.ctv6mtdqk.18; Michael W. Galbraith, ed., *Adult Learning Methods: A Guide for Effective Instruction*, 3rd ed. (Malabar, Florida: Krieger Publishing, 2004), 209-226.

[267] Michael W. Galbraith, ed., *Adult Learning Methods: A Guide for Effective Instruction*, 3rd ed. (Malabar, Florida: Krieger Publishing, 2004), 451-472.

[268] Michael W. Galbraith, ed., *Adult Learning Methods: A Guide for Effective Instruction*, 3rd ed. (Malabar, Florida: Krieger Publishing, 2004), 383-404.

[269] Binita Goswami, Anju Jain, and Bidhan Chandra Koner, "Evaluation of Brainstorming Session as a Teaching-learning Tool among Postgraduate Medical Biochemistry Students," *International Journal of Applied and Basic Medical Research* 7, Suppl 1 (December 2017): S15-S18, https://doi.org/10.4103/ijabmr.IJABMR_191_17.

Role-Playing. RI Assessment Score: 10/10 (All)
- Assigned roles are given to students to act out in a given scenario[270]
- Promotes experiential based learning[271]

Symposium. RI Assessment Score: 9 /10 (D, C, R, B, A, O, E, X, and T)
- A series of presentations by two to five persons with outstanding authority on different aspects of a topic or a closely related topic[272]
- Question time follows after the presentations[273]

Panel. RI Assessment Score: 10 /10 (All)
- A small group consisting of three to six people who sit around in front of an audience for purposeful engagement in specific conversations on a topic of their specialized expertise[274]

Forum. RI Assessment Score: 9/10 (D, C, R, B, A, O, E, X, and T)
- An open discussion conveyed by one or more resource persons with an entire group [275]
- characterized by a large size with twenty-five or more people for the group [276]

Simulation. RI Assessment Score: 10/10 (All)
- Enables adult learners to obtain knowledge, competencies, or skills by aiding them to be involved in situations that resemble real life scenarios [277]

---

[270] Nellie Munin and Yael Efron, "Role-Playing Brings Theory to Life in a Multicultural Learning Environment," *Journal of Legal Education* 66, no. 2 (Winter 2017): 309-331, https://www.jstor.org/stable/26402486; Bruce Joyce, Marsha Weil, and Emily Calhoun, *Models of Teaching*, 9th ed. (New York: Pearson Education, 2015), 257-278.

[271] Nellie Munin and Yael Efron, "Role-Playing Brings Theory to Life in a Multicultural Learning Environment," *Journal of Legal Education* 66, no. 2 (Winter 2017): 309-331.

[272] Michael W. Galbraith, ed., *Adult Learning Methods: A Guide for Effective Instruction*, 3rd ed. (Malabar, Florida: Krieger Publishing, 2004), 407.

[273] Michael W. Galbraith, ed., *Adult Learning Methods: A Guide for Effective Instruction*, 3rd ed. (Malabar, Florida: Krieger Publishing, 2004), 407.

[274] Michael W. Galbraith, ed., *Adult Learning Methods: A Guide for Effective Instruction*, 3rd ed. (Malabar, Florida: Krieger Publishing, 2004), 407.

[275] Michael W. Galbraith, ed., *Adult Learning Methods*, 407.

[276] Michael W. Galbraith, ed., *Adult Learning Methods: A Guide for Effective Instruction*, 3rd ed. (Malabar, Florida: Krieger Publishing, 2004), 407.

[277] Michael W. Galbraith, ed., *Adult Learning Methods: A Guide for Effective Instruction*, 3rd ed. (Malabar, Florida: Krieger Publishing, 2004), 361-382.

Demonstration. RI Assessment Score: 4/10 (A, E, X, and T)
- Shows how something works [278]
- Can be supplementary to content and can depict the descriptive content in the actual [279]

Action Learning. RI Assessment Score: 10/10 (All)
- Learning by doing real work [280]
- Synthesis of self-development with action for change [281]

Self-paced Online Courses (Asynchronous Formats). RI Assessment Score: 7/10 (D, C, B, O, E, X, and T)
- Utilizes documents and webpages
- Web computer-based training modules
- Electronic performance support systems(EPSS)
- Recorded live events
- Online learning communities [282]

Live E- Learning (Synchronous Online Formats). RI Assessment Score: 8/10 (D, C, R, B, O, E, X, and T)
- Online meetings
- Web seminars and broadcasts
- Coaching
- Instant messaging [283]

Self-Directed Learning (SDL). RI Assessment Score: 9 /10 (D, C, M, B, A, O, E, X, and T)
- A learner evaluates what he/she knows, needs to know, utilizes resources to fill in the knowledge holes or lacking skills, and evaluates the process on his/her own to meet his/her knowledge needs or skill acquisition [284]

---

[278] Michael W. Galbraith, ed., *Adult Learning Methods: A Guide for Effective Instruction*, 3rd ed. (Malabar, Florida: Krieger Publishing, 2004), 362.

[279] Michael W. Galbraith, ed., *Adult Learning Methods: A Guide for Effective Instruction*, 3rd ed. (Malabar, Florida: Krieger Publishing, 2004), 362.

[280] Judy O'Neil and Victoria J. Marsick, *Understanding Action Learning* (New York, NY: American Management Association, 2007), 1.

[281] Mike Pedler and John Burgoyne, "Action Learning," in Action Research, 3rd ed., ed. Hilary Bradbury (Los Angeles: Sage Publications, 2015), chap. 17.

[282] Harvey Singh, "Building Effective Blended Learning Programs," *Educational Technology* 43, no. 6 (November-December 2003): 52, https://www.jstor.org/stable/44428863.

[283] Harvey Singh, "Building Effective Blended Learning Programs," *Educational Technology* 43, no. 6 (November-December 2003): 52, https://www.jstor.org/stable/44428863.

[284] Daniel Oswald, "Toward an Instructional-Design Theory for Fostering Self-Directed Learning," *Educational Technology* 44, no. 6 (November-December 2004): 31-38, published by Educational Technology Publications, Inc.

Lecture-Based Instruction. RI Assessment Score: 6/10 (D, A, O, E, X, and T)
- An expert in a particular subject presents an informative speech to a group of learners with the goal of information transfer at the cognitive level.[285]

Field Trip. RI Assessment Score: 9/10 (D, C, R, M, B, O, E, X, and T)
- A trip with associated peers to an area outside of the classroom for concrete learning and reflective observation.
- Advantageous especially for students with diverging and assimilating learning styles[286]

Group Project (Project- Based Learning/PBL). RI Assessment Score: 10/10 (All)
- A cooperative educational assignment which requires students to plan, discuss, coordinate, and utilize their various relevant skills with other students for learning and the completion of the assignment[287]
- Its effectiveness can depend heavily on collectivism and individualism cultural tendencies.

Individual Project.[288] RI Assessment Score: 7/10 (M, B, A, O, E, X, and T)
- A project which is designed for an individual student to explore, reflect, engage, and apply relevant skills and knowledge for a deep learning regarding a subject.
- Requires student-centered learning and may have reduced effectiveness for high teacher dependent culture

While all the ten specific teaching methods delineated can be useful and be advantageous for relational teaching in various contexts, hybridization of a few select methods are commendable due to its ability to enhance relational interactions and to increase the actualization of the relational aspects from the potentials the teaching methods inherently possess. These enhancements and increased actualization grow from the methods' complementarity nature

---

[285] Michael W. Galbraith, ed., *Adult Learning Methods: A Guide for Effective Instruction,* 3rd ed. (Malabar, Florida: Krieger Publishing, 2004), 227-252.

[286] Alice Y. Kolb & David A. Kolb, The Kolb Learning Style Inventory 4.0: A Comprehensive Guide to the Theory, Psychometrics, Research on Validity and Educational Application (n.p.: Experience Based Learning Systems, 2013): 9-17, www.learningfromexperience.com.

[287] Vorawat Boondee, Pachoen Kidrakarn, Worawat Sa-Ngiamvibool, "A Learning and Teaching Model using Project-Based Learning (PBL) on the Web to Promote Cooperative Learning," *European Journal of Social Sciences* 21, no. 3 (2011): 498-506.

[288] Jonathan N. Thigpen, *Teaching Techniques: Revitalizing Methodology* (Wheaton Il: Evangelical Training Association, 2001), 36.

and the synergistic effects that follow after certain sequential ordering of the methods diachronically.

The following are two such examples of how to selectively utilize and synthesize the twenty-one teaching methods for more effective relational teaching practice.

Example 1: Mentorship/Simulation/Role-Playing/Group Discussion Iterative Method

Although oral learners [learners who prefer to learn through oral means, remember visually, and communicate concretely and affectively] learn by observation and imitation, it is important that the teacher becomes relationally knowable and relatable to the learners before the utilization of the simulation teaching method due to oral learners' usual tendency to learn from someone they know.[289] In the relational space provided by mentorship, a teacher is empowered to empathize with the learners, engage in dialogue through sharing personal narratives, and expand common ground by showing patience, perseverance, humility, inclusivity, and love. Such interactions and strengthening of connections are crucial in relational teaching since relational teaching prioritizes relationships over the acts and the processes of teaching itself. Moreover, by demonstration of empathy, engaging dialogues, and through expanding common ground by showing Christlike characters, a teacher not only can reflect His character but also can bring His manifest Presence to the learners. Such demonstration and the presence of Christ in mentorship not only can strengthen the trust, depth, and closeness of the relationships necessary for effective learnings to occur in the learners, but can also prepare them to enter into a saving relationship with Christ or to deepen their connections and relationships with Him Who gives a new heart and enables learning through interactions with Himself, Who enlightens, guides, and instructs in the Holy Spirit. Such empowerment to feel and perceive through a new heart, enlightening of the inner eyes, the progression of belonging toward becoming, and the learnings brought about through Christ go beyond a simple paradigm shift or a meaning perspective change brought about by an autonomous critical reflection confined and limited to oneself. Such relationally engaging and connecting mentorship will create room in the learners for the level of trust and the volitional, affective, and cognitive readiness necessary for the oral learners' participation in learning during the implementation of the simulation teaching method.[290]

Utilizing role-playing method after simulation is advisable due to its ability to provide a concrete experience for oral learners beyond the observation gained through the simulation. Such a concrete experience is highly beneficial

---

[289] Tom Steffen and William Bjoraker, *The Return of the Oral Hermeneutics*, 69, 72.
[290] Tom Steffen and William Bjoraker, *The Return of the Oral Hermeneutics*, 70.

for oral learners because oral learners give emphasis on concrete experience for their theoretical formulations and accumulations of learning.[291] With the prior strong relationship established between a teacher and the learners with increased trust and increased understanding of their common grounds, the learners are ready to address questions more openly, express their opinions more comfortably with greater sense of security, and be more transparent about areas where they find implementation challenging based on observations from the simulation stage. Such enhanced horizontal relationship connections between the teacher and the learners with increased rapport are not only beneficial for further cognitive, affective, and behavioral learning, but provides a platform for spiritual impact and influence for gospel-centered transformations and experience of God which is primal and fundamental for all learning.[292]

After a concrete experience gained with the role-playing method, discussions can be employed to enhance the overall learning process of the learners by providing a community of relational learning and knowledge construction. Since oral learners have a strong focus on relationships with people, allowing learners within a community to interact, to reflect on what they have learned communally, to create the narratives of their learning, and to preserve the communal narratives of learning, are crucial. After the implementation of the three prior teaching methods, the learners can dialogically engage with other learners in the learning community, reflect upon what they have learned through relational matrices, and construct or consolidate their theoretical frameworks and learning narratives in light of such reflection.[293]

Iteration of the sequence of the hybridized four teaching methods is beneficial for the enhancement of learning for the oral learners due to oral learners' iterative learning style.[294] Having gone through the discussions with other oral learners in the community, the learners can approach the mentorship with more confidence regarding their learning and can appreciate more regarding the teachings the mentor has provided in the past. Through the iterative process, the teacher is not only open to feedback about the learners' experiences with each component of the hybridized method but is also ready to build upon the learning that took place in the learners, undetached from the various learnings that occurred in each part of the method. Such broader view of the learnings that took place in the learners

---

[291] Tom Steffen and William Bjoraker, *The Return of the Oral Hermeneutics*, 67.
[292] Although general revelation is accessible to all learners, experiencing gospel-centered transformations and encountering God through Christ are necessary for individuals to hold particular knowledge and learning within an appropriate boundary and order framed by the proper overarching metanarrative.
[293] Tom Steffen and William Bjoraker, *The Return of the Oral Hermeneutics*, 72.
[294] Tom Steffen and William Bjoraker, *The Return of the Oral Hermeneutics*, 71.

can help the teacher to stay more connected to the learners, to build relationships, and be more relational by acknowledging and celebrating the learners' achievements beyond the confines of his teaching. Additionally, such process of iteration will create space for the teacher to evaluate the fruit of his teaching, and help him to evaluate his teaching pedagogy, teaching strategy, teaching techniques, the goals of teaching, and the focus of education more in relational terms.

Example 2: Mentorship/Group Discussion/Group Project Iterative Method

Sequentially arranging group discussions after mentorship is highly advantageous for oral learners because mentorship can prepare the learners to participate in the group discussion session more actively and more meaningfully. Mentorship can prepare the learners for group discussions by providing a structural framework regarding a topic, key terms, key concepts, and questions to reflect upon prior to a group discussion session. As mentors guide the learners relationally, with empathy, gentleness, kindness, patience, love, and building upon the learners' responses building on the relationship, the learners will have increased interest in the topic of learning. Furthermore, such mentorship is likely to increase the learners' inclusive attitude of other learners in the discussion session, increase the learners' confidence and motivation to engage in more meaningful dialogues and fruitful learning during the discussion session, and more likely to influence the learners to engage more relationally with other learners to the effect of shaping and impacting them to be more relational in their approach to education.

The implementation of the group discussion before group project complements the project by providing the learners another learning experience with echoes of past learnings and to collectively associate their learning.[295] Although the learners are likely to participate and share various knowledge they have acquired regarding the topics or the subjects involved in the group project due to their collectivistic tendency, the group discussion provides a place for the learners to dialogue and refine their knowledge regarding specific topics or subjects prior to the implementation of the group project. This tuning process will not only provide many echoes of what they have learned in the past for further internal reflections, but also foster greater collective unity, greater cognitive consensus, and smoother execution of the group project, with no participant losing face and preventing impendences or impediments in the future learnings.

The iterative aspect of the three teaching methods will provide the iteration necessary for oral learners for their learning process. Furthermore,

---

[295] Tom Steffen and William Bjoraker, *The Return of the Oral Hermeneutics* (Eugene, OR: Wifi&Stock, 2020), 69.

the iterative process can strengthen the mutual connection through an increase in shared memory, expansion of shared interest, and diachronic transformation which cannot be obtained through a brief lapse of time. It will ensure and reinforce the relational priority in teaching through the repetition of relational mentorship method in the sequence.

Conclusion and Suggestion for Future Research

Based on the procedural analysis carried out as outlined in this chapter, the study's findings are two-fold: firstly, on the scriptural ground, it was demonstrated that RI is scripturally approved educational framework while disapproving positivism, relativism, constructivism, and critical theory, and secondly, after considering ten essential distinctives (markers) from RI for ICE, and analyzing twenty-one teaching methods based on these distinctives, it was determined that problem-based learning, discussion, mentorship, case study, brainstorming, role-playing, panel, simulation, action learning, and group projects best align for RI framework as its teaching methods based on the number of qualifications of the RI distinctives. Additionally, after this analysis, a few methods from the twenty-one were selected and combined as illustrative examples to demonstrate their use in relational teaching practices.

Although there are many possible hybridizations of teaching methods (binary -420, ternary-8400, quaternary-168000), further explorations and research are advisable on different hybridizations of teaching methods for more transformative learning inducive relational teaching practices across various cultural contexts.[296] Furthermore, the extent of the contribution of each RI marker (distinctive) for the whole, each distinctive's relationship with the other(s) for the overall teaching effectiveness, and delineation of other possible RI factors such as the cognitive, psychological, affective, biological, and spiritual maturity of both learners and teachers, are areas in relational teaching methods that require further research.

Works Cited

Boondee, Vorawat, Pachoen Kidrakarn, and Worawat Sa-Ngiamvibool. "A Learning and Teaching Model Using Project-Based Learning (PBL) on the Web to Promote Cooperative Learning." *European Journal of Social Sciences* 21, no. 3 (2011): 498-506.

Burruss, Jill D. "Problem-Based Learning." *Science Scope* 22, no. 6 (March 1999): 46-49. https://www.jstor.org/stable/43179798.

Galbraith, Michael W., ed. *Adult Learning Methods: A Guide for Effective Instruction.* 3rd ed. Malabar, FL: Krieger Publishing, 2004.

---

[296] These numbers represent different sequential approaches to hybridizations based on just twenty-one methods that were personally selected for discussion purposes in this chapter.

Goswami, Binita, Anju Jain, and Bidhan Chandra Koner. "Evaluation of Brainstorming Session as a Teaching-Learning Tool among Postgraduate Medical Biochemistry Students." *International Journal of Applied and Basic Medical Research* 7, Suppl 1 (December 2017): S15-S18. https://doi.org/10.4103/ijabmr.IJABMR_191_17.

Kerr, Orin S. "The Decline of the Socratic Method at Harvard." *Nebraska Law Review* 78, no. 1 (1999): 113-118.

Knowles, Malcolm. "Andragogy—Not Pedagogy." *Adult Leadership* 16, no. 10 (April 1968): 350-352, 386.

Kolb, Alice Y., and David A. Kolb. *The Kolb Learning Style Inventory 4.0: A Comprehensive Guide to the Theory, Psychometrics, Research on Validity and Educational Application.* Experience Based Learning Systems, 2013. www.learningfromexperience.com.

Merriam-Webster Online, s.v. "Socratic method," accessed November 21, 2023, https://www.merriam-webster.com/dictionary/Socratic%20method.

Merriam-Webster Online, s.v. "debate," accessed November 21, 2023, https://www.merriam-webster.com/dictionary/debate.

Munin, Nellie, and Yael Efron. "Role-Playing Brings Theory to Life in a Multicultural Learning Environment." *Journal of Legal Education* 66, no. 2 (Winter 2017): 309-331. https://www.jstor.org/stable/26402486.

Oswald, Daniel. "Toward an Instructional-Design Theory for Fostering Self-Directed Learning." *Educational Technology* 44, no. 6 (November-December 2004): 31-38.

O'Neil, Judy, and Victoria J. Marsick. *Understanding Action Learning.* New York, NY: American Management Association, 2007.

Pedler, Mike, and John Burgoyne. "Action Learning." In *Action Research*, 3rd ed., edited by Hilary Bradbury. Los Angeles: Sage Publications, 2015.

Polya, George. "On Learning, Teaching, and Learning Teaching." *The American Mathematical Monthly* 70, no. 6 (June - July 1963): 605-619. https://doi.org/10.2307/2311629.

Rachlin, Marjorie B. "Discussion Method." In *Labor Education for Women Workers*. Philadelphia: Temple University Press, 1981. https://doi.org/10.2307/j.ctv6mtdqk.18.

Rosato, Jennifer L. "The Socratic Method and Women Law Students: Humanize, Don't Feminize." *Southern California Review of Law and Women's Studies* 7 (1997): 37-40.

Singh, Harvey. "Building Effective Blended Learning Programs." *Educational Technology* 43, no. 6 (November-December 2003): 51-54. https://www.jstor.org/stable/44428863.

Steffen, Tom, and William Bjoraker. *The Return of Oral Hermeneutics: As Good Today as It Was the Herew Bible and First-Century Christianity*. Eugene, OR: Wipf & Stock, 2020.

Thigpen, Jonathan N. *Teaching Techniques: Revitalizing Methodology*. Wheaton, IL: Evangelical Training Association, 2001.

Wan, Enoch, and Ryan Gimple. *Covenant Transformative Learning: Theory and Practice for Mission*. Portland, OR: Western Academic, 2021.

Wan, Enoch, and Jon Raibley. *Transformational Change in Christian Ministry*. 2nd ed. Portland, OR: Western Academic, 2022.

CHAPTER 11
Case Study #3 – Christ-Centered Transformational Education for Second-Generation Chinese Adolescents.

Jessie Yin

Introduction

Christ-centered transformational education is a pedagogical model I developed from the relational interactionist framework. It aims to foster holistic growth in individuals through their relationships with God and others by integrating Spiritual Formation, Ministry Training, Outreach and Mission from a Christ-centered scope. This model emphasizes relational transformation and Christ-centered character development, preparing individuals to embrace the indwelling of Christ vertically and reflect the splendor of Christ horizontally.

This chapter will examine the essence of Christ-Centered Transformational Education and its application to Relational Intercultural Education (RICE), particularly within the youth ministry context. By reviewing recent interviews and insights gathered from a Christian youth camp in an intercultural setting, the efficacy of this model will be validated through a comprehensive case study analysis among Second-generation Chinese adolescents and their parents.

Definition of Key Terms

Youth Ministry
Refers to the church's tailored ministry for individuals aged 11 to 17, encompassing various programs and activities within a church context. Youth ministry has emerged as a relatively recent addition to the church's strategy worldwide.

Adolescents/Youth
Individuals within the age range of 11 to 17.

First-generation Chinese
Individuals born in a region culturally rooted in Chinese traditions who have migrated to America as the initial generation of their family undergo this immigration experience.

Second-generation Chinese Adolescents / Chinese-American Adolescence
Adolescents with at least one parent who is a first-generation Chinese immigrant.

Christ-Centered Transformational Education
Christ-centered transformational education integrates relational interactionism and transformational growth principles to nurture holistic growth. It emphasizes spiritual formation, ministry training, outreach, and mission within a Christ-centered framework, focusing on relational transformation and character development.

Chinese congregations
Christian gatherings in America comprised of first-generation Chinese immigrants who speak Chinese as their native language and second-generation Chinese who speak English.

RICE for Second-generation Chinese Adolescents

Most second-generation Chinese-American adolescents in the United States receive education in America. In contrast, most first-generation Chinese immigrants received education in Asia before adulthood, resulting in significant cultural differences. Within Chinese congregations in America which are composed mainly of first-generation Chinese immigrants, educating second-generation constitutes intercultural education.

From a relational transformation perspective, intercultural youth ministry involves Christians from different cultures and ages interacting with others to develop and enhance their Christ-like character and behavior together.[297] As Christ transcends generations and cultures, embracing His likeness encourages individuals from different backgrounds to increasingly mirror Him, ultimately bridging the gap between people's differences.

Beyond cultural differences, adolescent education also differs significantly from adult education due to ongoing brain development and cognitive differences, despite their physical similarities with adults.[298] Understanding these biological traits provides insight into adolescents' cognitive capacities and their developmental diversities.[299] It is also notable that peer relationships play a more significant role in adolescent education, as peers are a primary source of information outside the family. Peer interactions can

---

[297] Enoch Wan, Mark Hedinger, and Jon Raibley, *Transformational Growth: Intercultural Leadership/Discipleship/Mentorship* (Western Academic Publishers, 2023), 33.

[298] Frances E. Jensen and Amy Ellis Nutt, *The Teenage Brain: A Neuroscientist's Survival Guide to Raising Adolescents and Young Adults*, Reprint edition (Harper Paperbacks, 2016), 13–15.

[299] John Santrock, *Adolescence,* 17th edition (McGraw-Hill Education, 2018), 92.

have both positive and negative impacts, particularly affecting adolescents' self and social identity. Therefore, adolescent education requires adjusting teaching methods and environments according to the characteristics specific to this group.

As mentioned in Chapter 4, effective education across cultures requires using teaching methods that fit the learners, even if they do not match the preferences of the educators. According to the critical concept of RICE, education is relational, and we should not just see adolescents as objects to teach. Instead, we need to understand their interactions and culture by entering their world and attempt to build relationships beyond the existing culture gap. When designing a curriculum for second-generation adolescents in Chinese congregations, it is crucial to carefully consider cultural and age differences and involve the second generation in the whole church body.

Christ-Centered Transformational Education

RICE contains a dynamic interconnection of interactions between teachers and students, among fellow students, and among teachers, students, and God. When exploring the transformational change brought about by Christian education, the impact of these relational interactions on individual transformation inevitably comes into play. Individuals are no longer isolated entities, and education is not merely self-development but rather the result of mutual interactions with others.

Colossians 1:27-28 summarizes the core of transformational education, emphasizing Christ as the center of everything: " To them God chose to make known how great among the Gentiles are the riches of the glory of this mystery, which is Christ in you, the hope of glory. Him we proclaim, warning everyone and teaching everyone with all wisdom, that we may present everyone mature in Christ. " "Christ in you" underscores the experience of Christ dwelling within, signifying an intimate vertical relationship with God. "The hope of glory" not only encompasses the individual's vertical relationship with God but also, in the first half of the sentence, implies that the glorious riches of Christ can be manifested through believers' lives, serving as a testimony to others. "All wisdom" indicates the flexibility in employing various teaching methods according to students' needs, with the ultimate goal of bringing individuals into an intimate relationship with Christ and growing in His likeness.

Paul serves as a model in Christian education, leaving us valuable insights. Based on Paul's teachings, we can summarize seven Christ-centered characteristics of transformational education: Character like Christ (1 Cor 11:1), involves one person with a Christ-like character influencing another to imitate Christ. Confidence in Christ (1 Tim 4:12), the confidence in Christ stems not from accumulated credentials but from Christ's character. Competence from Christ (Rom 12:6), we receive spiritual gifts from Christ and must exercise them wisely and diligently. Commitment to Christ (Gal 6:9), serving the Lord requires perseverance and not giving up easily. Courage through Christ (2 Tim 1:12), to courageously face suffering and persecution in Christ, without fear, knowing that Christ guards us. Collaboration under Christ (Eph 4:16), the growth of Christians is not independent but within the context of a complete body of Christ, where each part contributes to mutual growth and beneficial interaction with others. In Communication of Christ (Mark 16:15 / 2 Tim 2:2), Jesus taught his disciples, emphasizing that the life of Christ within us is meant to reach out to all people. Paul also explicitly instructs Timothy regarding the intergenerational transmission of education.

These Christ-centered characteristics are not just markers of leadership but a Christian's inevitable expressions of experiencing Christ's indwelling, that he/she will naturally manifest Christ's glory. They are also the goals we pursue in transformational education. I propose the educational process of developing these seven Christ-centered characteristics as Christ-Centered Transformational Education, with three stages, A to C to achieve these goals, as displayed in Figure 11-1.

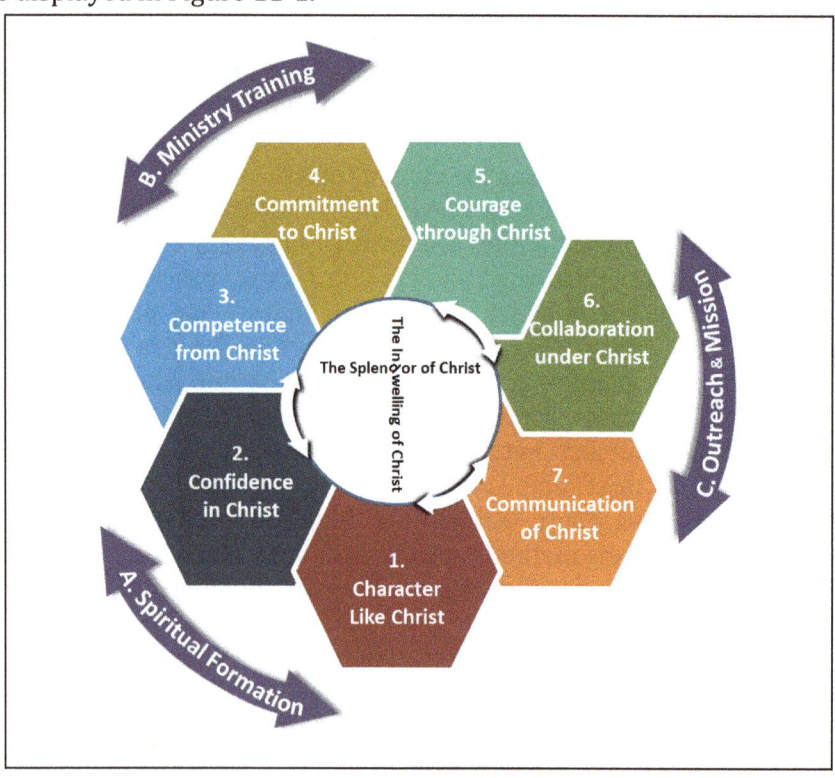

Figure 11-1. Christ-Centered Transformational Education

Stage A, Spiritual Formation, focuses on enhancing students' internal character and confidence through biblical teachings and spiritual development. This stage is guided by spiritual mentors within the framework of relational interactionism. Stage B, Ministry Training, develops students' abilities and capacities through practical ministry experiences, strengthening their character within a community and fostering transformational change. Stage C, Outreach and Mission, helps students cross boundaries, spread the gospel, become witnesses, and impact more lives. These three stages echo and emphasize the transformative journey of God's work in us (Being), God's work among us (Belonging), and God's work through us (Becoming).[300]

These three stages, with overlapping timelines, can cycle continuously, built towards Christ-centered qualities. This educational model enables experiencing Christ's indwelling vertically and manifesting His glory horizontally in relationships. It shapes the Christian community internally and its relationships with society, emphasizing the church's unity with Christ as its head. In the context of youth ministry, these three steps can be conducted interchangeably or simultaneously, blending to help adolescents achieve comprehensive development in faith, service abilities, and intercultural experiences. Such an educational model can help adolescents establish a solid foundation of faith and prepare them to be future servants and soldiers of God's kingdom.

Application in Youth Ministry as a youth camp design

There are diverse teaching methods in the Bible, and there is no absolutely correct way, although many churches tend to insist that only lecturing from the pulpit is the most orthodox form.[301] When we return to the Bible, we can see that Jesus attached great importance to creatively designing teaching activities according to the needs of students in their specific culture. He would tell stories, use real-life examples, and have a practical hidden curriculum.[302] As a teacher, Jesus' example helps us think about what teaching methods are suitable for the context of RICE, especially for Chinese-American adolescents.

Young people need contact with faithful individuals who can influence them to make godly decisions in real encounters and see hope in a broken world—something that cannot be provided online.[303] At the same time, we

---

[300] Enoch Wan and Jon Raibley, *Transformational Change in Christian Ministry*, Second Edition (Western Academic Publishers, 2022), 12.

[301] George M. Hillman Jr and Sue Edwards, eds., *Invitation to Educational Ministry: Foundations of Transformative Christian Education* (Kregel Academic, 2018), 68.

[302] Mark A. Maddix and James Riley Jr. Estep, *Practicing Christian Education: An Introduction for Ministry*, Illustrated edition (Grand Rapids, Michigan: Baker Academic, 2017), 116–17.

[303] Hillman and Edwards, *Invitation to Educational Ministry*, 412.

should give adolescents the "ownership" of serving, allowing them space to lead ministries in the real world while providing sufficient support and protection.[304] When they are more involved, the learning process goes deeper.[305] We can also educate through stories because not only was this frequently used by Jesus, but it has also been a long-standing teaching method in different cultures for different ages.[306] After considering these factors, Los Alamos Chinese Christian Fellowship (LACCF) attempted a new teaching activity in early 2024 through an interactive youth camp to practice and explore, meeting the needs of adolescents and promoting their growth. This camp invited a Taiwan Christian organization, "YaTong Theater," to bring their design of scenario-based theater games and invited their coworkers to serve as directors and mentors for the camp. I was responsible for designing and leading morning worship and messages each day and also served as a mentor.

The "Prince, Princess, Dragon" youth camp was a five-day daytime event held at LACCF for adolescents in grades six and above. The camp structure focused on a story where a prince and princess, overcoming past conflicts, joined forces to defeat a fire dragon using Nerf Guns. Campers spent the first four days setting up large-scale scenery for the battles they designed. During the first four days, they were divided into two groups: the drama team rehearsed the story of the prince and princess uniting to defeat the dragon, integrating live performances of their conflicts and growth. The scenery design team used church props to create scenes, control lighting, and manage sound effects for the final interactive game. On the final day, the entire church community, including adults and children from both the Chinese congregation and the affiliated American church, and campers' peers from the community, were invited to join a 1.5-hour interactive Nerf game together. Campers also shared their preparations and spiritual insights with the guests afterward.

Our teaching approach of the camp emphasized building relationships through experiential learning and promoting collaboration among adolescents. With a mentor-to-adolescent ratio of 1:2, all mentors who guided students through the tasks were first-generation Chinese, forming intercultural relationships and education. Collaboration was also encouraged, with drama performances requiring line memorization and group cooperation, while construction projects involved group design competitions. In designing the camp curriculum, I incorporated biblical teachings aligned with the camp's theme. Each day started with morning worship and thematic

---

[304] Kara Powell, Brad M. Griffin, and Cheryl A. Crawford, *Sticky Faith, Youth Worker Edition: Practical Ideas to Nurture Long-Term Faith in Adolescentsagers* (Zondervan, 2011), 156.

[305] Howard Hendricks, *Teaching to Change Lives: Seven Proven Ways to Make Your Teaching Come Alive*, Reprint edition (Multnomah, 2003), 46.

[306] Hillmann and Edwards, *Invitation to Educational Ministry*, 390.

messages to empower adolescents to overcome challenges, drawing inspiration from biblical lessons and personal stories. Additionally, activities such as scenery construction, Nerf game design, and drama performances were integrated into the curriculum, offering students opportunities to engage in teamwork, leadership, and spiritual growth.

Feedback from Adolescents' and Parents' Interview

The interview content from both adolescents and parents was analyzed deductively, focusing on the three stages of Christ-centered transformational education: Spiritual Formation, Ministry Training, and Outreach & Mission, encompassing aspects such as personal and spiritual growth, development of social and leadership skills, and reflections on mentorship and community involvement.

Spiritual Formation:

Parents noted adolescents' personal growth, citing increased confidence and responsibility, attributing these changes to their participation in the winter camp. They also observed a deepening of their children's spiritual understanding, influenced by thematic Bible teachings and live worship experiences. Adolescents echoed these observations, expressing personal and spiritual growth through newfound boldness and insights gained from camp activities and Bible studies.

- **Parent:** "I think her confidence has developed, and she was very introverted and wouldn't express herself."
- **Youth:** "We had Bible studies in the morning. I think it was good, sort of using our story of the dragon prince and the princess as a metaphor for living as a Christian."

Ministry Training:

Parents highlighted adolescents' development of teamwork, communication, and leadership skills during performances, emphasizing their children's positive attitude and ability to work together effectively. Adolescents recognized the importance of teamwork and communication skills, acknowledging the trust and understanding fostered among peers. Furthermore, parents and adolescents alike appreciated the opportunities for creativity and problem-solving, which enhanced their courage and competence in facing challenges.

- **Parent:** "No one seems to complain... he feels good about himself, they are very proud of themselves."
- **Youth:** "I learned that in order to make something work, you have to really have good teamwork and communication skills and also leadership..."

Outreach & Mission:

Parents commended mentors from YaTong Theater for their positive influence on adolescents and their dedication to the camp activities. They also valued the opportunity for family and community involvement, seeing it as a means to strengthen familial bonds and faith-sharing. Adolescents similarly appreciated the mentors' guidance and the chance to collaborate with parents and community members, though they noted some challenges in coordination and communication.

- **Parent:** "The brothers (YaTong's coworkers) are role models for them, influencing them by example."
- **Youth:** "I felt a sense of accomplishment because it looked like the parents and community members were having fun and it was because of the thing that we created..."

Conclusion

In Christ-centered transformational education, the three steps of spiritual formation, ministry training, and outreach and mission closely follow the process of transformative change: divine aid, the input of godly teachers, and the Christian learner's response. From the case study, we observe the following:

Firstly, spiritual formation is deeply connected to divine aid. God's guidance and intervention are crucial in nurturing the character and faith of adolescents. This step focuses on personal spiritual growth and developing a Christ-like character through daily worship and Bible study. This represents the "being" phase, grounding individuals in their identity in Christ.

Secondly, ministry training involves the guidance of godly teachers who mentor students through practical ministry experiences. Mentors from YaTong Theater and LACCF provide essential support, helping adolescents translate Biblical teachings into actionable skills. This stage embodies the "belonging" phase, where adolescents build relationships within the community of believers, reinforcing their sense of belonging to the body of Christ.

Lastly, the outreach and mission phase highlights the Christian learner's response. Students actively engage in spreading the gospel and participating in mission work. This engagement reinforces their learning and demonstrates their growth in faith, ministry skills, and leadership. By leading activities like Nerf games and storytelling, adolescents apply their training in real-world contexts. This is the "becoming" phase, where they step into their roles in God's mission, growing into their calling and impacting others to follow Christ.

In summary, the case study illustrates how Christ-centered transformational education, applied through the lens of Relational

Intercultural Education (RICE), positively impacts second-generation Chinese adolescents. Through a youth camp experience, we have observed how this approach nurtures holistic growth, deepens spiritual understanding, and cultivates essential social and leadership skills. The camp's emphasis on fostering Christ-centered character development and building cross-cultural relationships with God and others, including peers and first-generation Chinese, highlights its effectiveness in promoting transformational growth among the youth.

Works Cited

Banks, James A. "Approaches to Multicultural Curriculum Reform." *Trotter Institute Review* 3, no. 3, Article 5 (June 1989): 17–19.

———. "Diversity, Group Identity, and Citizenship Education in a Global Age." *Educational Researcher* 37, no. 3 (April 2008): 129–39. https://doi.org/10.3102/0013189X08317501.

———. "Multicultural Education: Characteristics and Goals." In *Multicultural Education: Issues and Perspectives*, 3–30. John Wiley & Sons, 2010.

Banks, James A. "Teaching for Social Justice, Diversity, and Citizenship in a Global World," 68:296–305. Taylor & Francis, 2004.

Benet-Martínez, Verónica, and Ying-yi Hong, eds. *The Oxford Handbook of Multicultural Identity*. Oxford University Press, 2014. https://doi.org/10.1093/oxfordhb/9780199796694.001.0001.

Bennett, Milton J. "A Short Conceptual History of Intercultural Learning in Study Abroad." In *A History of U.S. Study Abroad: 1965 - Present*, 419–49. Forum on Education Abroad, 2010. https://www.idrinstitute.org/wp-content/uploads/2018/02/short_conceptual_history_ic_learning.pdf.

Berben, Kenneth J. "Social Pragmatics and the Origins of Psychological Discourse (Chapter 6)." In *The Social Construction of the Person*, n.d. https://www.researchgate.net/publication/290002177_Social_Pragmatics_and_the_Origins_of_Psychological_Discourse#fullTextFileContent.

Berne, Eric. *Games People Play: The Psychology Of Human Relationships*, 2010.

Boud, David. "Experience and Learning: Reflection at Work. EAE600 Adults Learning in the Workplace: Part A," n.d. https://www.academia.edu/29435057/Experience_and_Learning_Reflection_at_Work_EAE600_Adults_Learning_in_the_Workplace_Part_A.

Bradley, Akirah. "A Time to Intervene: A Historical Overview of Pedagogical Responses to an Unjust Society." *The Vermont Connection* 28, no. 1 (January 1, 2007): 70–79.

Brookfield, Stephen D. "Transformative Learning as Ideology Critique." In *Learning as Transformation: Critical Perspectives on a Theory in Progress*, 125–48. San Francisco: Jossey-Bass, 2000.

Cartwright, John, Gabriel Etzel, Christopher Jackson, and Timothy Paul Jones. *Teaching the World: Foundations for Online Theological Education*. Nashville: B&H Academic, 2017.

Cavalier, Robert J. "Introduction to Habermas's Discourse Ethics," n.d.

Chan, Siu Kuen Sonia. "A Relational Model of Intercultural Learning and Interactions." Dissertation, Western Seminary, 2023.

Chiu, Ai Chen (Noel). "Key Parameters of Establishing Frontline LGBTQ Outreach." PhD Thesis, Western Seminary, 2021.

Constable, Thomas L. "Notes on Genesis," Edition 2024. https://www.planobiblechapel.org/tcon/notes/html/ot/genesis/genesis.htm.

Cross, K. Patricia. "Why Learning Communities? Why Now?" *About Campus* 3, no. 3 (July 1, 1998): 4–11. https://doi.org/10.1177/108648229800300303.

Cummins, Jim, Joanne Tompkins, and Sonia Nieto. "The Light in Their Eyes: Creating Multicultural Learning Communities." *TESOL Quarterly* 35, no. 1 (2001): 200. https://doi.org/10.2307/3587870.

Cushner, Kenneth, and Jennifer Mahon. "Intercultural Competence in Teacher Education: Developing the Intercultural Competence of Educators and Their Students: Creating the Blueprints." In *The SAGE Handbook of Intercultural Competence*, 304–20. Thousand Oaks, CA: SAGE Publications, Inc, 2009.

Dewey, John. "John Dewey My Pedagogic Creed." *School Journal* 54 (January 1897): 77–80.

Eugenics at Stanford. "Ellwood Cubberley | Stanford Eugenics History Project." Accessed December 28, 2023. https://www.stanfordeugenics.com/ellwood-cubberley.

Everist, Norma Cook. *The Church as Learning Community: A Comprehensive Guide to Christian Education*. Nashville, TN: Abingdon Press, 2002.

Freire, Paolo. "Pedagogy of the Oppressed (Revised)." *New York: Continuum*, 1996.

Gay, Geneva. "Preparing for Culturally Responsive Teaching." *Journal of Teacher Education* 53, no. 2 (March 2002): 106–16. https://doi.org/10.1177/0022487102053002003.

Gibson, Margaret Alison. "Approaches to Multicultural Education in the United States: Some Concepts and Assumptions." *Anthropology & Education Quarterly* 7, no. 4 (1976): 7–18.

Gleason, Philip. "The Odd Couple: Pluralism and Assimilation." In *Speaking of Diversity: Language and Ethnicity in Twentieth-Century America.*, 47–90. Johns Hopkins University Press, 2019. https://muse.jhu.edu/pub/1/oa_monograph/chapter/2412200.

Guan, Shu-Sha Angie, Afaf Nash, and Marjorie Faulstich Orellana. "Cultural and Social Processes of Language Brokering among Arab, Asian, and Latin

Immigrants." *Journal of Multilingual and Multicultural Development* 37, no. 2 (February 17, 2016): 150–66. https://doi.org/10.1080/01434632.2015.1044997.

Hargrave, Susan. *Doing Anthropology*. Kangaroo Ground, Vic.: South Pacific Summer Institute of Linguistics, 1993.

Hatcher, Tim. "Towards Culturally Appropriate Adult Education Methodologies for Bible Translators: Comparing Central Asian and Western Educational Practices," n.d.

Hedinger, Karen. "A Relational Language Acquisition Approach for Global Kingdom Workers." Dissertation, Western Seminary, 2020.

Hedinger, Karen, Mark Hedinger, and Lauren Wells. *LanguageCourse*. Portland, OR: CultureBound, 2020.

Hendricks, Howard. *Teaching to Change Lives: Seven Proven Ways to Make Your Teaching Come Alive*. Reprint edition. Multnomah, 2003.

Hiebert, Paul G. *Anthropological Insights for Missionaries*. Grand Rapids, Mich: Baker Book House, 1985.

———. *Anthropological Reflections on Missiological Issues*. Grand Rapids, Mich: Baker Books, 1994.

———. *The Gospel in Human Contexts: Anthropological Explorations for Contemporary Missions*. Grand Rapids, Mich: Baker Academic, 2009.

———. *The Missiological Implications of Epistemological Shifts : Affirming Truth in a Modern/Postmodern World*. Christian Mission and Modern Culture. Harrisburg, Pa: Trinity Press International, 1999. https://search.ebscohost.com/login.aspx?direct=true&db=e000xna&AN=242967&site=ehost-live&scope=site.

History. "A Century of Trauma at U.S. Boarding Schools for Native American Children," July 9, 2021. https://www.nationalgeographic.com/history/article/a-century-of-trauma-at-boarding-schools-for-native-american-children-in-the-united-states.

IDRInstitute. "DMIS Model." Accessed April 8, 2024. https://www.idrinstitute.org/dmis/.

"Intercultural Education | DICE Project." Accessed February 27, 2019. http://www.diceproject.ie/de-ice/intercultural-education/.

Jang, Sujin. "Cultural Brokerage and Creative Performance in Multicultural Teams." *SSRN Electronic Journal*, 2017. https://doi.org/10.2139/ssrn.3056274.

Jensen, Frances E., and Amy Ellis Nutt. *The Teenage Brain: A Neuroscientist's Survival Guide to Raising Adolescents and Young Adults*. Reprint edition. Harper Paperbacks, 2016.

Johnson, Lauri D., and Yoon K. Pak. "Teaching for Diversity: Intercultural and Intergroup Education in the Public Schools, 1920s to 1970s." In *Review of*

Research in Education, 1–31. SAGE Publications, 2019. https://doi.org/10.3102/0091732X18821127.

Jr, George M. Hillman, and Sue Edwards, eds. *Invitation to Educational Ministry: Foundations of Transformative Christian Education*. Kregel Academic, 2018.

Jung, Joanne J. *Character Formation in Online Education: A Guide for Instructors, Administrators, and Accrediting Agencies*. Grand Rapids: Zondervan Publishing House, 2015.

"Kallen, Horace Meyer." In *Jewish Virtual Library*. jewishvirtuallibrary.com. Accessed December 26, 2023. https://www.jewishvirtuallibrary.org/kallen-horace-meyer.

Knight, George R. *Philosophy & Education: An Introduction in Christian Perspective*. Fourth. Berrien Springs, MI: Andrews University Press, 2006.

Knight, Jane. "Updating the Definition of Internationalization," n.d., 2.

Krass, Alfred C. "Contextualization for Today." *Gospel in Context* 2, no. 3 (July 1979): 27–30.

"Larry Cuban on School Reform and Classroom Practice: Schools as Factories: Metaphors That Stick | National Education Policy Center." Accessed December 28, 2023. https://nepc.colorado.edu/blog/schools-factories.

Li, Ci-Rong, Chen-Ju Lin, Yun-Hsiang Tien, and Chien-Ming Chen. "A Multilevel Model of Team Cultural Diversity and Creativity: The Role of Climate for Inclusion." *The Journal of Creative Behavior* 51, no. 2 (June 2017): 163–79. https://doi.org/10.1002/jocb.93.

Lowe, Stephen D., and Mary E. Lowe. *Ecologies of Faith in a Digital Age: Spiritual Growth through Online Education*. Downer's Grove: IVP Academic, 2018.

Luna, David, Torsten Ringberg, and Laura A. Peracchio. "One Individual, Two Identities: Frame Switching among Biculturals." *Journal of Consumer Research* 35, no. 2 (August 1, 2008): 279–93. https://doi.org/10.1086/586914.

Lurie, Howard, and Richard Garrett. "Deconstructing Competency-Based Education: An Assessment of Institutional Activity, Goals, and Challenges in Higher Education." *The Journal of Competency-Based Education* 2, no. 3 (2017): e01047. https://doi.org/10.1002/cbe2.1047.

Maddix, Mark A., and James Riley Jr. Estep. *Practicing Christian Education: An Introduction for Ministry*. Illustrated edition. Grand Rapids, Michigan: Baker Academic, 2017.

Morgan, Christopher. "The Nature of Sin." The Gospel Coalition. Accessed July 8, 2024. https://www.thegospelcoalition.org/essay/the-nature-of-sin/.

Neuner, Gerhard. "The Dimensions of Intercultural Education." In *Intercultural Competence for All: Preparation for Living in a Heterogeneous World*, 11–50. Council of Europe Pestalozzi Series, 2. Council of Europe, 2012.

Nickerson, Charlotte. "False Consensus Effect: Definition and Examples," November 3, 2022. https://www.simplypsychology.org/false-consensus-effect.html.

Ong, Walter J. *Orality and Literacy: The Technologizing of the Word*. 2nd Edition. New Accents. New York: Routledge, 2002.

Pekerti, Andre A, Miriam Moeller, David C Thomas, and Nancy K Napier. "N-Culturals, the next Cross-Cultural Challenge: Introducing a Multicultural Mentoring Model Program." *International Journal of Cross Cultural Management* 15, no. 1 (April 2015): 5–25. https://doi.org/10.1177/1470595814559532.

Plueddemann, James E. *Teaching Across Cultures: Contextualizing Education for Global Mission*. Downers Grove, IL: IVP Academic, 2018.

Pollock, David C., and Ruth E. Van Reken. *Third Culture Kids: Growing up among Worlds*. Revised edition. 1 online resource (xiv, 306 pages) : illustrations vols. Boston: Nicholas Brealey Publishing Boston, 2009.

Powell, Kara, Brad M. Griffin, and Cheryl A. Crawford. *Sticky Faith, Youth Worker Edition: Practical Ideas to Nurture Long-Term Faith in Teenagers*. Zondervan, 2011.

Raibley, Jon. "Experiencing Communities of Learning: A Phenomenological Study of Students Enrolled in Western Seminary's Online Master of Divinity Program." Western Seminary, 2021.

"Research Paradigms – Methodologies, Methods, and Practices," January 19, 2023. https://writeprofessionally.org/research-methods/2023/01/19/research-paradigms/.

Richards, Jack C, and Theodore S Rodgers. *Approaches and Methods in Language Teaching*. Cambridge: Cambridge University Press, 2017.

Santrock, John. *Adolescence*. 17th edition. McGraw-Hill Education, 2018.

Sherpa, Dawa. "Socio Cultural Diversity Interplays on Motivational and Learning." *Sotang, Yearly Peer Reviewed Journal* 1, no. 1 (August 1, 2019): 65–71. https://doi.org/10.3126/sotang.v1i1.45743.

Sleeter, Christine E. "Multicultural Education as a Form of Resistance to Oppression." *Journal of Education* 171, no. 3 (1989): 51–71.

Smith, James K. A. *You Are What You Love: The Spiritual Power of Habit*. Grand Rapids: Brazos Press, 2016.

Sparks, Sarah D. "Why Teacher-Student Relationships Matter." Education Week, March 12, 2019. https://www.edweek.org/ew/articles/2019/03/13/why-teacher-student-relationships-matter.html.

Stewart, James E. "A Snapshot of the Student Experience - Pre-Interview Questionnaire," October 25, 2011.

Taylor, Edward W, and Patricia Cranton. "A Content Analysis of Transformative Learning Theory," n.d.

Verywell Mind. "The Psychology of What Motivates Us." Accessed October 29, 2024. https://www.verywellmind.com/what-is-motivation-2795378.

Volf, Miroslav. *Exclusion and Embrace, Revised and Updated: A Theological Exploration of Identity, Otherness, and Reconciliation*. Updated edition. Nashville: Abingdon Press, 2019.

Wan, Enoch. "A Critique of Charles Kraft's Use/Misuse of Communication and Social Sciences in Biblical Interpretation and Missiological Formation." *Global Missiology, Research Methodology*, October 2004, 29.

———. "Critique of Functional Missionary Anthropology." *His Dominion* 8, no. 3 (April 1982).

———. "Global People and Diaspora Missiology." Presentation at Plenary session presented at the Tokyo 2010—Global Mission Consultation, Tokyo, Japan, May 13, 2010.

———. "Relational Theology and Relational Missiology." *Occasional Bulletin* 21 (2007): 1–8.

———. "Rethinking Urban Mission in Terms of Spiritual and Social Transformational Change." Presented at the Missiological Society of Ghana/WAMS Biennial International Conference, Virtual, October 26, 2021.

Wan, Enoch, and Siu Kuen Sonia Chan. "CONTEXTUALIZATION THE ASIAN WAY: RELATIONAL CONTEXTUALIZATION." *Asian Missions Advance*, no. 78 (Winter 2023). https://www.asiamissions.net/asian-missions-advances/amadvance-52-60/asian-missions-advance-78/.

Wan, Enoch, and Mark Hedinger. "Transformative Ministry for the Majority World Context: Applying Relational Approaches." *EMS Occasional Bulletin*, Spring 2018. https://www.emsweb.org/images/occasional-bulletin/volume-31/OB_Spring_2018.pdf.

Wan, Enoch, Mark Hedinger, and Jon Raibley. *Transformational Growth: Intercultural Leadership/Discipleship/Mentorship*. Western Academic Publishers, 2023.

Wan, Enoch, and Natalie Kim. *Relational Intercultural Training for Practitioners of Business As Mission: Theory and Practice*. Western Academic Publishers, 2022.

Wan, Enoch, and Jon Raibley. *Transformational Change in Christian Ministry*. 2nd edition. Portland, OR: Western Academic Publishers, 2022.

———. *Transformational Change in Christian Ministry Second Edition*. Western Academic Publishers, 2022.

———. *Transformational Change in Christian Ministry Second Edition*. Stanford: Western Academic Publishers, 2022.

———. "Transforming Meaning Perspectives and Intercultural Education." In *Covenant Transformative Learning Theory and Practice for Mission*, 147–62. Western Seminary Press, 2021.

Weibel-Orlando, Joan, Frances E. Karttunen, and Margaret Connell Szasz. "Between Worlds: Interpreters, Guides, and Survivors." *Ethnohistory* 42, no. 4 (1995): 659–62. https://doi.org/10.2307/483151.

Wiles, Jerry. "Digital Orality: New Signs of Spiritual Opportunities." *International Orality Network* (blog). Accessed January 6, 2024. https://orality.net/content/digital-orality-new-signs-of-spiritual-opportunities/.

Zilliacus, Harriet, and Gunilla Holm. "Multicultural Education and Intercultural Education: Is There a Difference?" In *Dialogues on Diversity and Global Education*, 11–28, 2009.

CHAPTER 12
Case Study #4 – The Importance of Names.

Robert Aguayo

Introduction

    I clearly remember the moment at the graduation ceremony when I received my Ed.D. in Education, and as I was preparing to walk to receive my diploma, the person calling my name pronounced it incorrectly. It is odd to think that this is the main thing I remember about my graduation ceremony, especially after so many years of study in order to walk across that stage. Names are important and growing up between two sociocultural contexts with one last name from my father which is hard to pronounce in the United States, and a second last name from my mother that was hard to pronounce in Mexico (which uses both parents' last names), I automatically ended up spelling out my last names when introducing myself to others. Knowing a person's name and learning how to pronounce it correctly has always been important to me not only personally, but also as an educator, as I find it an essential connection with the students I am teaching.

    The importance of names became even clearer to me in the last years as I worked teaching adults in Uganda. As I joined a ministry that was training pastors and leaders, I was introduced to some of the local leaders and even some of the students with their name and a number, for example James 1 or James 2. The reason behind this was that the original teacher, because of the difficulty with the local names, did not take the time to learn the students' full name and since there were a lot of repeated names, decided to number them in order to be able to know to which one he was referring. This did not sit well with me as a teacher, especially after all the classes in intercultural education for my current Ph.D. program. Karen Pennesi tells us that, "a person's name is seen as somehow continuous with a person's value, so nowhere can names be used in an absurd or irresponsible way without that having implications on the bearer."[307]

---

[307] Karen Pennesi, "'They can learn to say my name': Redistributing Responsibility for Integrating Immigrants to Canada." *Anthropologica 58,* no. 1 (2016): 52, https://www.jstor.org/stable/26350524

This issue with names became even more important on my last trip to Uganda for a medical outreach, where I was in charge of doing the malaria tests and the first question I asked them was, "what is your name?" What I found as I heard their answers and began to ask more questions on the names themselves and their significance was something that has given me new insights into the importance of names in intercultural education. I found it true as Pennesi tells us that, "personal names carry multiple social meanings that may associate a particular name with a language, gender, age, range, ethnicity, socio-economic status, marital status, religion, or kin group. These categorical associations adhere to names through historical use and contribute to the formation of the name bearer's social identity..."[308]

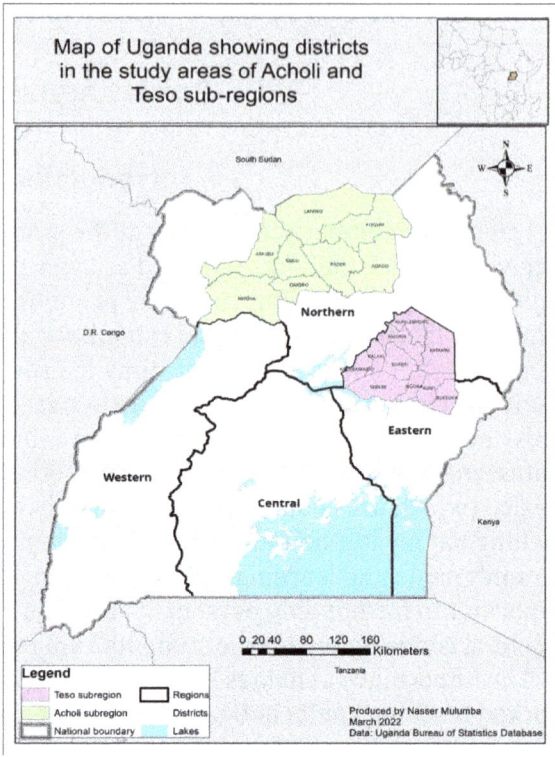

Figure 12-1. Teso sub-region of Uganda

Cultural Background

My first visit to Uganda was in 2014 and in the last 10 years I have been privileged to be able to go and train pastors to study and teach God's Word. The area where we have been called to work is in the eastern part of Uganda among the Teso (Iteso) people. The national language of Uganda is English but there are 41 different local languages that are spoken in the different areas of Uganda. Ateso is the local language in our area of ministry and is taught alongside English in school in the Teso sub-region seen in Figure 12-1.

As I got to know the people that we were working with in the province of Ngora, I was introduced to them by their "Christian" name. Norah Orawanga, tells us, "Uganda's sustaining legacies of colonialism include one's "first name" not being their "family name"; and in many cases not a Ugandan name. Our colonizers required that we have their names as our "religious names";

---

[308] Ibid.

and it is those names, for example, one's "Christian name" that they elevated as the "first name."³⁰⁹ I found out as I began to ask questions that in the Teso tribal cultures each person has several names. There is their Christian name which can change depending on the local church influences, for example you can have a name from a Christian or Anglican church tradition like James, George, Samuel, or Isaac, or from a Catholic tradition like Boniface or Emmanuel. We would see these variations as we were doing medical missions in different areas in the sub-region where names would vary from one place to another. We also had Islamic names in some areas but they were not as prevalent. Along with these names each person had a traditional name (like Oselle, Omoding, Eboku, Maraka, Oromait, Agiru, Amunyelet, Odeke, Ilima, Atim, Acan, etc.) which are family names. These were the names that were given to me first when we were doing medical missions and as I asked questions about these names, I found out that they had a very important meaning behind them. Susan Suzman tells us that "children in many African societies have meaningful names – unlike their Western counterparts, whose names are primarily labels. In Zulu, Xhosa, Sotho, Tswana, and many other cultures, name givers traditionally chose personal names that pointed to a range of people and circumstances that were relevant at the time of the child's birth."³¹⁰ As I began to ask questions, I found that people are named by their families depending on the time of year or season that they were born, or for a special event that took place, or according to their family birth order, if they were firstborn or twins. We see some examples of names that I found in figure 12-2.

    I found while asking for their names during the medical clinics, that there is no special order as to how to place their names and no concept of first or last name, but usually the family name is mentioned first and then the Christian/Islamic name. Ben Jones tells us that, "in Iteso tradition a child is named when the umbilical cord is cut. This name will be one of a number of names available to the "*ateker*" (the extended family of aunts, uncles, cousins). This is why children almost never share the same name as a parent." ³¹¹ This is why as he continues to tell us that, "for many in the village, this *ateker* name functions as a first name and it is usual to refer to people by their *ateker* name rather than their Christian name, which only comes at baptism." ³¹²

---

    ³⁰⁹ Norah Orawanga. 2020. "Expat Gaze Part 4 – Ugandan Names." (blog) October 15, 2020, https://nowaraga.com/2020/10/15/expat-gaze-part-4-ugandan-names/
    ³¹⁰ Susan M. Suzman, "Names as pointers: Zulu personal naming practices." *Language in Society 23*, no. 2, (June 1994): 253, https://www.jstor.org/stable/4168516
    ³¹¹ Ben Jones. 2009. "What's in a name?" *The Guardian* (International Edition) February 23,2009. https://www.theguardian.com/society/katineblog/2009/feb/23/how-names-chosen-meaning-katine
    ³¹² Ibid.

Event or Special Occasion	Names Associated (male/female)
Born during the rainy season	Okiru/Akiru, Ekidon/Ikidon
Born during a drought	Okolong/Ocakolong
Born during a famine	Otenge/Atenge
Born during planting season	Ayiet/Ikinyom
Born during harvest	Odwenyat/Adwenyat
Born during war, disaster,	Emariat/Amariat Acanit
Born after previous children died	Etyang/Atyang, Emodo, Etawoi/Atawoi.
Born by the roadside	Orot/Arot
Born at night	Okware
Born at dawn	Ojore
Born twins (firstborn)	Opio/Apio or Odongo/Adongo (2 set of
Born twins (second born)	Ochen/Achen
First born	Okia/Akia
Born after twins	Okello/Akello

Figure 12-2. Ateso Names

In learning some of the names I also noticed that special names have also come into use through a Christian influence. You have many names, especially for girls that reflect Christian characteristics such as Blessing, Mercy, Fortunate, or Constance. These are not only used in English but also in an Ateso version as Mario Cisternino, tells us that, "research shows the different kinds of individual names (which are more precisely called birth names); their meanings, their value, and their development caused by the Christian faith. It shows in a self-evident manner their better, autonomous development in achieving and showing a Christian mentality..."[313]

Intercultural Education Implications

As we have seen, Intercultural education promotes the understanding of different peoples and cultures. Enoch Wan and Jon Raibley present us with the model of "being," "belonging," and "becoming" as a relational process of transformational change. In this model they, "see change as a process of understanding who we are as individual beings, seeing how we interact in social networks we belong to, and deliberately shaping those interactions to help the process of transformation and growth."[314] This is explained further in Figure 12-3.

---

[313] Mario Cisternino, "Evolution of Birth Names among the Kiga of Western Uganda." *Anthropos* Bd.72, H. 3./4. (1977): 467, https://www.jstor.org/stable/40459133

[314] Enoch Wan and Jon Raibley. *Transformational Change in Christian Ministry*. Portland, OR.: Western Academic Publishers, 2022: 27.

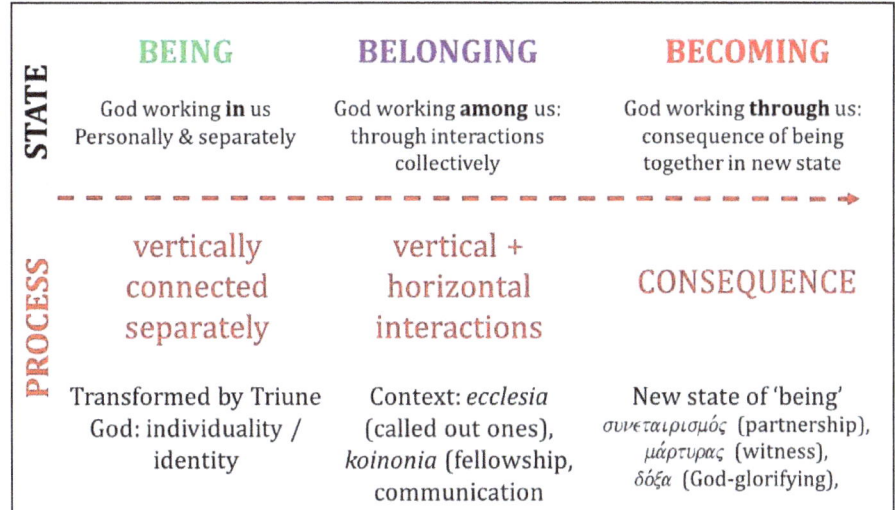

Figure 12-3. Relational Realism and Transformational Change[315]

Names and name usage is an important part in this process. As we have seen names, especially in the African traditions, are not simply labels but describe our being and this is the initial connection that God uses for the transformational process. In all cultures names have a special meaning, Rita Kohli and Daniel K. Solórzano show that, "as a baby, identity and self-concept are developed through a family's repeated use of a child's name... additionally, names frequently carry cultural and family significance. Names connect children to their ancestors, country of origin or ethnic group, and often have deep meaning or symbolism for parents and families."[316] This is where our "Being" begins to be formed. They continue to tell us that, "when a child goes to school and their name is mispronounced or changed, it can negate the thought, care and significance of the name and thus the identity of the child."[317] On the other hand, Pennesi tells us that, "having one's name recognized, remembered, accepted, and correctly pronounced and spelled contributes to a sense of belonging."[318] Brandon Bosch tells us,

---

[315] Enoch Wan, Mark Hedinger, and Jon Raibley. *Transformational Growth: Intercultural Leadership, Discipleship, Mentorship*. Portland, OR: Western Academic Publishers, 2023: 68.

[316] Rita Kohli and Daniel G. Solórzano, "Teacher, please learn our names!: racial microaggressions and the K-12 classroom." *Race Ethnicity and Education 15*, no. 4, (September 2012): 444, http://dx.doi.org/10.1080/13613324.2012.674026

[317] Ibid.

[318] Karen Pennesi, "'They can learn to say my name': Redistributing Responsibility for Integrating Immigrants to Canada." *Anthropologica 58,* no. 1 (2016): 48, https://www.jstor.org/stable/26350524

There are several reasons for instructors to invest the cognitive and temporal resources necessary to recognize their students by name. First, learning names may help teachers better connect with their students. Second, names are "emotional loaded" and can have important cultural, familial, and racial/ethnic meanings to an individual. Third, failure to call students by the correct name can leave students feeling humiliated and undervalued. Finally, our brains respond uniquely to the sound of our own names compared to hearing the names of others, which can be seen with functional magnetic resonance imaging... knowing student names can also enable an instructor to create an environment that is more likely to increase student engagement. [319]

Belonging is the second aspect whereas Enoch Wan, Mark Hedinger, and Jon Raibley tell us that we are, "originally from different cultures but entering the 'belonging' phase: interacting with one another within an intercultural context, vertically submitting to the sovereignty of the Father, under the lordship of Christ and indwelt by the Holy Spirit."[320] As intercultural educators, taking the time to learn our students' names is foundational to all the other teaching and learning that will happen afterwards. As we bring about these vertical and horizontal interactions we will, as Wan, Hedinger, and Raibley tell us, "become members of the faith community (the Church) and bless one another horizontally through fellowship and God-centered communication. Despite cultural differences and possible language barriers, they interact with humility, mutuality, and unity horizontally."[321] We see this in the figure below where the process of intercultural discipleship is seen in action.

---

[319] Brandon Bosch, "Does being known matter? Analyzing the Effects of Name Recognition by Instructor and Student." *College Teaching* (2023): 2, https://doi.org/10.1080/87567555.2023.2203893

[320] Wan, Enoch, Mark Hedinger, and Jon Raibley. *Transformational Growth*, 68.

[321] Wan, Enoch, Mark Hedinger, and Jon Raibley. *Transformational Growth*, 68.

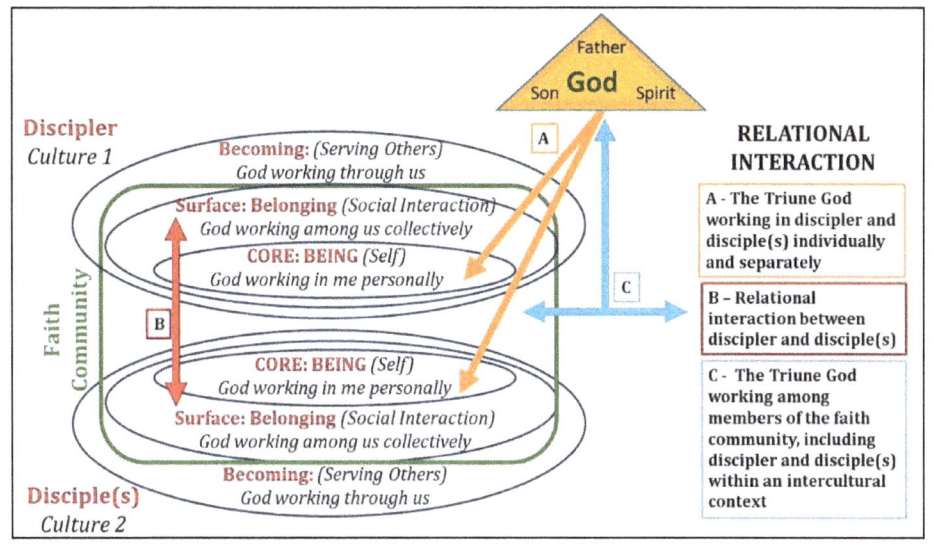

Figure 12-4. Intercultural Discipleship in Action[322]

As we take this one step further and we focus on becoming, we find the importance of names in the relational interaction between our Creator and His creation and His plans and purposes for us. One of the first things we see that God does is to give His creation a name that reflects his creation as being made from the dust of the earth. In Genesis 2:18-19 we are introduced to Adam whose name means earth or soil and later God calls him to give names to the other creatures around him, "And the LORD God said, 'It is not good that man should be alone; I will make him a helper comparable to him.' Out of the ground the LORD God formed every beast of the field and every bird of the air, and brought them to Adam to see what he would call them. And whatever Adam called each living creature, that was its name."[323] Adam later names his wife Eve as we see in Genesis 3:20, "Adam called his wife's name Eve, because she was the mother of all living."[324] Names have great importance in Scripture and we even see cases of God changing someone's name such as the case of Abram to Abraham and Saul to Paul, but in each case the name change reflected the change that God had brought about in them and the implications of the plans and purposes for their lives. We are also promised a new name as we come into the presence of our Creator, but it will be His name that will be given to us. In Revelation 3:12 we see that, "He who overcomes, I will make him a pillar in the temple of My God, and he shall go out no more. I will write on him the name of My God and the name of the city

---

[322] Ibid, 107.
[323] NKJV
[324] NKJV

of My God, the New Jerusalem, which comes down out of heaven from My God. And I will write on him My new name."[325]

Conclusion

Wan, Hedinger and Raibley show us that, "the importance of that two-way relationship is that, on a horizontal plane, both discipler and disciple will be impacted by their interaction… In the same way, God works in both the disciple-maker and the disciple. He brings growth and increasing maturity and the joy of His Spirit to all who are serving and growing."[326]

Many times as educators we can fall into a pragmatic mindset and put aside the relational interaction, as we want to reach the goal of educational transformation. This is especially true in an intercultural setting where learning the names and correct pronunciation can be a difficult process for the teacher and thus not seen as an important aspect of education. In order to reach an intercultural mindset, we need to value and take the time to connect relationally to our students and make that initial connection with their names. This will lay a foundation for a greater intercultural understanding that will allow us to bring about the transformative changes that we are working towards in ICE. This is not only a transformation of thought and action that we need to go through as Intercultural Educators, but it is also part of the transformation process that God works in our lives to make us more into His image. We are transformed through "becoming" and in His name letting Him work through us to serve others. Isaiah 62:2 tells us, "The Gentiles shall see your righteousness, and all kings your glory. You shall be called by a new name, which the mouth of the LORD will name. You shall also be a crown of glory in the hand of the LORD, and a royal diadem in the hand of your God."

Works Cited

Bosch, Brandon. "Does being known matter? Analyzing the Effects of Name Recognition by Instructor and Student." *College Teaching* (2023): 2, https://doi.org/10.1080/87567555.2023.2203893

Cisternino, Mario. "Evolution of Birth Names among the Kiga of Western Uganda." *Anthropos* Bd.72, H. 3./4. (1977): 465-485, https://www.jstor.org/stable/40459133

Jones, Ben. 2009. "What's in a name?" *The Guardian* (International Edition) February 23, 2009. https://www.theguardian.com/society/katineblog/2009/feb/23/how-names-chosen-meaning-katine

---

[325] NKJV
[326] Wan, Enoch, Mark Hedinger, and Jon Raibley. *Transformational Growth*, 108.

Kohli, Rita and Daniel G. Solórzano. "Teacher, please learn our names!: racial microaggressions and the K-12 classroom." *Race Ethnicity and Education 15*, no. 4, (September 2012): 441-462, http://dx.doi.org/10.1080/13613324.2012.674026

Orawanga, Norah. 2020. "Expat Gaze Part 4 – Ugandan Names." (blog) October 15, 2020, https://nowaraga.com/2020/10/15/expat-gaze-part-4-ugandan-names/

Pennesi, Karen. "'They can learn to say my name': Redistributing Responsibility for Integrating Immigrants to Canada." Anthropologica 58, no. 1 (2016): 46-59, https://www.jstor.org/stable/26350524

Suzman, Susan M. "Names as pointers: Zulu personal naming practices." *Language in Society 23,* no. 2, (June 1994): 253-272, https://www.jstor.org/stable/4168516

Wan, Enoch, Mark Hedinger, and Jon Raibley. 2023. *Transformational Growth: Intercultural Leadership, Discipleship, Mentorship*. Portland, OR: Western Academic Publishers.

Wan, Enoch, and Jon Raibley. 2022. *Transformational Change in Christian Ministry*. Portland, OR.: Western Academic Publishers.

CHAPTER 13

Case Study #5: International Student Ministry (ISM) Workers as Relational Intercultural Educators (RICE-R) in Discipleship of International Students.

Estera Piroşcă Escobar

Introduction

In Scripture we can see clearly how Jesus, the master educator, called and made disciples by utilizing a variety of creative educational methods. These methods were crafted such that they would be understandable from the perspective of the learners' cultural patterns. As His followers, believers are called to be His witnesses and make disciples of all peoples, which includes crossing cultural boundaries. One of the avenues for Relational Intercultural Education (RICE) is discipleship of international students where God calls International Student Ministry (ISM) workers to be relational intercultural educators (RICE-R) used by Him in the life of international students in an intercultural setting.

This chapter will examine a model for intercultural relational discipleship in the context of ISM and its application to RICE.

Definition of Key Terms

A few definitions are listed before advancing with a discussion of an intercultural relational discipleship model.

- **International student ministry (ISM)** – "Christians relationally carrying out *missio Dei* and Christian ministry to students from other countries."[327]
- **International student ministry (ISM) workers** – Full-time practitioners/vocational ministers who are employed at a Christian church or para-church organization, such as a nonprofit entity, serving in Christian ministry among the diaspora group of international students.

---

[327] Enoch Wan, "Introduction," in *Diaspora Missions to International Students*, ed. Enoch Wan (Portland: Western Seminary Press, 2019), 8.

- **International students** – "The diaspora category of those who voluntarily leave their homeland to reside in a host country, usually temporarily, for educational and professional advancement."[328]

Intercultural Relational Discipleship Process

In the context of ISM, the discipleship of international students is an important component of the ministry and is also a relational educational process in an intercultural context. I will utilize the model of Intercultural Relational Discipleship Process (see Figure 1) to outline the process of discipleship in the context of ISM and its application to RICE. The model is based on the theory of RICE (see Chapter 3).

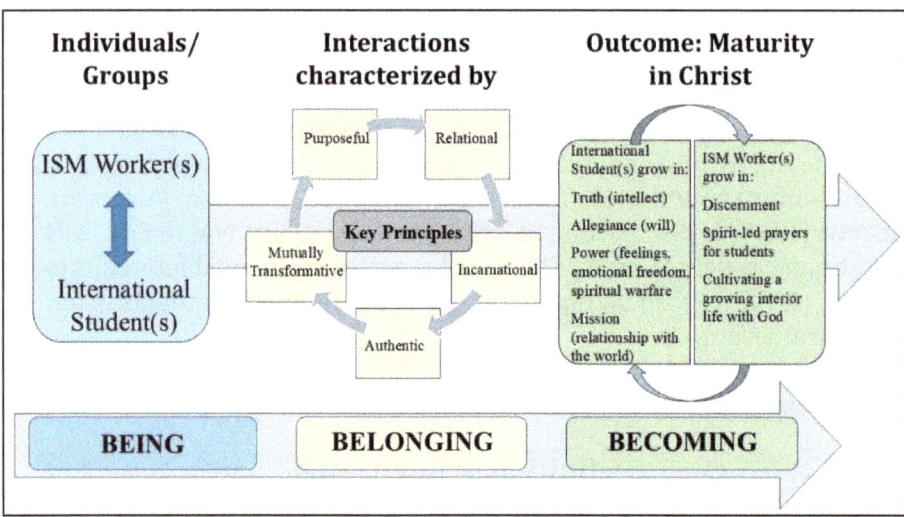

Figure 13-1. Intercultural Relational Discipleship Process in ISM as an Application of RICE

Both ISM worker and international student as individual "beings" embark on a relational intercultural educational process led by the Triune God who uses the godly ISM worker in this process. The process is graphically displayed by the grey arrow in the background. They form connections with each other and others, indicated by the up-down arrow in "being" phase, interacting in various ways in an intercultural educational context of "belonging" that is relational, incarnational, authentic, mutually transformative, and purposeful. The goal is for them to "become" mature in

---

[328] Leiton Edward Chinn, "The Global ISM Movement Emerging From Diaspora Missions On Campuses: From John R. Mott to Lausanne," in *Diaspora Missions to International Students*, ed. Enoch Wan (Portland: Western Seminary Press, 2019), 119.

Christ and to be used by God in the transformation of others. The change does not take place solely in the international student, but in the ISM worker as well. This is indicated by the right and left arrows in the "becoming" phase.

"Being:" ISM Workers and International Students

There are several themes that highlight who ISM workers are as individual beings entering the discipleship process and relational elements that allow them to form connections.

ISM Workers as "beings"	Relational Elements
Immigration status	The ISM workers born in the US minister in their home country among international students. The foreign-born ISM workers minister outside of their home country among international students.
Roles associated with ISM workers	ISM workers find modes of connection with international students. Specifically, there are three areas that reflect their roles in connecting, such as "showing hospitality, meeting physical and social needs, and, most importantly, discussing the spiritual side of life. A common denominator is building friendships with students."[329]
Transcultural workers	The attitudes that characterize ISM workers as transcultural workers are those of learning, postponing judgment, and inquisitiveness.[330]

Figure 13-2. Themes of ISM Workers as "beings" and Relational Elements

I will cover three experiences that highlight who international students are as individual beings entering the discipleship process and relational elements that allow them to form connections.

---

[329] Jack Burke, *Paradigm Shift: Why International Students Are So Strategic to Global Missions*, (Bloomington: Westbow Press: 2019), 210.

[330] Denis LaClare, "Wearing Different Hats: The Attitudes, Behaviors, and Experiences of Six Transcultural Workers," (PhD diss., Biola University, 2018), 140.

Experiences of International Students as "beings"	Relational Elements
Acculturative experiences	When international students leave their homelands and spend time pursuing higher education in the US, they will go through changes that impact the discipleship journey. Some students can adjust well to life in the US while others' experiences lead them to reject and remain outsiders to the local society.
Academic experiences	International students arrive with expectations to obtain a degree, to excel academically, and to eventually be accomplished in their career.
Religious experiences	International students who willingly join a discipleship journey are already followers of Jesus. Some of them come as believers from their home countries, while others become Christians in the US.

Figure 13-3. Experiences of International Students as "beings" and Relational Elements

"Belonging:" Key Principles of Discipleship

The next phase in the model of Intercultural Relational Discipleship Process is "belonging." The ISM worker and the international student interact by following some key principles: relational, incarnational, authentic, mutually transformative, and purposeful.

Relational

The first principle is relational. There are seven possible relationships that could be involved in the discipleship process.[331] The table below provides a brief description for each relationship.

Relationships in the Discipleship Process	Brief Description
Within the Trinity	The Triune God is relationship and He desires to relate to His creation.
God and the ISM worker	Before any discipleship techniques and methods, the ISM worker relates to God vertically first (John 15:4).

---

[331] This is an adaptation of the seven missionary relationships within a relational paradigm of intercultural ministry training proposed by Enoch Wan and Mark Hedinger in Chapter 6 of their book, *Relational Missionary Training* (Skyforest: Urban Loft Publishers, 2017).

Relationships in the Discipleship Process	Brief Description
God and the international student	God is actively relating to the international student.
ISM worker and international student	There are several elements of interpersonal relationships that are vital: sharing of one's life, serving as example, and balancing love and truth.[332]
ISM worker in culture	ISM workers minister to and along international students in their home country, within their host culture. Yet they minister within a diaspora setting.
International student and his/her culture	The international students come from different countries and cultures than the ISM workers. ISM workers need to understand "what is going on when people leave their home culture, go to a completely different culture, profess faith in Christ, and then return to the original culture"[333] or wherever God might lead them after graduation.
Involvement of other created beings	Other created beings are angels and demons. God in His mercy transferred ISM workers and international students from the Kingdom of Darkness into the Kingdom of Light. However, they must be on their guard, realize they are engaged in spiritual warfare and could experience harassment from Satan (John 10:10).

Figure 13-4. Seven Relationships in the Intercultural Discipleship Process in ISM

Incarnational

The second key principle in interactions between an ISM worker and an international student is to be incarnational. Fernando argued that "there is something to be said about intimate friends, such as those in a discipling relationship, being in each other's homes."[334] The impact of being in such an place of importance in people's lives, such as their home, is that it "fosters an openness and depth in the relationship."[335] Through mundane activities international students experience a godly lifestyle in relationships.

---

[332] Robert W. Pazmiño, *Foundational Issues in Christian Education: An Introduction to Evangelical Perspective* (Grand Rapids: Baker Academic), 44.

[333] Debbie D. Philip, *Heading Home with Jesus: Preparing Chinese Students to Follow Christ in China* (Pasadena: William Carey Library, 2018), 4.

[334] Ajith Fernando, *Discipling in a Multicultural World*, (Wheaton, Illinois: Crossway, 2019), 146.

[335] Fernando, *Discipling in a Multicultural World*, 146.

Authentic

Third, the discipleship process is authentic. ISM workers recognize the price of commitment, the privilege of spending significant time together with the international students, the intentionality of being open about their lives with their strengths and weaknesses, and the benefits of challenging the students to do the same.

Mutually Transformative

The fourth key principle is that the discipleship journey is mutually transformative. As acknowledged in Chapter 7, within discipleship, there is a mutual exchange of learning and teaching between members of learning communities, as God directs, guides and works among the participants. For ISM workers, this involves affirming the dignity of international students and "listening to them, learning from them, cheering them on in their challenges, and affirming them in their strengths, accomplishments and dreams."[336]

Purposeful

The final principle is purposeful. The ISM worker is focused on utilizing specific discipleship methods in the context of RICE. The methods include creating an environment where an intercultural learning community can thrive. In Chapter 7 the concept of intercultural learning communities is unpacked, as well as educational implications.

Additionally, the ISM worker is purposeful by considering pedagogical dimensions of discipleship in an intercultural context and as indicated in Chapter 4, shapes educational plans to fit the learner's cultural patterns. Some of these dimensions are learning styles, and teaching methods. In terms of learning styles, for example, East Asian students employ a circular rather than linear thinking pattern, they prefer a reflective learning style and opt for group collaborative learning. [337]

In terms of teaching methods, for example, professors in Western Christian graduate institutions found that, unlike North American evangelical theology approaches, international students use concerns in culture as catalyst for theological reflection and then apply Scripture to those concerns, rather than starting with Scripture and seeing how it speaks to cultural

---

[336] Nate Mirza, *Home Again: Preparing International Students to Serve Christ in Their Home Countries*, Home Again Publishing, 2018, 23.

[337] Arthur David Howard, "The Role of Learning Styles in the Discipleship of East Asian University Students" (DMin diss., Carey Theological College, 2013), 143-4, Theological Research Exchange Network.

needs[338]. Additionally, these professors encountered differences in how they interpret the Biblical text and how international students approach it.

"Becoming:" Maturity in Christ

The Triune God's purpose through the intercultural relational discipleship process is for both ISM worker and international student to "become" mature in Christ. With God as the primary influencer, He uses the ISM worker as RICE-R in this process.

Two important aspects in transformational change are the timing of the change and transgressional change. ISM workers need to consider the timing of the change and the readiness of the students. These elements are influenced by various factors such as God's sovereignty and the obedience of the students. It is possible that the international student might not respond to God's work in their lives in a positive way. This regression away from God is indicated in Chapter 1 through the concept of transgressional change.

International Student: Four Dimensions of Maturity in Christ

For international students, transformational growth happens in four dimensions: in truth, in allegiance, in power, and in mission.

The truth dimension has to do with the mind, with thinking and intellect. International students are transformed in truth when they are "learning to read, pray, and trust God's Word, rather than ours,"[339] when they realize that their lives are secure in Christ and that "regardless of the culture we are in, we are only truly at home when we are in Christ,"[340] and when they "know Christ, not just as one who helps us with our problems, but as the very essence of our lives."[341]

The allegiance dimension refers to the will. Obedience and humility are part of being transformed in one's allegiance. For international students, obedience involves realizing that they are living under a new authority, and that will lead to "changing attitudes and behavior in our relationships, habits, priorities, what we feed our minds, or how we serve Him."[342] Additionally, developing humility is part of growing in Christ.

The power dimension focuses on feelings, as well as emotional freedom and engaging in spiritual warfare. Transformed feelings and emotions are

---

[338] Cheryl A. Guth, "Teaching International Students: Cultural Challenges Experiences by Professors in Christian Graduate Education" (PhD diss., Trinity International University, 2014), 89, ProQuest.
[339] Philip, *Heading Home with Jesus*, 152.
[340] Mirza, *Home Again*, 46.
[341] Ibid.
[342] Ibid, 49.

healthy and reflect a deep relationship with God, through Christ and led by the Spirit. However, the ability to have mature and godly emotions is often constrained by past hurt or trauma. This requires spiritual and emotional healing. Along with experiencing emotional freedom, transformational growth in power has to do with engaging in spiritual warfare. Wan asserts that to be victorious in spiritual warfare, "the best way is to be preventive by the leaders' modeling, teaching, and discipling and by the followers' watching carefully against the enemies, and walking daily in the Spirit."[343]

The mission dimension has to do with one's relationship with the world. For international students, transformational growth in mission is embracing their ethnic identity given by God and knowing who they are and what they are to do with their lives. With the influence of the ISM workers and involvement in ministry, they develop a vision to "see our part in God's overarching story of history, and what God may be planning to do in and through us in the future."[344]

ISM Worker: Three Aspects of Maturity in Christ

For ISM workers, transformational growth happens in three aspects: discernment, Spirit-led prayers for students, and cultivating a growing interior life with God.

The discernment aspect has to do with ISM workers' "lived knowledge of God in the midst of the ambiguities of" discipling international students[345]. ISM workers grow in their approach to discipleship, realizing that the intercultural relational discipleship process is a journey guided by godly principles rather than a one-size-fits-all formula. Thus, ISM workers practice discernment in perceiving what steps of spiritual growth are most appropriate for the international students they disciple.

The second aspect of growth for ISM workers is to pray Spirit-led prayers that are most suitable for the international students they disciple. ISM workers have the mind of Christ (1 Corinthians 2:16) and "are seated with him in the heavenly places" (Ephesians 2:6). As they listen to the Holy Spirit's leading, they learn to bring specific petitions that are in accord with God's will.

---

[343] Enoch Wan, "Spiritual Warfare and Victorious Christian," Articles, Enoch Wan, accessed July 2, 2024, 5, https://www.enochwan.com/english/articles/pdf/Spiritual%20Warfare%20&%20Victorious%20Christian.pdf.

[344] Enoch Wan, Mark Hedinger, and Jon Raibley, *Transformational Growth: Intercultural Leadership, Discipleship, Mentorship*, (Portland: Western Academic Publishers, 2023), 157.

[345] Evan B. Howard, *A Guide to Christian Spiritual Formation: How Scripture, Spirit, Community, and Mission Shape Our Souls*, (Grand Rapids: Baker Academic, 2018), 179.

Finally, the third aspect of growth is to cultivate a growing interior life with God. Discipling international students is hard work and involves experiencing pain and emotional stress. ISM workers learn to cultivate a growing interior life with God in order to meet the demands of discipling as well as all other responsibilities in their lives.

Conclusion

This chapter exemplifies how the theory of RICE can be applied to a model of intercultural relational discipleship process in the context of ISM. The vertical relationship between ISM worker and God, international student and God, and horizontally the relationship between the ISM worker and international student, as well as with the wider body of Christ are vital connections in the intercultural context of discipleship of international students. Recognizing the vertical and horizontal relationships does not mean separating them in pedagogy at horizontal level but demands the interplay of all these connections in the various dimensions of RICE, to be able to achieve the maturity in Christ that ISM workers and international students seek.

Works Cited

Burke, Jack. *Paradigm Shift: Why International Students Are So Strategic to Global Missions.* Bloomington: Westbow Press, 2019.

Chinn, Leiton Edward. "The Global ISM Movement Emerging From Diaspora Missions On Campuses: From John R. Mott to Lausanne," in *Diaspora Missions to International Students*, ed. Enoch Wan, 119-138. Portland: Western Seminary Press, 2019.

Fernando, Ajith. *Discipling in a Multicultural World*. Wheaton, Illinois: Crossway, 2019.

Howard, Arthur David. "The Role of Learning Styles in the Discipleship of East Asian University Students." DMin thesis, Carey Theological College, 2013. Theological Research Exchange Network.

Howard, Evan B. *A Guide to Christian Spiritual Formation: How Scripture, Spirit, Community, and Mission Shape Our Souls*. Grand Rapids: Baker Academic, 2018.

LaClare, Denis. "Wearing Different Hats: The Attitudes, Behaviors, and Experiences of Six Transcultural Workers." PhD diss., Biola University, 2018.

Mirza, Nate. *Home Again: Preparing International Students to Serve Christ in Their Home Countries*. Home Again Publishing, 2018.

Pazmiño, Robert. *Foundational Issues in Christian Education: An Introduction to Evangelical Perspective.* Grand Rapids, Michigan: Baker Academic, 2008.

Philip, Debbie. *Heading Home with Jesus*. Littleton: William Carey Library, 2018.

Wan, Enoch. "Introduction," in *Diaspora Missions to International Students,* ed. Enoch Wan, 7-10. Portland: Western Seminary Press, 2019.

—. "Spiritual Warfare and Victorious Christian." Enoch Wan. Accessed April 2, 2024. https://www.enochwan.com/english/articles/pdf/Spiritual%20Warfare%20&%20Victorious%20Christian.pdf.

Wan, Enoch, and Mark Hedinger. *Relational Missionary Training*. Skyforest: Urban Loft Publishers, 2017.

Wan, Enoch, Mark Hedinger, and Jon Raibley. *Transformational Growth : Intercultural Leadership, Discipleship, Mentorship*. Portland: Western Academic Publishers, 2023.

CHAPTER 14
Case Study #6
Relational Competency-Based Intercultural Theological Education

Enoch Wan and Tin Nguyen

Introduction

The **purpose** of this paper is to introduce relational competency-based education and use the training of leaders from the ethnic minority groups in Vietnam as a case study of relational competency-based intercultural education.

The **organization** of this chapter is as follows: It begins with presenting CBE characteristics and the primary difference between Traditional Education (TE) and Competency-based Education (CBE). We then discuss the relevance of CBE within the paradigm of relational interactionism. It will be concluded with a proposal of educational process of design and implementation CBE interculturally within the framework of relational interactionism for the training of leaders from ethnic minority groups in Vietnam.

Traditional Education and Competency-Based Education

The diagram below depicts the difference between Traditional Education (TE) and Competency-Based Education (CBE). First, as competency is the primary focus of CBE, outcomes are emphasized during the course of design and implementation of a CBE program. In fact, outcomes become a basis for success.

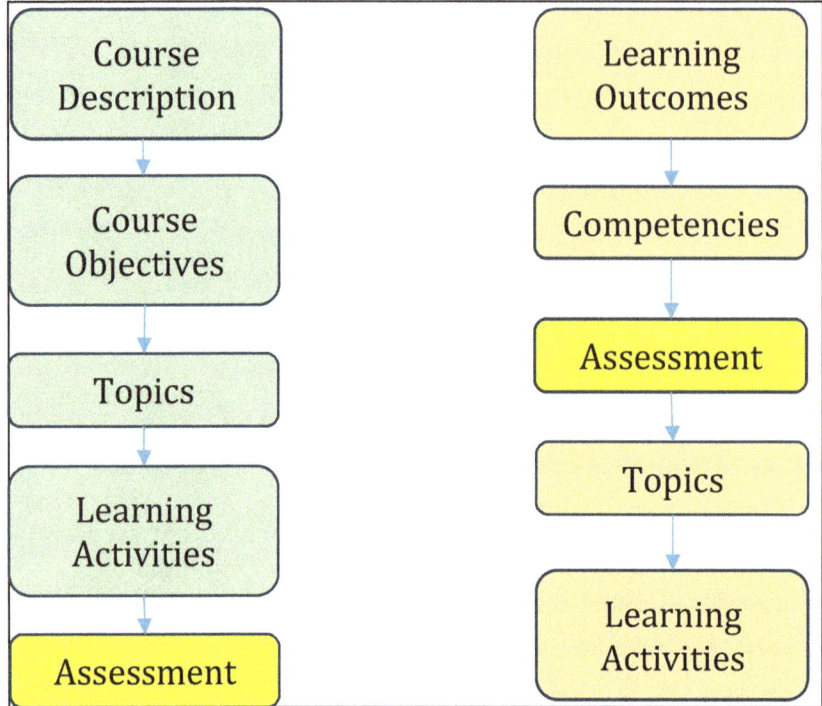

Figure 14-1. Comparison between Traditional Education and Competency-Based Education

CBE Characteristics

Definition of CBE

"CBE is a teaching and learning approach that focuses on demonstrated student learning and the application of that learning rather than time spent in class or on material."[346]

> "A competency is a focused learning experience within a learning domain that is related to a well-defined content area. The content areas are identified as domains, and each domain is broken down into subdomains as a way to categorize learning concepts. The subdomains are then divided into competencies, which are organized into objectives. Each objective is further broken down into topics."[347]

---

[346] CBEN, Competency Based Education Network Conference, Jacksonville, FL, October 2023.

[347] Strut Learning, https://www.strutlearning.com/. Accessed 9/9/2024.

CBE Core Characteristics

Competency-based education has the following core characteristics:[348]
1. Student progress marked by demonstrated proficiency.
2. Competencies include explicit, measurable, transferable learning objectives that empower students.
3. Assessment is meaningful and a positive learning experience for students.
4. Students receive timely, differentiated support based on their individual learning needs.
5. Learning outcomes emphasize competencies that address behaviors, attitudes, skills, and dispositions.

The Role of Assessment in CBE

It should be obvious that assessment plays a significant role in CBE because the bottom line of CBE is demonstrated competencies. The question at hand is how to do assessment to ensure that students indeed possess the competencies the program promises to deliver.

The Role of Mentors in CBE

Mentors play a vital role in CBE. Due to the nature of CBE, where the role of formal education in the forms of fixed-time classroom is diminished and self-study becomes the norm, students need other people to interact with for both emotional encouragement and academic support.

CBE within the Paradigm of Relational Interactionism

The philosophy and practices of CBE fit naturally within the paradigm of relational interactionism, and therefore can be incorporated effortlessly into any educational programs developed in a framework of relational interactionism.

---

[348] CBEN, Competency Based Education Network Conference, Jacksonville, FL, October 2023.

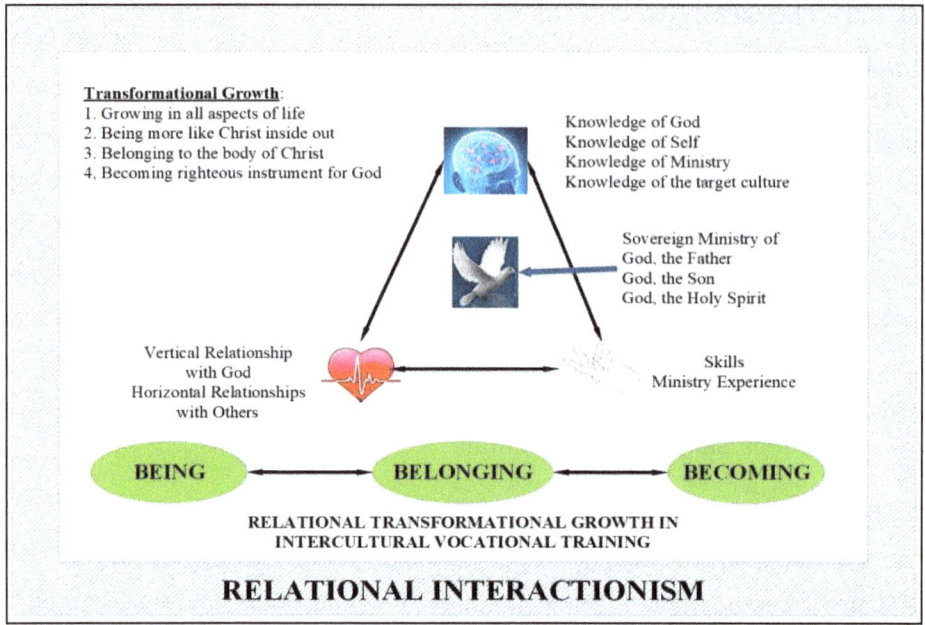

Figure 14-2. CBE-oriented Intercultural Education within Relational Interactionism[349]

Before going any further, it would be instructive to review the theoretical framework of transformational change that happens within a relational context that Wan proposes in his paper.[350] Wan identifies three steps in transformational change: being, belonging, and becoming. Nguyen summarizes those three steps as follows:

> "Being represents personal transformation as a result of a vertical relationship with the Being and the sanctifying work of the Holy Spirit. Belonging represents the redeemed relationships with family, with a local body of Christ, and with the global church. Becoming is the outcome of change during the stage in which children of God become Christ-like."[351]

In this section, the relevance of CBE within the framework of relational interactionism is discussed.

---

[349] Figure14-2 is adapted from Nguyen's dissertation: Tin Nguyen, "An Intercultural Vocational Training Program for Kingdom Workers in Northern Vietnam," Unpublished EdD dissertation, Western Seminary, 2022:209.

[350] Enoch Wan, "Rethinking Urban Mission in Terms of Spiritual and Social Transformational Change", 10.

[351] Tin Nguyen, Ed.D. Dissertation, "An Intercultural Vocational Training Program for Kingdom Workers in Northern Vietnam," Western Seminary, 2022.

The Ultimate Goal of Education

The holistic goal of education within the framework of relational interactionism encompasses the CBE three-fold goal which includes content, skills, and behavior to cover spiritual growth and community engagement for the purpose of the body of Christ. The holistic goal of education starts with establishing and strengthening our vertical relationship with God. That is just the beginning. Education proceeds to the stage of becoming when the student develops horizontal relationships with brothers and sisters in the faith. The CBE fruits are evident at the final stage of becoming when the student exhibits transformational outcomes.

The concept of CBE behavior is enlarged within the framework of relational interactionism to extend beyond human goodness and cultural appropriateness to cover Christ-like behavior which goes much deeper than just words and deeds. Consequently, a CBE relational training program must be prepared to deal with abstract things such as how to facilitate and measure humility and the matters of the heart. These things can be challenging as one determines to implement CBE practices in a paradigm of relational interactionism.

The CBE-Inspired Interactionism

There are several types of interactions happening in competency-based education within the framework of relational interactionism.

First, there are intentional interactions between students and their advisors. There are two kinds of advisors: non-academic and academic. Non-academic advisors are sometimes called mentors. Non-academic advisors encourage students and help them with daily life issues while academic advisors assist with learning activities. The existence of non-academic advisors highlights the holistic nature of relational interactionism. It recognizes that students are in school not just to gain knowledge and skills but also to grow as a person. The role of academic advisors emphasizes the student's needs for academic assistance beyond the classroom. This requires a mental shift in instructors who may be accustomed to delivering prepared lectures and holding fixed office hours. They must become flexible and available to offer students the help they need. This can be seen as a formalization of the idea of student-centered education proposed by many educators in traditional education.

Second, there are frequent interactions between students. The CBE philosophy implicitly requires students to learn from one another. Before they reach out to advisors, they tend to ask one another. Within the framework of relational interactionism, this facilitates the belonging stage of the students where they help one another. This also creates opportunities for those who are more mature and more advanced academically to aid their classmates. By doing so, they propel along their becoming stage to become an instrument of grace within their community.

Peer support is the main reason CBE schools intentionally create self-study hours so that students can interact with one another. Advisors are also present in self-study halls to offer help if required.

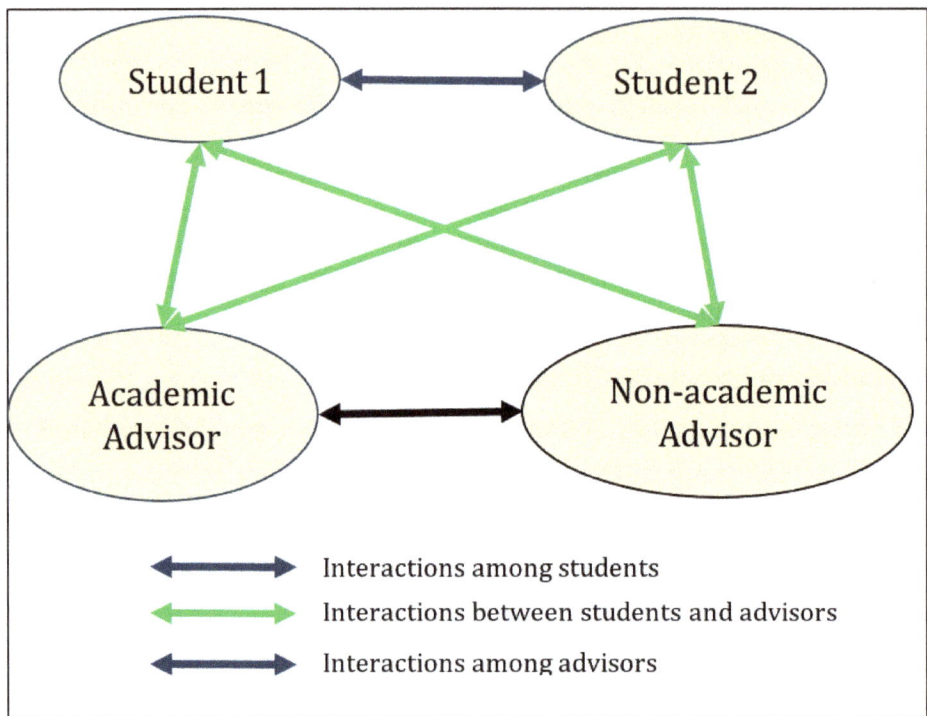

Figure 14-3. Interactions in a CBE framework of Relational Interactionism

Third, there are also interactions among advisors. There may be interdisciplinary issues that require more than one advisor to manage. There may be issues that need to be discussed between mentors and academic advisors. For example, a student struggling in class may be pinpointed to an emotional issue that goes beyond what a math professor can do. In that case, the professor would require non-academic advisors to help. As another example, a student may have an issue with their professor which needs a mentor to advocate for them. The professional interactions among advisors display the nature of collaborative mission as advisors realize their key role in shaping the lives of their students.

In summary, within the framework of relational interactionism, there are constant interactions happening at multiple levels, formal, nonformal and informal, all of which benefit the development of the students and bring about integrative outcomes at the completion of the program.

CBE Assessment

As competencies are the focus of competency-based education, the design of CBE programs begins with the end in mind. As a result, assessment plays a key role in the design process of CBE programs, at lot more than in traditional education (TE). TE assessment is at the end of a top-down instructional design flow decided by the instructor based on their designed learning activities to make sure students have met their expectations. CBE assessment is tied directed to the communicated competencies, designed to ensure that the course has accomplished its promises for the students. The bottom line of assessment is to make sure education indeed delivers, regardless of the approaches, TE or CBE. Quality of education is sought earnestly by educators, both TE and CBE.

Within the framework of relational interactionism, assessment is not limited to the duration of the learning process but expanded to cover the pre-learning process to offer advanced standing, during the learning process to provide timely feedback to students, and after the learning process to assess the program success.

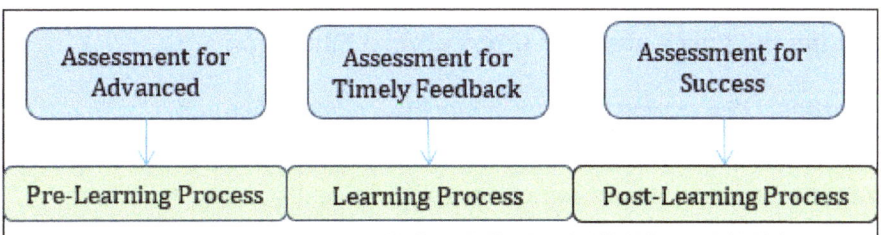

Figure 14-4. CBE Assessment

CBE Program Design Process

The CBE program design process employs the principles of backward design to layout learning materials for the competency, including syllabus, summative assessment, formative assessment questions, and learning activities for each topic.

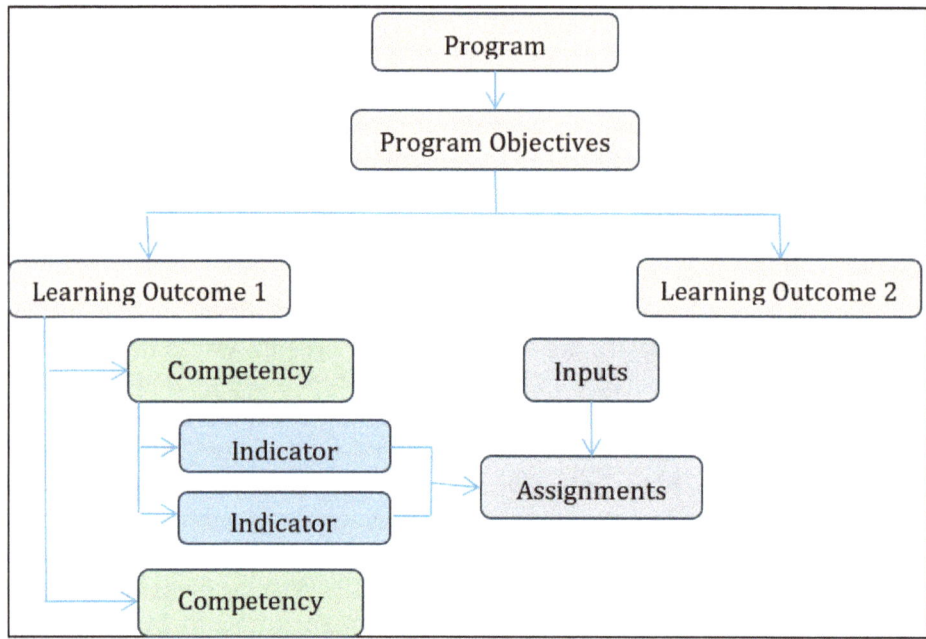

Figure 14-5. The CBE Program Design Process

Process of Intercultural Education

In this section, we will explain the design and implementation CBE interculturally within the framework of relational interactionism for the training of leaders from ethnic minority groups in Vietnam.

Designing the Curriculum for Intercultural Education

Ethnographic description of ethnic minority groups in Vietnam

Vietnam is a multiethnic country. Even though they share the official language of the land, ethnic minority groups have distinct cultures and languages. For the present case study, only the Hmong and Mien groups are considered. Below is an ethnographic description of these two people groups. As in the major culture of Vietnam, the Hmong and Mien cultures are built on a complex network of relationships. As a result, Hmong and Mien students are highly relational. They live and work together in small villages scattered the hillsides of northern Vietnam. The communal trait among their leaders manifests itself in their preference to be in small group discussions with their friends as opposed to those they do not know. Once in a trusted environment, they are much more animated. Each Hmong and Mien village functions as a large family. Your neighbors would take care of your children when you are away from a few days to even two weeks of time with no questions asked. As far as learning styles are concerned, Hmong and Mien students are passive in class. However, they listen attentively and follow the lecture closely. They would not strike up conversations with the instructor during the lecture or openly disagree with them. If they have questions, they will approach the instructor privately and ask timidly. Once they know the instructor is open to them, they will share their personal stories. A majority of them prefer printed materials over videos and other high-tech sources such as PDF files and PowerPoint presentations even though some of them appear tech savvy. Hmong and Mien students are self-motivated. They treasure the opportunity to learn to be effective for the Kingdom. Many of them have been in ministry for a few years without being trained formally. They laboriously work on class assignments to show their earnestness. Many of them would go back to their respective ministries and quickly share what they have learned with those at home.

Ethnographic studies among leaders of Hmong and Mien people groups also show that integrity, teamwork, and a fervent desire for learning communities are their anthropological characteristics. For a comprehensive educational anthropology of these two people groups, the reader is referred to Nguyen's work.[352]

Designing the curriculum to train leaders from ethnic minority groups in Vietnam

Ethnographic description of ethnic minority groups in Vietnam in the previous section serves as guideposts to the designing of the curriculum to train leader from the Hmong and Mien ethnic minority group in Vietnam.
- The curriculum must be intercultural.
- The target students are highly relational and self-motivated.
- The target students are communal.
- The target students are passive but are truly thoughtful learners.
- The target students value integrity and teamwork.

As a result, the curriculum for intercultural education encompasses the following characteristics:

---

[352] Tin Nguyen, Ed.D. Dissertation, "An Intercultural Vocational Training Program for Kingdom Workers in Northern Vietnam," Western Seminary, 2022.

- The learning environment is friendly and communal. Open discussions, group projects, self-study with supervision are encouraged.
- Learning activities are multi-sensory with many forms of education: lectures, testimonies, group discussions, videos, and projects.
- Assessment is meant to be a means of reenforcing education, not that of punishment.

Implementing Intercultural Education

The following diagram depicts a curriculum for intercultural education to train leaders of Hmong and Mien ethnic minority people groups in northern Vietnam.

Figure 14-6. Intercultural Leadership Training Program in Relational Interactionism

The curriculum presented above starts with a course or a track consisting of many courses on the topic of **Spiritual Formation**. The purpose for this track is to help establish the **Being** within the student. The second track is **Discipleship** which facilitates the **Belonging** stage. The third track, **Ministerial Ethics and Church Leadership,** helps the student to graduate from the Belonging stage to the Becoming stage. The remaining three tracks on Exegetical Bible Study and Preaching, Christology and Practical Theology, and Evangelism help the student to blossom in their **Becoming** stage to become an effective leader in strengthening the church through teaching, preaching, protecting and growing the church via evangelism. The whole educational process happens within a framework of relational interactionism. The curriculum is then implemented according to the CBE course design flow discussed in a previous section. Feedback from the students and instructors is then used to improve the curriculum.

Conclusions

In this chapter, core characteristics of competency-based education are presented, followed by a comparison of major differences between traditional education (TE) and competency-based education (CBE). Then the relevance of competency-based education within the framework of relational interactionism is analyzed. Core elements of CBE relational interactionism such as assessment and interactions are discussed. An educational program design process following CBE is proposed. Finally, we concluded by presenting the process of implementing intercultural education, including curriculum design for training leaders of Hmong and Mien ethnic minorities living interculturally in the highlands of northern Vietnam.

Works Cited

Competency-Based Education Conference Proceedings, Jacksonville, FL, October 2023.

Tin Nguyen, Ed.D. Dissertation, "An Intercultural Vocational Training Program for Kingdom Workers in Northern Vietnam," Western Seminary, 2022.

Enoch Wan, "Rethinking Urban Mission in Terms of Spiritual and Social Transformational Change," 2022.

CHAPTER 15
CONCLUSION

In the multicultural and dynamic world in which we live, people from multiple cultures meet at many places, at many levels, and with varying levels of healthy or unhealthy interaction. For centuries, people have tried to understand how cultures work so that these interpersonal cross-cultural interactions could be better understood and better managed. As humans, we want to navigate cultural differences well – achieving mutually beneficial outcomes and enjoying the differences that exist between us.

Those noble desires, though, go unfulfilled more often than not. The techniques that we think should give us tools for healthy interactions turn out to cause more misunderstanding. The desire to understand one another degenerates into stereotyping and ethnocentrism.

The approach of looking only at people and the approach of finding cultural clues to help us design methods for interaction have frustrated us as humans for generations. This book has presented another way to understand and navigate the differences that exist across human cultures, especially in terms of educational contexts. Our focus in RICE has been to understand intercultural education from a relational interactionist perspective.

How does this relational interaction perspective lead us to understand intercultural situations?

To put it in briefest terms, we understand the cross-cultural educational context to be relational in ways that includes vertical relationships as well as horizontal. We understand God is active in the classroom or around the fireplace as one generation passes on wisdom, skills, knowledge, stories, and attitudes to another. We believe God is active in the digital environment where people from numerous cultures are interacting. Perhaps they are separated by hundreds of miles, and yet the Spirit of God is more than able to span that distance. We believe that God is present in the classroom where a human teacher is leading students from another culture through reading exercises. God is present. He is relational. He opens hearts, and He allows one culture to work well with another for His glory. He is active in the "teacher" as well as the "learner." He is active in the one learning how to move to another culture, just as He is active in those who are welcoming the stranger to live among them.

We also see horizontal relationships as fostering learning and teaching. When those relationships cross cultures, the participants must find new ways to understand and be understood. One of the strongest tools for them to use is to carefully learn the rules of relationship within the "other" culture. How do followers respond to leaders? How do older people respond to younger? How do men and women interact? It is in those relationships between people that we best learn what it means to bring educational ministry into a culture different from our own. Just as we learn to hear a new language, so we learn to see and appreciate the interactions between people in a new culture. By learning how to observe, analyze and adapt to those different relational patterns we become the "grafted plant root" that ties together one culture with another.

How does this relational interactionist approach lead us to navigate the cultural differences we find in our educational contexts?

It is one thing to grow in understanding, but how do we grow in application? How do we live differently in a new cultural environment? How do teachers go about their classroom management or their preparation of coursework as they grow in understanding of the relational approaches that they have observed?

The Case Studies section gave us numerous examples. We adapt to a new culture through a mixture of cultural humility on one hand, and allowing ourselves to be uncomfortable for the sake of the Gospel. We do not demand that people in the new culture adapt to us; we learn to adapt to them. It is awkward and uncomfortable at first, but like a grafted rootstock eventually ties into the tissues of the new host, soon enough the discomfort reduces and the ability to be "a Greek to the Greeks and a Jew to the Jews" (1 Cor 9:20 ff) takes its place.

Learning to understand and navigate differences across cultures is no small task, and it is no easy task. But in a world where migration is bringing millions of cross-cultural relationships into existence, it is a task that the Church must master. The good news is that we do not need to master this task alone. "I will never leave you, nor forsake you" (Heb 13:5) says our Lord. He will open our understanding about those we need to reach, and He will open their understanding of working with us. He will guide us as we learn to navigate relational interactions across cultures. Our prayer as the authors of this textbook is that God would be glorified and His people edified by seeing intercultural education in terms of relational interactionism.

Appendix 1: Two Series of Publication by Enoch Wan

Series on Diaspora Missiology

- Diaspora Missiology E. Wan
- Diaspora Missiology (EMS)
- Church Planting among Immigrants in US Urban Centers (Second Edition): The "Where", "Why", And "How" of Diaspora
- Engaging Chinese diaspora in the ministry of Bible translation
- Diaspora Missions to International Students
- Missions beyond the diaspora: local cross-cultural ministry of Chinese congregations in the San Francisco bay area
- Wu Chang Church: An Action-research Case Study of Multiethnic Ministries in Taiwan
- The Hispanic Hybrid Identity in Miami: Ethnographic Description and Missiological Implications
- Scattered Africans Keep Coming
- Mobilizing Vietnamese Diaspora for the Kingdom
- Chinese Diaspora Kingdom Workers: In Action and With Guidance
- Wandering Jews and Scattered Sri Lankans: Viewing Sri Lankans of the Gulf Cooperation Council through the Lens of the Old Testament Jewish Diaspora

Series on Relational Paradigm

Marketplace Transformation: Motivating and Mobilizing Chinese Churches in the Silicon Valley for Gospel Transformation
by Enoch Wan & Howard Shauhau Chen

In this book, you will find: (1) an ethnographic description of marketplace professionals in the Silicon Valley; (2) practical suggestions for motivating and mobilizing local Chinese churches in the Silicon Valley to engage marketplace professionals for marketplace transformation.

Publication Date: August 12, 2021

Covenant Transformative Learning: Theory and Practice for Mission
by Ryan Gimple & Enoch

This book is a presentation of covenant transformative learning theory and its application to basic tasks of cross-cultural missions. Covenant transformative learning theory is a derivative of Mezirow's transformative learning theory, but is reformed by the application of Meek's epistemological framework and practical in the use of "relational realism" paradigm.

Publication Date: August 19, 2021

Engaging the Secular World through Life-on-life Disciple-making in the British Context: Relational Paradigm in Action
by Enoch Wan & Shane Mikeska

As the first volume in the "Relational Series," this book is a contemporary approach to engage the secular world through relational "life on life disciple-making" in the British context as a way to illustrate relational paradigm in action.

Publication Date: January 14, 2020

A Theology of Spirit-Anointed Witness in Holistic Christian Mission Framed in the Relational Paradigm
by Enoch Wan & Mathew Karimpanamannil

In this book, a theology of Spirit-anointed witness in holistic Christian mission is articulated with an emphasis on "relational paradigm." The thesis is that the church be authorized, enlightened, enriched, equipped, and empowered to proclaim, practice, and demonstrate the power of God's Kingdom.

Publication Date: December 20, 2019

Missionary Preparation in the Gospel of Matthew In Light of 28:16-20
by Enoch Wan & Rob Penner

In this book, the authors propose an alternative to the popular understanding that Matthew 28:18-20 is the "Great Commission" passage.

Publication Date: February 18, 2022

Holistic Mission Through Mission Partnership
by Enoch Wan & John Jay Flinn

This book is about mission partnership, between Total Health (US-based) with the La Ceiba GCLA church in Honduras that offers unique opportunities for transformation in both patients at the clinic and the mission workers at the same time. In this case study of holistic mission, through mutuality and reciprocity, God is at work spiritually and physically among both patients in the clinic and the mission workers.

Publication Date: August 19, 2021

The Cross and the Kaleidoscope
by Alex Early & Enoch Wan

The purpose of this book is to integrate the doctrine of Penal Substitutionary Atonement with the relational paradigm for Christian ministry in the 21st century employing a kaleidoscopic perspective..

Publication Date: November 2, 2021

Doxological Missiology: Theory, Motivation, and Practice
by Enoch Wan & Jace Cloud

This book makes the case that the imago Dei can only be properly understood in connection with the missio Dei and the gloria Dei. "Glorifying God" is accomplished as the image-bearers of God are sent on the missio Dei in order to spread the glory of God throughout the earth as they live out God's truth, goodness, and beauty in the world. In this sense, the integration of the image of God, mission of God, and glory of God are combined into the new paradigm of "Doxological Missiology" and applied in theory, motivation, and practice.

Publication Date: February 29, 2022

Establishing Frontline LGBTQ Outreach
by Noel Chiu & Enoch Wan

This book is an exploratory study dedicated in searching for key parameters which can be systematically followed as guidelines and will positively contribute to Christian leaders seeking to establish Frontline LGBTQ Outreach, in order to witness to those within LGBTQ communities.

Publication Date: February 21, 2022

A Holistic and Contextualized Mission Training Program
by Enoch Wan & Tin Nguyen

In this book, the readers will find a detailed presentation of mission training programs for contemporary Vietnam that is contextually appropriate in term of their cultural background and contemporary living surroundings. The design of the mission training program is based on an educational and anthropological understanding of Vietnamese lay leaders with the goal of motivating and mobilizing them for Christian mission.

Publication Date: March 22, 2022

Relational Leadership Development: An Ethnological Study in Inuit Contexts
by Enoch Wan & John Ferch

By using existing ethnographic data on the Inuit, the authors in this book propose a relational, orality-based model for ministry leadership development that is "glocalized" to Inuit contexts.

Publication Date: February 19, 2022

Transformational Change in Christian Ministry, Second Edition
by Enoch Wan & Jon Raibley

We explore the concept of "relational interactionism" to describe this process of interactions that take place within relational networks, influencing who we are, what we do, and who we are becoming. We have also included chapters by 10 practitioners of relational ministry, demonstrating the application of the principles in practice.

Publication date: July 28, 2022

Motivations for Mission: A Relational-Covenantal Perspective
by Enoch Wan & Christopher M. Santiago

The purpose of this book is to explore motivations for mission from a covenantal perspective within a relational framework in three steps: exploring the topic theologically, examining it theoretically, and deriving missiological implications.

This book is a contribution to an underrepresented perspective to the missiological research on motives for mission.

Publication Date: August 17, 2022

Relational Partnerships for Missions Mobilization
by Enoch Wan & Joshua Paxton

This book explores a relational approach to building partnerships through the Synergy process at Calvary University. Our prayer is that it will help pastors, educators, and mission agency leaders think Scripturally about how to build relational partnerships for mobilizing the next generation of missionaries.

Publication date: Aug. 17, 2022

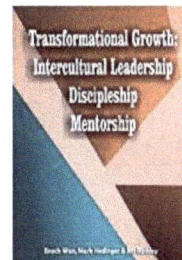

Transformational Growth: Intercultural Leadership, Discipleship, Mentorship
by Enoch Wan, Mark Hedinger, Jon Raibley

This book is a sequel to an earlier publication by Enoch Wan & Jon Raibley, Transformational Change in Christian Ministry (2022) which provided the theoretical framework for this book.

While the focus of the earlier work is on "transformational change" generally, this one is on "transformational growth" specifically dealing with the practice of leadership, discipleship, and mentorship within intercultural context.

Publication date: May 8, 2023

Appendix 2: Resources for Further Studies

Transformative Learning

- Jack Mezirow, Learning as Transformation: Critical Perspectives on a Theory in Progress.
- Jack Mezirow, Edward W. Taylor (eds), Transformative Learning in Practice: Insights from Community, Workplace, and Higher Education.
- Edward Taylor, Fostering Mezirow's Transformative Learning Theory in the Adult Education Classroom: A Critical Review
- Andrew Kitchenham, The Evolution of John Mezirow's Transformative Learning Theory
- Daniel Harbecke, Following Mezirow: A Roadmap through Transformative Learning

Outcome-Based Education

- Gwennis McNeir, Outcomes-Based Education
- Roy Killen, Outcomes-Based Education: Principles and Possibilities
- Michael J. Lawson and Helen Askell-Williams, Outcomes-Based Education
- Yuzainee Md Yusoff, Achievement of the Program Outcomes in Outcomes-Based Education Implementation – A Meta-Analysis
- M.R. Anala, et al. Outcome Based Education: An Empirical Approach

Andragogy

- Malcolm S. Knowles, The Adult Learner
- Sharan B. Merriam, Laura L. Bierema, Adult Learning, Linking Theory and Practice.
- Stephen Pew, Andragogy and Pedagogy as Foundational Theory for Student Motivation in Higher Education

BIBLIOGRAPHY

Banks, James A. "Approaches to Multicultural Curriculum Reform." *Trotter Institute Review* 3, no. 3, Article 5 (June 1989): 17–19.

———. "Diversity, Group Identity, and Citizenship Education in a Global Age." *Educational Researcher* 37, no. 3 (April 2008): 129–39. https://doi.org/10.3102/0013189X08317501.

———. "Multicultural Education: Characteristics and Goals." In *Multicultural Education: Issues and Perspectives*, 3–30. John Wiley & Sons, 2010.

Banks, James A. "Teaching for Social Justice, Diversity, and Citizenship in a Global World," 68:296–305. Taylor & Francis, 2004.

Benet-Martínez, Verónica, and Ying-yi Hong, eds. *The Oxford Handbook of Multicultural Identity*. Oxford University Press, 2014. https://doi.org/10.1093/oxfordhb/9780199796694.001.0001.

Bennett, Milton J. "A Short Conceptual History of Intercultural Learning in Study Abroad." In *A History of U.S. Study Abroad: 1965 - Present*, 419–49. Forum on Education Abroad, 2010. https://www.idrinstitute.org/wp-content/uploads/2018/02/short_conceptual_history_ic_learning.pdf.

Berben, Kenneth J. "Social Pragmatics and the Origins of Psychological Discourse (Chapter 6)." In *The Social Construction of the Person*, n.d. https://www.researchgate.net/publication/290002177_Social_Pragmatics_and_the_Origins_of_Psychological_Discourse#fullTextFileContent.

Berne, Eric. *Games People Play: The Psychology Of Human Relationships*, 2010.

Boud, David. "Experience and Learning: Reflection at Work. EAE600 Adults Learning in the Workplace: Part A," n.d. https://www.academia.edu/29435057/Experience_and_Learning_Reflection_at_Work_EAE600_Adults_Learning_in_the_Workplace_Part_A.

Bradley, Akirah. "A Time to Intervene: A Historical Overview of Pedagogical Responses to an Unjust Society." *The Vermont Connection* 28, no. 1 (January 1, 2007): 70–79.

Brookfield, Stephen D. "Transformative Learning as Ideology Critique." In *Learning as Transformation: Critical Perspectives on a Theory in Progress*, 125–48. San Francisco: Jossey-Bass, 2000.

Cartwright, John, Gabriel Etzel, Christopher Jackson, and Timothy Paul Jones. *Teaching the World: Foundations for Online Theological Education*. Nashville: B&H Academic, 2017.

Cavalier, Robert J. "Introduction to Habermas's Discourse Ethics," n.d.

Chan, Siu Kuen Sonia. "A Relational Model of Intercultural Learning and Interactions." Dissertation, Western Seminary, 2023.

Chiu, Ai Chen (Noel). "Key Parameters of Establishing Frontline LGBTQ Outreach." PhD Thesis, Western Seminary, 2021.

Constable, Thomas L. "Notes on Genesis," Edition 2024. https://www.planobiblechapel.org/tcon/notes/html/ot/genesis/genesis.htm.

Cross, K. Patricia. "Why Learning Communities? Why Now?" *About Campus* 3, no. 3 (July 1, 1998): 4–11. https://doi.org/10.1177/108648229800300303.

Cummins, Jim, Joanne Tompkins, and Sonia Nieto. "The Light in Their Eyes: Creating Multicultural Learning Communities." *TESOL Quarterly* 35, no. 1 (2001): 200. https://doi.org/10.2307/3587870.

Cushner, Kenneth, and Jennifer Mahon. "Intercultural Competence in Teacher Education: Developing the Intercultural Competence of Educators and Their Students: Creating the Blueprints." In *The SAGE Handbook of Intercultural Competence*, 304–20. Thousand Oaks, CA: SAGE Publications, Inc, 2009.

Dewey, John. "John Dewey My Pedagogic Creed." *School Journal* 54 (January 1897): 77–80.

Eugenics at Stanford. "Ellwood Cubberley | Stanford Eugenics History Project." Accessed December 28, 2023. https://www.stanfordeugenics.com/ellwood-cubberley.

Everist, Norma Cook. *The Church as Learning Community: A Comprehensive Guide to Christian Education*. Nashville, TN: Abingdon Press, 2002.

Freire, Paolo. "Pedagogy of the Oppressed (Revised)." *New York: Continuum*, 1996.

Gay, Geneva. "Preparing for Culturally Responsive Teaching." *Journal of Teacher Education* 53, no. 2 (March 2002): 106–16. https://doi.org/10.1177/0022487102053002003.

Gergen, Kenneth J. "Social Pragmatics and the Origins of Psychological Discourse (Chapter 6)." In *The Social Construction of the Person*, n.d. https://www.researchgate.net/publication/290002177_Social_Pragmatics_and_the_Origins_of_Psychological_Discourse#fullTextFileContent.

Gibson, Margaret Alison. "Approaches to Multicultural Education in the United States: Some Concepts and Assumptions." *Anthropology & Education Quarterly* 7, no. 4 (1976): 7–18.

Gleason, Philip. "The Odd Couple: Pluralism and Assimilation." In *Speaking of Diversity: Language and Ethnicity in Twentieth-Century America.*, 47–90. Johns Hopkins University Press, 2019. https://muse.jhu.edu/pub/1/oa_monograph/chapter/2412200.

Guan, Shu-Sha Angie, Afaf Nash, and Marjorie Faulstich Orellana. "Cultural and Social Processes of Language Brokering among Arab, Asian, and Latin

Immigrants." *Journal of Multilingual and Multicultural Development* 37, no. 2 (February 17, 2016): 150–66. https://doi.org/10.1080/01434632.2015.1044997.

Hargrave, Susan. *Doing Anthropology*. Kangaroo Ground, Vic.: South Pacific Summer Institute of Linguistics, 1993.

Hatcher, Tim. "Towards Culturally Appropriate Adult Education Methodologies for Bible Translators: Comparing Central Asian and Western Educational Practices," n.d.

Hedinger, Karen. "A Relational Language Acquisition Approach for Global Kingdom Workers." Dissertation, Western Seminary, 2020.

Hedinger, Karen, Mark Hedinger, and Lauren Wells. *LanguageCourse*. Portland, OR: CultureBound, 2020.

Hendricks, Howard. *Teaching to Change Lives: Seven Proven Ways to Make Your Teaching Come Alive*. Reprint edition. Multnomah, 2003.

Hiebert, Paul G. *Anthropological Insights for Missionaries*. Grand Rapids, Mich: Baker Book House, 1985.

———. *Anthropological Reflections on Missiological Issues*. Grand Rapids, Mich: Baker Books, 1994.

———. *The Gospel in Human Contexts: Anthropological Explorations for Contemporary Missions*. Grand Rapids, Mich: Baker Academic, 2009.

———. *The Missiological Implications of Epistemological Shifts : Affirming Truth in a Modern/Postmodern World*. Christian Mission and Modern Culture. Harrisburg, Pa: Trinity Press International, 1999. https://search.ebscohost.com/login.aspx?direct=true&db=e000xna&AN=242967&site=ehost-live&scope=site.

History. "A Century of Trauma at U.S. Boarding Schools for Native American Children," July 9, 2021. https://www.nationalgeographic.com/history/article/a-century-of-trauma-at-boarding-schools-for-native-american-children-in-the-united-states.

IDRInstitute. "DMIS Model." Accessed April 8, 2024. https://www.idrinstitute.org/dmis/.

"Intercultural Education | DICE Project." Accessed February 27, 2019. http://www.diceproject.ie/de-ice/intercultural-education/.

Jang, Sujin. "Cultural Brokerage and Creative Performance in Multicultural Teams." *SSRN Electronic Journal*, 2017. https://doi.org/10.2139/ssrn.3056274.

Jensen, Frances E., and Amy Ellis Nutt. *The Teenage Brain: A Neuroscientist's Survival Guide to Raising Adolescents and Young Adults*. Reprint edition. Harper Paperbacks, 2016.

Johnson, Lauri D., and Yoon K. Pak. "Teaching for Diversity: Intercultural and Intergroup Education in the Public Schools, 1920s to 1970s." In *Review of Research in Education*, 1–31. SAGE Publications, 2019. https://doi.org/10.3102/0091732X18821127.

Jr, George M. Hillman, and Sue Edwards, eds. *Invitation to Educational Ministry: Foundations of Transformative Christian Education*. Kregel Academic, 2018.

Jung, Joanne J. *Character Formation in Online Education: A Guide for Instructors, Administrators, and Accrediting Agencies*. Grand Rapids: Zondervan Publishing House, 2015.

"Kallen, Horace Meyer." In *Jewish Virtual Library*. jewishvirtuallibrary.com. Accessed December 26, 2023. https://www.jewishvirtuallibrary.org/kallen-horace-meyer.

Knight, George R. *Philosophy & Education: An Introduction in Christian Perspective*. Fourth. Berrien Springs, MI: Andrews University Press, 2006.

Knight, Jane. "Updating the Definition of Internationalization," n.d., 2.

Krass, Alfred C. "Contextualization for Today." *Gospel in Context* 2, no. 3 (July 1979): 27–30.

"Larry Cuban on School Reform and Classroom Practice: Schools as Factories: Metaphors That Stick | National Education Policy Center." Accessed December 28, 2023. https://nepc.colorado.edu/blog/schools-factories.

Li, Ci-Rong, Chen-Ju Lin, Yun-Hsiang Tien, and Chien-Ming Chen. "A Multilevel Model of Team Cultural Diversity and Creativity: The Role of Climate for Inclusion." *The Journal of Creative Behavior* 51, no. 2 (June 2017): 163–79. https://doi.org/10.1002/jocb.93.

Lowe, Stephen D., and Mary E. Lowe. *Ecologies of Faith in a Digital Age: Spiritual Growth through Online Education*. Downer's Grove: IVP Academic, 2018.

Luna, David, Torsten Ringberg, and Laura A. Peracchio. "One Individual, Two Identities: Frame Switching among Biculturals." *Journal of Consumer Research* 35, no. 2 (August 1, 2008): 279–93. https://doi.org/10.1086/586914.

Lurie, Howard, and Richard Garrett. "Deconstructing Competency-Based Education: An Assessment of Institutional Activity, Goals, and Challenges in Higher Education." *The Journal of Competency-Based Education* 2, no. 3 (2017): e01047. https://doi.org/10.1002/cbe2.1047.

Maddix, Mark A., and James Riley Jr. Estep. *Practicing Christian Education: An Introduction for Ministry*. Illustrated edition. Grand Rapids, Michigan: Baker Academic, 2017.

Morgan, Christopher. "The Nature of Sin." The Gospel Coalition. Accessed July 8, 2024. https://www.thegospelcoalition.org/essay/the-nature-of-sin/.

Neuner, Gerhard. "The Dimensions of Intercultural Education." In *Intercultural Competence for All: Preparation for Living in a Heterogeneous World*, 11–50. Council of Europe Pestalozzi Series, 2. Council of Europe, 2012.

Nickerson, Charlotte. "False Consensus Effect: Definition and Examples," November 3, 2022. https://www.simplypsychology.org/false-consensus-effect.html.

Ong, Walter J. *Orality and Literacy: The Technologizing of the Word*. 2nd Edition. New Accents. New York: Routledge, 2002.

Pekerti, Andre A, Miriam Moeller, David C Thomas, and Nancy K Napier. "N-Culturals, the next Cross-Cultural Challenge: Introducing a Multicultural Mentoring Model Program." *International Journal of Cross Cultural Management* 15, no. 1 (April 2015): 5–25. https://doi.org/10.1177/1470595814559532.

Plueddemann, James E. *Teaching Across Cultures: Contextualizing Education for Global Mission*. Downers Grove, IL: IVP Academic, 2018.

Pollock, David C., and Ruth E. Van Reken. *Third Culture Kids: Growing up among Worlds*. Revised edition. 1 online resource (xiv, 306 pages) : illustrations vols. Boston: Nicholas Brealey Publishing Boston, 2009.

Powell, Kara, Brad M. Griffin, and Cheryl A. Crawford. *Sticky Faith, Youth Worker Edition: Practical Ideas to Nurture Long-Term Faith in Teenagers*. Zondervan, 2011.

Raibley, Jon. "Experiencing Communities of Learning: A Phenomenological Study of Students Enrolled in Western Seminary's Online Master of Divinity Program." Western Seminary, 2021.

"Research Paradigms – Methodologies, Methods, and Practices," January 19, 2023. https://writeprofessionally.org/research-methods/2023/01/19/research-paradigms/.

Richards, Jack C, and Theodore S Rodgers. *Approaches and Methods in Language Teaching*. Cambridge: Cambridge University Press, 2017.

Santrock, John. *Adolescence*. 17th edition. McGraw-Hill Education, 2018.

Sherpa, Dawa. "Socio Cultural Diversity Interplays on Motivational and Learning." *Sotang, Yearly Peer Reviewed Journal* 1, no. 1 (August 1, 2019): 65–71. https://doi.org/10.3126/sotang.v1i1.45743.

Sleeter, Christine E. "Multicultural Education as a Form of Resistance to Oppression." *Journal of Education* 171, no. 3 (1989): 51–71.

Smith, James K. A. *You Are What You Love: The Spiritual Power of Habit*. Grand Rapids: Brazos Press, 2016.

Sparks, Sarah D. "Why Teacher-Student Relationships Matter." Education Week, March 12, 2019.

https://www.edweek.org/ew/articles/2019/03/13/why-teacher-student-relationships-matter.html.

Stewart, James E. "A Snapshot of the Student Experience - Pre-Interview Questionnaire," October 25, 2011.

Taylor, Edward W, and Patricia Cranton. "A Content Analysis of Transformative Learning Theory," n.d.

Verywell Mind. "The Psychology of What Motivates Us." Accessed October 29, 2024. https://www.verywellmind.com/what-is-motivation-2795378.

Volf, Miroslav. *Exclusion and Embrace, Revised and Updated: A Theological Exploration of Identity, Otherness, and Reconciliation*. Updated edition. Nashville: Abingdon Press, 2019.

Wan, Enoch. "A Critique of Charles Kraft's Use/Misuse of Communication and Social Sciences in Biblical Interpretation and Missiological Formation." *Global Missiology, Research Methodology*, October 2004, 29.

———. "Critique of Functional Missionary Anthropology." *His Dominion* 8, no. 3 (April 1982).

———. "Global People and Diaspora Missiology." Presentation at Plenary session presented at the Tokyo 2010—Global Mission Consultation, Tokyo, Japan, May 13, 2010.

———. "Relational Theology and Relational Missiology." *Occasional Bulletin* 21 (2007): 1–8.

———. "Rethinking Urban Mission in Terms of Spiritual and Social Transformational Change." Presented at the Missiological Society of Ghana/WAMS Biennial International Conference, Virtual, October 26, 2021.

Wan, Enoch, and Siu Kuen Sonia Chan. "CONTEXTUALIZATION THE ASIAN WAY: RELATIONAL CONTEXTUALIZATION." *Asian Missions Advance*, no. 78 (Winter 2023). https://www.asiamissions.net/asian-missions-advances/amadvance-52-60/asian-missions-advance-78/.

Wan, Enoch, and Mark Hedinger. "Transformative Ministry for the Majority World Context: Applying Relational Approaches." *EMS Occasional Bulletin*, Spring 2018. https://www.emsweb.org/images/occasional-bulletin/volume-31/OB_Spring_2018.pdf.

Wan, Enoch, Mark Hedinger, and Jon Raibley. *Transformational Growth: Intercultural Leadership/Discipleship/Mentorship*. Western Academic Publishers, 2023.

Wan, Enoch, and Natalie Kim. *Relational Intercultural Training for Practitioners of Business As Mission: Theory and Practice*. Western Academic Publishers, 2022.

Wan, Enoch, and Jon Raibley. *Transformational Change in Christian Ministry*. 2nd edition. Portland, OR: Western Academic Publishers, 2022.

———. *Transformational Change in Christian Ministry Second Edition*. Western Academic Publishers, 2022.
———. *Transformational Change in Christian Ministry Second Edition*. Stanford: Western Academic Publishers, 2022.
———. "Transforming Meaning Perspectives and Intercultural Education." In *Covenant Transformative Learning Theory and Practice for Mission*, 147–62. Western Seminary Press, 2021.
Weibel-Orlando, Joan, Frances E. Karttunen, and Margaret Connell Szasz. "Between Worlds: Interpreters, Guides, and Survivors." *Ethnohistory* 42, no. 4 (1995): 659–62. https://doi.org/10.2307/483151.
Wiles, Jerry. "Digital Orality: New Signs of Spiritual Opportunities." *International Orality Network* (blog). Accessed January 6, 2024. https://orality.net/content/digital-orality-new-signs-of-spiritual-opportunities/.
Zilliacus, Harriet, and Gunilla Holm. "Multicultural Education and Intercultural Education: Is There a Difference?" In *Dialogues on Diversity and Global Education*, 11–28, 2009.

www.ingramcontent.com/pod-product-compliance
Lightning Source LLC
Chambersburg PA
CBHW050903160426
43194CB00011B/2265